DAILY

REPRIEVE

DAILY REPRIEVE

A.A. FOR ATHEISTS & AGNOSTICS

ALEX M.

ISBN-10   1974024571

ISBN-13   978-1974024575

Cover photo by Jeon Sang O

Cover design by J. Bourge Hathaway

Printed by CreateSpace, An Amazon.com Company

"The atoms of our bodies are traceable to stars that manufactured them in their cores and exploded these enriched ingredients across our galaxy, billions of years ago. For this reason, we are biologically connected to every other living thing in the world. We are chemically connected to all molecules on Earth. And we are atomically connected to all atoms in the universe. We are not figuratively, but literally stardust."

Neil deGrasse Tyson

PREFACE

I wrote *Daily Reprieve* to share my personal experience as a sober, passionate, and grateful member of Alcoholic Anonymous. As a life-long atheist, I find parts of the book *Alcoholics Anonymous* a most frustrating read, since author Bill Wilson, despite a few perfunctory disclaimers, constantly and continually implies that God is the Higher Power I must choose as the solution for my alcoholism. I had always heard that we had an option in A.A.—a religious God, or a secular Higher Power that's anything but us. The Big Book strongly suggests otherwise, as does most A.A. approved literature.

Even after the Big Book added "God as we understood Him," two of the most popular early A.A. publications supplementing the Big Book clearly and repeatedly stated that God was the required Higher Power for sobriety. They were *The Little Red Book* (1946) by Ed Webster, containing Step 12 insights, partially edited and blessed by Dr. Bob, and the *Twenty-Four Hours a Day* (1954) book by Richmond Walker, which was based on the daily devotional *God Calling* by A. J. Russell and used by the Christian Evangelical Oxford Group. Today's popular A.A. meditation book, the *Daily Reflections*, remains a deeply Christian centered, God as your Higher Power driven publication.

So is A.A. a religious Fellowship? Well, it's like trying to understand the difference between a mule and a horse—they are sort of the same—but not really. The Big Book subtext says on the one hand, "choose your own conception of God," but on the other hand, "your Higher Power needs to be God," a Hobson's choice at best.

Since A.A. has only one primary text, the book *Alcoholics Anonymous*, and only one recovery program, the 12 Steps, neither of which are ever going to change, I asked myself "Now that I'm sober, what is the best way for this atheist to carry the spiritual message of A.A. to the still suffering alcoholic using the standard A.A. literature?"

So I decided to write a Big Book based daily meditation book that was secular in nature, hoping to broaden the gateway of A.A. to everyone, but especially to atheists, agnostics, freethinkers, and all those who have a problem with the "God stuff" in their recovery.

In *Daily Reprieve*, much of the text of the first 164 pages of the Big Book [2nd ed.] is presented sequentially, covering each day of the year. Below each day's citation is a Consideration and meditative Question taken from my experience. Although not always possible, I made every effort to keep my writing gender neutral.

In my Considerations and Questions, I tried to differentiate the term God from Higher Power as best I could. Since there is no universal consensus on the meaning of Higher Power or Spirituality, this was a very difficult task. It was even more difficult and confusing because in the Big Book God is always the Higher Power of choice, but the book also concedes one's Higher Power may not always be God.

I suspect Bill Wilson knew exactly what he was doing when he intertwined, overlapped and appeared to intentionally entangle the terms God and Higher Power, making it almost impossible for the reader to reject God as the Higher Power essential for recovery.

In my practical view, God refers to religion, and Higher Power refers to the power of whatever non-religious, spiritual beliefs a person has, which can be described as a spiritual Power, Force, Energy, Purpose or Principles of one's own choosing, understanding and experience. In my mind, God means religion; Higher Power means anything other than religion.

When I stopped drinking for good, I entered the Fellowship of Alcoholics Anonymous, received my only 24 hour chip, completed my 12 Step work, ironically, with a loving, kind, capable born-again Christian sponsor, and adopted the design for living suggested in the Big Book. But recovery did not come easily.

I drank all my life. As my illness progressed, I became less able to control my drinking. Eventually the time came whenever I started drinking I never knew where I would end up, and when I really wanted to quit for good, I couldn't. That's the best definition of an alcoholic I know.

On the day I reached my jumping off place I had a shotgun in my mouth, fully convinced I would never be able to drink or live normally again. I was beat and I was done. I was truly powerless over alcohol and my life was a mess. All my efforts to control my drinking had failed. Lack of power was my dilemma. I couldn't fix my problem on my own. I had to find some type of power, other than my own self-reliance and self-sufficiency, to help me treat my disease.

I washed up on the shores of A.A. eleven years ago, drunk, desperate and dying. All I remember hearing through the haze was that God will get me sober. God is the only Higher Power able to guide me to a new life. Since I had never believed in any god, much less the Christian God I grew up with, I was ready to turn around, stumble out, keep drinking, and never return.

But I was dying, and felt I had nothing left to lose, so why not give A.A. a try? If it didn't work, I could try something else. Besides, no one was going to tell me I couldn't get sober in A.A. if I really wanted to, so I'd prove all of them wrong, just for spite.

I learned I needed to exchange alcohol, a Higher Power definitely greater than I was for a very long time, for two new powers to change my life.

The first was the people power of the A.A. Fellowship, easily found in A.A. meetings and through a sponsor. The second was some type of power greater than me that wasn't me; a spiritual power of my experience and understanding, as suggested in the 12 Steps and the book *Alcoholics Anonymous*, upon which I could draw motivation to change, and the strength and direction to adopt a new design for living.

When I read the Big Book for the first time, I had many questions about God and the Higher Power references. Members kept insisting that A.A. was not a religious program, but a spiritual one, whatever spiritual means, despite almost every A.A. group's habit of reciting the Lord's Prayer at the end of each meeting. You could have fooled me. Everything I read in the Big Book screamed Christianity.

Bill Wilson's repetitive and not so subtle hints that only those who came to believe in God were the only genuine A.A. members, and the only ones who could truly recover, was beginning to get on my nerves.

After Bill added the "Appendix II—Spiritual Experience" section, presumably due to confusion and complaints from his early readers, it did little to lessen the book's Christian bias in my eyes.

Thanks to A.A. pioneer Jim Burwell and a few other founding A.A. visionaries, the terms "Higher Power" and "God as we understood Him" forced their way into the Big Book, despite, one suspects, Wilson's objections. Additional secular references and God disclaimers, such as "Choose your own conception of God," and "Power greater than ourselves," barely cracked the door for atheists, agnostics, non-believers and freethinkers like myself.

In order to receive the full benefit of A.A., I had to overcome my prejudice against the Big Book's glum religious overtones. I had to let go of my anger and resentment over the condescending attitude expressed toward non-believers in the chapter "We Agnostics," in other sections of the Big Book, and by a surprising number of members in the rooms of A.A. I had to put aside my contempt prior to investigation when it seemed to me that "praying it away" was A.A.'s go to solution for any problem that cropped up.

To get over my aversion to the God focus of the Big Book, I decided to learn all I could about A.A., so I read dozens of books about Bill Wilson and A.A., including historical articles from the 1930s to the present, and listened to A.A. audio tapes from the 1940s on the early history of A.A. and its founders. I watched blurry home movies of Bill Wilson describing his role in the birth of A.A.

I read as much as I could tolerate of William James' mind-numbing *Varieties of Religious Experience*, and much of the same tedious Oxford Group literature that Wilson had read, since A.A. had deep roots in that non-denominational Evangelical Christian movement.

I learned all I could about Dr. Bob and his amazing wife Anne, and how Akron and Cleveland strongly influenced the growth and direction of A.A. I tried to understand the core of A.A. and the influence of other pioneer founders, especially in relation to the early debates and struggles A.A. experienced leading up to 1939 when the Big Book was published.

Was A.A. meant to be a dog whistle Christian religious program, or a truly secular spiritual program, despite any disclaimers to the contrary? If A.A. was a spiritual program, what does spiritual really mean, and how best could it lead me into sobriety and a new way of living?

It was important for me to resolve any disputes I had with the Big Book not only to stay sober, but most importantly, to be able to experience a spiritual awakening so I could try to carry the message of A.A. to others in an honest, helpful, effective, objective and unbiased manner. It was a real struggle for me, and took a long time to resolve.

As an atheist in A.A., I felt I had two choices on how to try to carry our message of recovery to the newcomer. I could stick to the God, Higher Power and 12 Step terminology exactly as written in the Big Book, since that is what newcomers and all A.A. members read, focusing instead on the meaning and importance of the individual choice each of us has in how we create and use our innate spiritual energy.

Or, I could dismiss, refuse to discuss, denigrate, replace, or never use the words God or Higher Power in my writings, or when discussing our need for some type of spiritual Power, Force, Purpose or Principles to aid us in recovery.

I could stay seated and refuse to participate in reciting the Lord's Prayer at the end of meetings. I could argue, mock and ridicule the distressing and overwhelmingly God-centric focus of A.A. during meeting discussions.

I really wanted to adopt the latter, more aggressive approach because I would be true to myself and my beliefs in doing so. But how effective would I be in carrying the message to all those faithful Christians and other religious folks, newcomers and old-timers alike, who make up the vast majority of the Fellowship?

In the end, right or wrong, I decided to use and follow the Big Book text exactly as written, since that is what all A.A. members read and it is what got me sober. In *Daily Reprieve* I frequently use the Big Book term Higher Power as my own spiritual power experience.

When I refer to my own Higher Power, it is never God. It is the spiritual Force within me that motivates and enables me to live a life based on the Higher Purpose of being less selfish and self-centered, while trying to practice the Higher Principles of the 12 Steps: Honesty, Hope, Faith, Courage, Integrity, Willingness, Humility, Forgiveness, Justice, Perseverance and Service.

When taking a newcomer through the Steps, I do not shy away from any discussion of God or Higher Power. Whatever beliefs a newcomer may have about God or their Higher Power, I explain that nothing in the Big Book should dissuade them from embracing their 12 Step work by taking whatever actions are necessary for them to find, define, and use their own Higher Power.

My suggestion to the newcomer is to ignore what others think, do, or say, and seek their own motivating power to change themselves, calling it God, Higher Power, Spiritual Power, Door Knob, Greater Good, Good Orderly Direction, Group of Drunks, or whatever they want. I don't care anymore. I just want them to get sober and find a wonderful new way of living, using the power of the Fellowship and the power of their religious or spiritual values, with the Big Book as their guide.

Today, I view the Big Book in three ways.

First, it is a textbook that literally saved my life. It is an owner's manual, or an instruction manual, on how I can recover from my hopeless state of mind and body. Through the 12 Steps, it leads me to a spiritual awakening that results in a profound change in my attitudes and actions.

If I study rather than browse the Big Book, it teaches me how to fit in with those around me, to form a connection with them, and find a new way of life that brings me some peace, dignity, integrity and happiness. It shows me how I can live in just this day to my fullest, regardless of the noise and chaos raging in my head and in the world about me.

Second, the Big Book is a historical document. It documents the beliefs of Bill Wilson and the experience of those that contributed to its creation. It is a historical record of how the first seventy-four members in A.A. got sober and mostly stayed sober. The Big Book reflects their religious and spiritual beliefs, their understanding of sobriety, and the actions they took which led them into a new life.

Third, the Big Book is really like one very long speaker meeting, in which the speaker tells the story of what they were like, what happened, and what they are like now.

By slowly changing my attitude towards the Big Book, my issues with the religious aspects of the book have diminished. Despite the incessant God references, the message in the book carries depth and weight, and the common sense suggestions it contains work for me each and every day.

In the Postscript section at the end of this book, I've shared various musings. I debated with myself whether or not to share my personal experience on these topics, but I said to myself, in true alcoholic fashion, "Well, it's my book and I'll do what I want with it, so there!"

My hope is that *Daily Reprieve* will help everyone in recovery, but especially the 31% of the population who identify themselves as atheist, agnostic or having no religious affiliation, and are trying to find a new design for living through the Fellowship of A.A. and its 12 Step program.

Enjoy.

ACKNOWLEDGEMENTS

First and foremost, I would like to thank A.A. for welcoming me and all alcoholics who have a desire to stop drinking, and for every A.A. member who continually tries to carry the message to the alcoholic who still suffers.

I would like to thank my exceptional family, especially my parents Cecile and Bill G., my sister Kyle C. and her husband Jeff, my late wife Anne H., my sister-in-law Jeanne H. and her wife Julia F., Cindy R. and Jeanie K., Kathy D. and Tom A., and Kathy D. and Joanne L., who all still love me unconditionally, as I do them.

I would like to thank my first sponsor, Dean J., who took me through all 12 Steps and the Big Book as a virgin, and to my current sponsor, Greg B., who shows me on a daily basis how to practice the principles of the 12 Steps like no one else I've ever met. I continue to want what he has. And thanks to all my sponsees, past and present, who keep me focused on the Big Book instructions, the A.A. solution, and the joy of living a sane and sober life.

Many thanks to Stephi W. for reviewing the first draft manuscript of this book and suggesting the book's title, and to Bonnie G. for reviewing multiple sections. Jeanne H. designed and created the book cover. She and her wife Julia F. provided content and editing assistance, suggested the book's subtitle, and kept me on track during the two and a half years it took me to write *Daily Reprieve*.

No acknowledgement would be complete without a warm thanks to Roger C., a member of Beyond Belief, an agnostic A.A. group in Toronto, Ontario, Canada. Roger has a Master's degree in Religious Studies from McGill University, and is the author and editor of numerous books and essays on recovery, including his most recent effort: *A History of Agnostics in AA* [aaagnostica.org]. His personal support, guidance, suggestions and writings have been invaluable to me, and his dedication to all those in recovery has helped a vast number of struggling alcoholics.

I would also like to thank several of my friends in the Fellowship, some of whom I know I have forgotten to list, but who will hopefully forgive me anyway.

These good folks and so many more help me stay on the beam in a variety of unexpected and surprising ways: Barney H., Bill H., Billy H., Bob T., W., Bob Z., Brad C., Brian F., Brian H., Bruce H., Camille F., Charlie S., Dan W., Don M., Fellon D., Frank H., Gerald R., Harold M., Harry N., Hazel B., Jack O., Jacque A., Jim M., Joe M., John B., John R., Keith L., Larry H., Lee B., Leon M., Lisa T., Lori C., Mark K., Mark L., Marvin S., Mike H., Pat R., Peyton S., Phil P., Rodney K., Ron K., Scott B., Skip B., Steve M., Suzanne N., Tim H., Tom C. and Vince J.

No words can ever express the depth of our thanks to Kasey and Burns B. for spending over four decades continuing to carry the message of hope and recovery to thousands in our community and beyond.

My appreciation goes to two of the best recovery authors I've ever read: Ernest Kurtz, author of *Not-God, A History of Alcoholics Anonymous*, as well as many other articles and books on A.A., and William White, author of *Slaying the Dragon, The History of Addiction Treatment and Recovery in America*, and multiple other publications.

And last, a deep and indescribable thanks to just a few of the A.A. pioneers who established our everlasting fellowship that has saved and transformed the lives of millions of alcoholics the world over: William James, The Oxford Group, Courtenay Baylor, Richard Peabody, Dr. Carl Jung, Rowland Hazard, Shep Cornell, Cebra Graves, Ebby Thacher, Bill & Lois Wilson, Dr. William Silkworth, Dr. Harry Tiebout, Father Ed Dowling, Rev. Sam Shoemaker, Dr. Robert & Anne Smith, Harvey & Bud Firestone, Jim Newton, Henrietta Seiberling, Rev. Walter Tunks, T. Henry & Clarace Williams, Sister Ignatia Gavin, Hank Parkhurst, Fitzhugh Mayo, Jim Burwell, Tom Uzzell, Dr. James W. Howard, Clarence Snyder, Jane Sturdevant, Sylvia Kauffmann, Florence Rankin, Marty Mann, and most fondly—to Victor and Lil.

DAILY
MEDITATION

JANUARY 1

FOREWORD

WE, of Alcoholics Anonymous, are more than one hundred men and women who have recovered from a seemingly hopeless state of mind and body. To show other alcoholics precisely how we have recovered is the main purpose of this book.

[Foreword 1st Edition]

CONSIDERATION

Can we really recover from alcoholism? Can we learn to drink like gentlemen again? Can we stop and start whenever we want? Not according to the experience of millions like us in A.A. All we can do is recover from our misconception that we have no way out of our alcoholic addiction. There is a way out, not out of alcoholism, but out of the desperation and despair which is all we have while drinking. Our textbook *Alcoholics Anonymous*, nicknamed the Big Book, instructs us how to work and use the program of A.A.'s 12 Steps as the solution for our daily malady. Recovering from a seemingly hopeless state of mind and body allows us to live a new life of choice and joy, and embrace a freedom we have never known before.

Am I willing to follow the recovery instructions in the Big Book?

JANUARY 2

FOREWORD

We are not an organization in the conventional sense of the word. There are no fees or dues whatsoever. The only requirement for membership is an honest desire to stop drinking. We are not allied with any particular faith, sect or denomination, nor do we oppose anyone. We simply wish to be helpful to those who are afflicted.

[Foreword 1st Edition p. xiii]

CONSIDERATION

We want to be able to drink relentlessly and enjoy the sense of ease and comfort it gives us, but never suffer any of the unpleasant consequences that come along with it. We want to have our cake and eat it too. When our disease progresses to the point where we must drink and can't stop, all we want is for the noise and pain to go away. We aren't sure stopping drinking will work, but sometimes we consider giving it a try because we can't find any other way out. This is Step Zero, having the desire to have the desire to stop drinking.

If I want to feel better, either because I can't stop drinking, or because of the damaging consequences of my drinking, am I willing to give A.A. a try?

JANUARY 3

FOREWORD

From this doctor, the broker had learned the grave nature of alcoholism. Though he could not accept all the tenets of the Oxford Groups, he was convinced of the need for moral inventory, confession of personality defects, restitution to those harmed, helpfulness to others, and the necessity of belief in and dependence upon God. Prior to his journey to Akron, the broker had worked hard with many alcoholics on the theory that only an alcoholic could help an alcoholic, but he had succeeded only in keeping sober himself. The broker had gone to Akron on a business venture which had collapsed, leaving him greatly in fear that he might start drinking again. He suddenly realized that in order to save himself he must carry his message to another alcoholic.

[Foreword 2nd Edition p. xvi]

CONSIDERATION

The key point A.A.'s founder Bill Wilson learns from Dr. William Silkworth is that alcoholism is a hopeless, fatal medical illness, and not caused by a lack of morals or insufficient will-power. Then, as now, there is no successful medical treatment that will prevent or cure alcoholism. However, there is an approach to our illness that can provide us with a daily reprieve from drinking. It is the Fellowship of Alcoholics Anonymous and their 12 Step program, drawn from Oxford Group practices, which becomes our new design for living. Stop drinking. Find and use a spiritual Higher Power, or God of your understanding. Clean house. Confess your wrongs. Change your behavior. Make amends. Pray and meditate. Carry the message. Practice the principles. Help others.

Am I willing to use the A.A. kit of spiritual tools to treat my illness?

FOREWORD

Could these large numbers of erstwhile erratic alcoholics successfully meet and work together? Would there be quarrels over membership, leadership and money? Would there be strivings for power and prestige? Would there be schisms which would split A.A. apart? Soon A.A. was beset by these very problems on every side and in every group. But out of this frightening and at first disrupting experience the conviction grew that A.A.'s had to hang together or die separately. We had to unify our Fellowship or pass off the scene.

[Foreword 2nd Edition p. xviii]

CONSIDERATION

We alcoholics, full of self-centeredness and self-righteousness, are a petulant lot. We insist on having our own way all the time, and rarely question our lofty thoughts, plans or actions. We relish attention, power, praise, money and approval. We demand to lead, never to follow. Soon we discover that we can accomplish few of our goals alone. A.A. teaches us how to play well with others, whether they are alcoholics or not. The Big Book says that our primary purpose in life is to fit ourselves to be of maximum service to God or our Higher Power, however we define it, and to those about us, so that we may be able to carry the A.A. message of recovery to the alcoholic who still suffers. If we can put aside our own ego, we will discover humility and responsibility, and finally relinquish our role as Director of the Universe. Only then will we have a chance of growing in the Fellowship and in our own lives.

Since I don't play well with others, am I willing to examine my role in my selfishness and self-centeredness, and take whatever actions are necessary to change my behavior?

JANUARY 5

FOREWORD

Of alcoholics who came to A.A. and really tried, 50% got sober at once and remained that way; 25% sobered up after some relapses, and among the remainder, those who stayed on with A.A. showed improvement. Other thousands came to a few A.A. meetings and at first decided they didn't want the program. But great numbers of these—about two out of three—began to return as time passed.

[Foreword 2nd Edition p. xx]

CONSIDERATION

If we want to recover from our hopeless state of mind and body, we first need hope. With hope we believe we have a chance, however small, of finding a new life free of alcohol. Once we believe that we have a chance, we can test the waters of recovery in A.A. If we stop drinking, take certain actions and stick with them, complete the suggested 12 Steps, and continue the maintenance work required for sobriety and emotional growth in our new life, our success can be 100%.

Do I have enough hope and courage to become willing to give A.A. a try?

JANUARY 6

FOREWORD

Another reason for the wide acceptance of A.A. was the ministration of friends—friends in medicine, religion, and the press, together with innumerable others who became our able and persistent advocates. Without such support, A.A. could have made only the slowest progress....Alcoholics Anonymous is not a religious organization. Neither does A.A. take any particular medical point of view, though we cooperate widely with the men of medicine as well as with the men of religion.

[Foreword 2nd Edition p. xx]

CONSIDERATION

Once we come to believe that we have a chance of recovery, we admit we need help. By ourselves, we are never able to stop drinking and get our life on track, despite trying for years to be self-reliant. Joining A.A. and reading the Big Book is a start, but we may also need support from our friends in other fields outside of A.A. Having a trusted A.A. sponsor and guide, who can show us how they got sober and found a new way of living, is also essential.

Am I willing to consult with other professionals if needed, and find an A.A. sponsor for help and guidance during my journey into recovery?

JANUARY 7

FOREWORD

Upon therapy for the alcoholic himself, we surely have no monopoly. Yet it is our great hope that all those who have as yet found no answer may begin to find one in the pages of this book and will presently join us on the high road to a new freedom.

[Foreword to 2nd Edition p. xxi]

CONSIDERATION

Once we start listening to other alcoholics tell their stories we no longer feel alone. The isolation of just me-and-my-bottle gives way to a new companionship with others just like us; others who have been through the pain and despair of dying, yet were reborn into a new life simply by sharing and doing what other alcoholics had done before them.

Am I willing to listen, share and follow the directions of those with solid sobriety in A.A.?

JANUARY 8

THE DOCTOR'S OPINION

We of Alcoholics Anonymous believe that the reader will be interested in the medical estimate of the plan of recovery described in this book.

[The Doctor's Opinion p. xxiii]

CONSIDERATION

Learning that we have a hopeless medical illness lessens the guilt we have over our drunken behavior and the shame of our inability to stop drinking on our own. We remain responsible for our actions, drunk or sober, but now we understand that we may be able to recover if we think of the Big Book as a prescription for better health, containing directions for a new way of living. Our Big Book with its 12 Step plan for recovery is not a philosophy book, but a textbook.

Am I studying the A.A. Big Book and trying to incorporate the A.A. instructions and principles into my life, rather than casually skimming through the book's chapters?

THE DOCTOR'S OPINION

In this statement he [Dr. Silkworth] confirms what we who have suffered alcoholic torture must believe that the body of the alcoholic is quite as abnormal as his mind. It did not satisfy us to be told that we could not control our drinking just because we were maladjusted to life, that we were in full flight from reality, or were outright mental defectives.

[The Doctor's Opinion p. xxiv]

CONSIDERATION

We have a three-fold disease of mind, body and spirit. We know we act crazy, and that our thinking becomes insane when drinking. We feel the physical damage that our drinking causes: sweating, shaking, nausea, vomiting, diarrhea, heart palpitations, swollen belly, numb feet, staggering gait, impotence and chronic insomnia, just to name a few. Our minds are mush. We are unable to concentrate or think straight, and can barely remember our own name. We are spiritually bankrupt and constantly suicidal. We have a medical illness, progressive and incurable, but not untreatable.

Do I accept that I have a three-fold disease beyond my control?

JANUARY 10

THE DOCTOR'S OPINION

We believe, and so suggested a few years ago, that the action of alcohol on these chronic alcoholics is a manifestation of an allergy; that the phenomenon of craving is limited to this class and never occurs in the average temperate drinker. These allergic types can never safely use alcohol in any form at all; and once having formed the habit and found they cannot break it, once having lost their self-confidence, their reliance upon things human, their problems pile up on them and become astonishingly difficult to solve.

[The Doctor's Opinion p. xxvi]

CONSIDERATION

For whatever reason, alcoholics are different from the normal drinker. Once we take that first drink, unlike most drinkers, we develop an uncontrollable allergic type reaction that triggers a craving for more and more alcohol. Obviously, if we never take that first drink, we will never crave alcohol. Why we have this allergy doesn't matter, nor does it matter if the term allergy is medically accurate. What matters is that we have our illness for life, and that it is not curable by magic shots, or pills, or surgery or anything else short of a spiritually driven change in our attitudes and actions toward life.

Do I understand that I have an obsession of the mind that drives me to drink, and an allergy of the body that will drive me to the grave unless I am completely abstinent?

JANUARY 11

THE DOCTOR'S OPINION

Frothy emotional appeal seldom suffices. The message which can interest and hold these alcoholic people must have depth and weight. In nearly all cases, their ideals must be grounded in a power greater than themselves, if they are to re-create their lives.

[The Doctor's Opinion p. xxvi]

CONSIDERATION

Dr. William Silkworth, a neuro-psychiatrist experienced in treating alcoholism, was unable to talk any of his patients into sobriety. The only alcoholics he saw improve had relied not on a medical solution, but a spiritual solution. These words may sound strange coming from a physician trained to treat patients through discourse, potions and pills, but he spoke from years of experience, not from some medical textbook.

Do I accept the fact that medical practitioners, skilled as they are, can never cure me of alcoholism or turn me into a normal drinker?

THE DOCTOR'S OPINION

Men and women drink essentially because they like the effect produced by alcohol. The sensation is so elusive that, while they admit it is injurious, they cannot after a time differentiate the true from the false. To them, their alcoholic life seems the only normal one. They are restless, irritable and discontented, unless they can again experience the sense of ease and comfort which comes at once by taking a few drinks—drinks which they see others taking with impunity.

[The Doctor's Opinion p. xxvi]

CONSIDERATION

"When I look out this window sober, it's cheap and it's dirty and it's ugly. But when I look out drunk it's beautiful."

[Days of Wine and Roses]

Drunk or sober, we will always be restless, irritable and discontented. Bill Wilson's spiritual guide, Father Ed Dowling, a non-alcoholic Jesuit priest from St. Louis that Bill met in 1940, described alcoholics as having been born with a permanent "divine dissatisfaction" in life. So we alcoholics seek relief. When drinking, alcohol liberates us from most of the disruptive feelings we don't know how to deal with by any other means. After a while, constantly drinking to change or bury unwanted feelings seems natural. Even when trouble occurs as a result of our drinking, we assume it's just a normal part of everyday living. If we suspect there might be something wrong with our distorted analysis, another drink will quickly return us to that illusory realm of well-being, where all we want to do is keep shutting off the noise in our head and find some peace.

Despite the relief I get from drinking, how much longer will it take me to acknowledge that what I'm doing is not normal or healthy, and that I'm paying a long term price for my addiction?

JANUARY 13

THE DOCTOR'S OPINION

After they have succumbed to the desire again, as so many do, and the phenomenon of craving develops, they pass through the well-known stages of a spree, emerging remorseful, with a firm resolution not to drink again. This is repeated over and over, and unless this person can experience an entire psychic change there is very little hope of his recovery.

[The Doctor's Opinion p. xxvii]

CONSIDERATION

Being forever restless, irritable and discontented, we naturally turn to what always gives us relief—King Alcohol. After a few drinks we feel better, but discover we can't stop drinking because the phenomenon of craving has been triggered. So we drink more. We do things we remember and things we don't remember. We find out afterwards how we harmed others. We feel guilty and are certain our drinking outcomes will be different next time. We pledge to change our ways. But things are never different next time, so once again we drink. Again we feel guilt and remorse, pledge to change our ways, and the infernal cycle continues.

Am I still running on that treadmill of delusion, depending on self-reliance, and believing that my self-will alone is sufficient to stop my drinking?

JANUARY 14

THE DOCTOR'S OPINION

On the other hand—and strange as this may seem to those who do not understand—once a psychic change has occurred, the very same person who seemed doomed, who had so many problems he despaired of ever solving them, suddenly finds himself easily able to control his desire for alcohol, the only effort necessary being that required to follow a few simple rules.

[The Doctor's Opinion p. xxvii]

CONSIDERATION

We are trapped in a deadly cycle of alcoholic obsession, drinking and craving more. It's like the old saying, "A man takes a drink, the drink takes a drink, the drink takes the man." Alcohol is the only way we know how to shut down the agony, clamor, and chaos of the crazy committee churning in our head. Our obsession drives us to drink, and the drink drives our craving for yet another, and at the end of the day nothing is different except that we are drunk or unconscious. We can't find a way out of this vicious cycle ourselves, despite years of trying. When we hear of others who have found a better way of living through some type of psychic change that we don't really understand, many of us, in a strange way, become curious and hopeful.

Can I admit that my way isn't working, and that another way might work if I'm willing to take suggestions and follow some rules, nutty as that sounds?

JANUARY 15

THE DOCTOR'S OPINION

I do not hold with those who believe that alcoholism is entirely a problem of mental control. I have had many men who had, for example, worked a period of months on some problem or business deal which was to be settled on a certain date, favorably to them. They took a drink a day or so prior to the date, and then the phenomenon of craving at once became paramount to all other interests so that the important appointment was not met. These men were not drinking to escape; they were drinking to overcome a craving beyond their mental control.

[The Doctor's Opinion p. xxvii]

CONSIDERATION

Early in our drinking career we drink to soothe feelings we don't know how else to deal with. We drink when agitated or calm, when happy or sad, when the sun is up and after it goes down. Even when we reach that point of satiation, we crave more when it makes no sense to drink more. We can't stop even after we begin to feel good and the noise in our head begins to quiet; our craving drives us on. We stop only when our liquor is gone, or we pass out, or get locked up, or die.

Do I remember the point in my drinking career when I changed from being a hard drinker to a real alcoholic—from just wanting to drink, to having to drink?

JANUARY 16

THE DOCTOR'S OPINION

All these, and many others, have one symptom in common: they cannot start drinking without developing the phenomenon of craving. This phenomenon, as we have suggested, may be the manifestation of an allergy which differentiates these people, and sets them apart as a distinct entity. It has never been, by any treatment with which we are familiar, permanently eradicated. The only relief we have to suggest is entire abstinence.

[The Doctor's Opinion p. xxviii]

CONSIDERATION

As real alcoholics, we are different from normal drinkers. Due to our alcoholic allergy, once we start drinking we will always crave more. We have no control over this—it just happens because we have a chemical brain illness. Trying to discover exactly why we have this malady will not change our bodily response to alcohol. Sometimes we can stop drinking after a few drinks and totter on home. Other times we drink to oblivion, which may result in incapacitation, jail or death. Before taking that first drink, we always believe we can predict where we will end up at the end of our spree, but those expectations are rarely realized.

Do I believe that if I never take that first drink, I'll never get drunk?

JANUARY 17

THE DOCTOR'S OPINION

Among physicians, the general opinion seems to be that most chronic alcoholics are doomed. What is the solution? Perhaps I can best answer this by relating one of my experiences. About one year prior to this experience a man was brought in to be treated for chronic alcoholism ....and seemed to be a case of pathological mental deterioration. He had lost everything worthwhile in life and was only living, one might say, to drink. He frankly admitted and believed that for him there was no hope. Following the elimination of alcohol, there was found to be no permanent brain injury. He accepted the plan outlined in this book. One year later he.....had emerged a man brimming over with self-reliance and contentment....A long time has passed with no return to alcohol.

[The Doctor's Opinion p. xxix]

CONSIDERATION

Dr. Silkworth reminds us that our alcoholic illness will eventually kill us. He had never seen alcoholics recover until 1935 when he met agnostic Henry Parkhurst, who was the second member to join A.A. in New York City. Unfortunately for Hank, he stayed sober for only four years, a reminder that just not drinking is not the same as recovery. We can recover from a hopeless state of mind and body, find a new way of living, live with dignity in our own skin and gain some peace and serenity in our lives if we follow the A.A. path and 12 Step principles. Bill Wilson and millions of others recovered in this way by accepting and following the instructions outlined in the Big Book.

Am I willing to follow the plan of action described in the Big Book to recover from my alcoholic illness?

JANUARY 18

THE DOCTOR'S OPINION

I often think of another case brought in......he had a talk with me in which he frankly stated he thought....treatment a waste of effort, unless I could assure him, which no one ever had, that in the future he would have the "will power" to resist the impulse to drink. His alcoholic problem was so complex and his depression so great, that we felt his only hope would be through what we then called "moral psychology" and we doubted if even that would have any effect. However, he did become "sold" on the ideas contained in this book. He has not had a drink for a great many years. I see him now and then and he is as fine a specimen of manhood as one could wish to meet.

[The Doctor's Opinion p. xxix]

CONSIDERATION

More testimony from Dr. Silkworth about A.A. number three from New York City, John Henry Fitzhugh Mayo, the religious son of an Episcopal clergyman who remained sober from 1935 until his death from cancer in 1943. Once again, Silkworth had never seen an alcoholic be cured of his illness, but believed that recovery was possible through not drinking and some type of major psychic change. Will power and moral psychology, meaning self-reliance and medical therapy, had never worked in the doctor's experience. However, when his patient Fitz followed the directions in the Big Book, Dr. Silkworth realized that recovery was possible after all.

What do I have to lose by giving the Big Book plan of action a try?

JANUARY 19

BILL'S STORY

My talent for leadership, I imagined, would place me at the head of vast enterprises which I would manage with the utmost assurance ......The drive for success was on. I'd prove to the world I was important.

[Bill's Story p. 1]

CONSIDERATION

Even though we never feel like we fit in, we need to show everyone that we do. So we convince ourselves not only that we fit in, but we are standing on top of the pile. We are number one. We have to be, and we'll prove it to the world. Alcohol only confirms what we already know—nobody is smarter, stronger, or more clever or qualified to be the Director of the Universe than we are. If only others would recognize this indisputable fact, we wouldn't have to keep trying to prove it.

Do I realize that my thinking problem started long before my drinking problem?

JANUARY 20

BILL'S STORY

We had long talks when I would still her forebodings by telling her that men of genius conceived their best projects when drunk; that the most majestic constructions of philosophic thought were so derived.

[Bill's Story p. 2]

CONSIDERATION

We love telling stories of great authors, artists, musicians, painters and sculptors who created immortal art and literature under the soft, snug blanket of alcohol. Whether the stories are true or not is irrelevant. They live in our heads and souls, and we yearn to become a part of them.

Do I realize that I started lying to myself long before I started lying to others?

JANUARY 21

BILL'S STORY

For the next few years fortune threw money and applause my way. I had arrived. My judgment and ideas were followed by many to the tune of paper millions. The great boom of the late twenties was seething and swelling. Drink was taking an important and exhilarating part in my life.

[Bill's Story p. 3]

CONSIDERATION

In time we reach that ethereal summit of perfection and admiration, or so we think. Nothing can go wrong and all is right in our world. Drink fuels our delusion, self-reliance and self-esteem. We ride that magic carpet of intoxication into oblivion and life cannot get any better.

Do I realize that it doesn't matter how I feel—depressed, elated or anywhere in between—that I'll always drink no matter what?

JANUARY 22

BILL'S STORY

My drinking assumed more serious proportions, continuing all day and almost every night. The remonstrances of my friends terminated in a row and I became a lone wolf.

[Bill's Story p. 3]

CONSIDERATION

Soon any fruits of our material success slip away, followed by delusion and denial over their whereabouts. Perhaps we aren't as successful as we pretend. Perhaps we aren't that benign Director of the Universe we claim to be. Is it possible the Emperor has no clothes after all? Overwhelmed by seeds of doubt fueled by comments from others, we disregard the committee in our head through more drink and isolation. Not being around others makes it easier to be around ourselves, as long as our alcohol lasts.

Do I become angry and isolate when people criticize my drinking?

JANUARY 23

BILL'S STORY

Liquor caught up with me much faster than I came up behind Walter [Hagen]. I began to be jittery in the morning.

[Bill's Story p. 3]

CONSIDERATION

A bit of alcohol here and there works for a while, until we find those nips and sips aren't enough to keep our bodies from waking us up in the middle of the night, shaking and trembling for more. Confused at first with these unwelcome interruptions, we quickly discover a few slugs of booze will let us slide back into our dreamless sleep.

Do I understand why I have the morning jitters?

JANUARY 24

BILL'S STORY

We went to live with my wife's parents. I found a job; then lost it as the result of a brawl with a taxi driver. Mercifully, no one could guess that I was to have no real employment for five years, or hardly draw a sober breath.

[Bill's Story p. 4]

CONSIDERATION

Once we become fully addicted to alcohol, we try numerous ways to convince ourselves otherwise. Maybe we need some new possessions to change the way we feel, like a new car or new furniture. Maybe getting a new house or apartment will help, or should we move to a new city? Perhaps a different job will allow us to sort everything out. We are almost certain that a new girlfriend, boyfriend or spouse will solve our problem. One thing is clear, that over time we become more and more dysfunctional and incapable—at home, at work and in the world at large.

Do I honestly think buying more stuff or running from my life and surroundings will solve my problem?

JANUARY 25

BILL'S STORY

Liquor ceased to be a luxury; it became a necessity.

[Bill's Story p. 5]

CONSIDERATION

When that dark day comes and we realize we are fully addicted to alcohol, everything in us cries out to deny it. It just can't be so. Even if we have to drink, it's not really that bad. So what if I need a little drink or two every day; lots of people do and they do just fine. We've still got our job, and our spouse and our house and our car, so it can't really be that bad. We've just got to work a bit harder to manage our situation.

Am I a real alcoholic?

JANUARY 26

BILL'S STORY

A tumbler full of gin followed by half a dozen bottles of beer would be required if I were to eat any breakfast. Nevertheless, I still thought I could control the situation.

[Bill's Story p. 5]

CONSIDERATION

For many of us, secret morning drinking is the best and only way to start the day. Rarely do we have a choice. Not only does drinking stop the nausea and shakes, but it reinforces our conviction that today will be different. Time is on our side. It will get better. Things will work out. We'll just take a few sips to steady our nerves and get us off on the right footing. If we have to take a shot or two after coming to and a few more throughout the day, it's a small price to pay to make it to cocktail hour when we can drink more openly.

Do I really believe that my secretive, all-day drinking is normal?

JANUARY 27

BILL'S STORY

Gradually things got worse. The house was taken over by the mortgage holder, my mother-in-law died, my wife and father-in-law became ill. Then I got a promising business opportunity. Stocks were at the low point of 1932, and I had somehow formed a group to buy. I was to share generously in the profits. Then I went on a prodigious bender, and that chance vanished. I woke up. This had to be stopped. I saw I could not take so much as one drink.

[Bill's Story p. 5]

CONSIDERATION

How many times does our drinking ruin our personal or business plans? How many times do we swear off, at least for a few days before an important engagement, whether it is family or business related? How many times does our excitement and enthusiasm lead us to believe we'll stay sober this time, at least until our obligations are fulfilled? How many times does all our careful planning dissolve into a drunken binge?

Have I ever destroyed situations or opportunities despite my best efforts to control my drinking beforehand?

JANUARY 28

BILL'S STORY

I had written lots of sweet promises, but my wife happily observed that this time I meant business. And so I did. Shortly afterward I came home drunk. There had been no fight. Where had been my high resolve? I simply didn't know. It hadn't even come to mind. Someone had pushed a drink my way, and I had taken it. Was I crazy?

[Bill's Story p. 5]

CONSIDERATION

We hope and wish and plan and plead and swear and know we'll get it right this time. With all the force of self-will that we can muster, we seize our resolve and forge ahead. Nothing and nobody will get us drunk until we're good and ready to get drunk. We'll choose the time and place. We're in charge. We glance at the bottle, then we stare at it. It tells us one little sip won't hurt. Just one, that's all. Suddenly, all our planning and promises go out the window and we reach for the bottle. We know we're going to drink, so we do. How crazy is this? Is it not insane to make our solemn plans of sobriety time after time, and expect a different outcome?

Do I understand that I'm probably not really crazy, but my behavior is always crazy whenever I start drinking?

JANUARY 29

BILL'S STORY

Renewing my resolve, I tried again. Some time passed, and confidence began to be replaced by cock-sureness. I could laugh at the gin mills. Now I had what it takes! One day I walked into a cafe to telephone. In no time I was beating on the bar asking myself how it happened.

[Bill's Story p. 5]

CONSIDERATION

Once in a blue moon we actually can control our drinking, at least for a while. As time passes without drinking we are convinced we've got it licked. Now that we thoroughly understand our problem, why not test it out by going to places where they serve liquor? The sights, sounds, smells and memories that pop up after entering those places suddenly overwhelm any rational thought of not drinking, and we're again thinking "Just one won't hurt." The insanity of our illness makes us believe that if we've ever stopped drinking before, then we've got our drinking under control. It's called The Great Lie.

Do I still believe The Great Lie?

JANUARY 30

BILL'S STORY

The remorse, horror and hopelessness of the next morning are unforgettable. The courage to do battle was not there. My brain raced uncontrollably and there was a terrible sense of impending calamity. I hardly dared cross the street, lest I collapse and be run down by an early morning truck, for it was scarcely daylight. An all-night place supplied me with a dozen glasses of ale. My writhing nerves were stilled at last. A morning paper told me the market had gone to hell again. Well, so had I. The market would recover, but I wouldn't. That was a hard thought. Should I kill myself? No—not now. Then a mental fog settled down. Gin would fix that. So two bottles, and—oblivion.

[Bill's Story p. 6]

CONSIDERATION

We slowly realize that after endless rounds of drinking and stopping and drinking and stopping, our life remains uncontrollable and unmanageable. We don't know how to live sober and we don't know how to live drunk. This is a horrible and deadly place to inhabit. We are boxed. There is no way out. We are as hopeless and helpless as we have ever been. We seem to have no choice left, other than to slowly drink ourselves to death or end our misery more quickly by our own hand. We think long and hard about suicide, but don't choose it yet; it's so messy and we can't muster enough mettle. Perhaps we fleetingly think of a loved one who might be hurt by our selfish action, so we hesitate in pulling the trigger or jumping off a building. Instead, we drink ourselves into another blackout. Over and over and over.

Do I feel my drinking has backed me into a corner with no way out?

JANUARY 31

BILL'S STORY

Again I swayed dizzily before an open window, or the medicine cabinet where there was poison, cursing myself for a weakling.

[Bill's Story p. 6]

CONSIDERATION

We want the pain to end. We want the insane racket of the unrelenting committee in our head to go away. We want peace. We think the only way out is suicide, and pray we'll be able to take that final step when we are drunk, since we could never do it those few times we tried when we were sober. How should I kill myself? What's my plan? Will it work, or will I mess it up? Can I make it look like an accident to avoid bringing shame upon my family? What if I don't do it right, and I survive only to become a cripple in a wheelchair? All these thoughts swirl through our sick soul. Why can't I pull the trigger or jump off the roof? Just let me die.

Do I really want to kill myself, or do I just want the noise and pain to stop?

FEBRUARY 1

BILL'S STORY

Then came the night when the physical and mental torture was so hellish I feared I would burst through my window, sash and all. Somehow I managed to drag my mattress to a lower floor, lest I suddenly leap. A doctor came with a heavy sedative. The next day found me drinking both gin and sedative. This combination soon landed me on the rocks. People feared for my sanity. So did I.

[Bill's Story p. 6]

CONSIDERATION

For so many of us suicide is rarely a fleeting thought. We carefully consider all the different ways we can end our lives without bringing disgrace on our family and friends. How can we make our suicide look like an accident? How can we kill ourselves painlessly? How can we be sure we'll be completely successful? How can we do the deed without making a mess? Should we jump to our death, pretending we fell? Maybe drown in a river? Accidentally shoot ourselves while cleaning our gun? Take rat poison by mistake? Perhaps an inadvertent overdose of that bottle of prescription pills in the medicine cabinet? All these thoughts swirl through our mind, each presenting its advantages and disadvantages.

Can I be unselfish, just for this one moment in my despair, or is my own pain enough justification for the perpetual heartache that will be suffered by all those who love me if I take my own life?

FEBRUARY 2

BILL'S STORY

It relieved me somewhat to learn that in alcoholics the will is amazingly weakened when it comes to combating liquor, though it often remains strong in other respects. My incredible behavior in the face of a desperate desire to stop was explained. Understanding myself now, I fared forth in high hope. For three or four months the goose hung high. I went to town regularly and even made a little money. Surely this was the answer—self-knowledge. But it was not, for the frightful day came when I drank once more.

[Bill's Story p. 7]

CONSIDERATION

We drink for relief until the relief no longer comes. We drink to get drunk, and we do get drunk, but the committee in our head gets louder and louder and no amount we drink can shut it up. Then we discover we can't stop drinking despite John Barleycorn's lack of effect. If we are lucky, we stumble into recovery and learn we have a medical illness manifested by an obsession of the mind and an allergy of the body to alcohol. We hear stories of how others have recovered by trudging a demanding spiritual path of action towards deliverance. Suddenly we feel restored, full of hope and promise. We've been educated, and have it all down. We've got it. Then, incredibly, we drink once again. Knowing is not doing. We can be full of all the book learning and education available, but on its own, this makes no difference. How soon we arrogantly dismiss the ominous experience of others because we know we're different, and what ultimately happened to them can't possibly happen to us.

Do I still believe that I'm different and that self-knowledge alone will successfully lead me into recovery?

FEBRUARY 3

BILL'S STORY

No words can tell of the loneliness and despair I found in that bitter morass of self-pity. Quicksand stretched around me in all directions. I had met my match. I had been overwhelmed. Alcohol was my master.

[Bill's Story p. 8]

CONSIDERATION

All of us come to that dark place where, sooner or later, we can fool ourselves no longer. We realize that every effort we make, mustering all of our might and will, again and again, will never prevent or postpone the certainty of our alcoholic demise and death. We are so alone, despondent and disillusioned, and know we are beat. Why bother to crawl out of the swamp just to get knocked back into it yet again? Let's just stay down here for a while and rest. We're done. We have no more strength in us. Drowning in the quicksand of addiction, we finally realize that the more we struggle the more we sink.

Am I able to stop struggling in the face of certain death?

FEBRUARY 4

BILL'S STORY

Fear sobered me for a bit. Then came the insidious insanity of that first drink, and on Armistice Day 1934, I was off again.

[Bill's Story p. 8]

CONSIDERATION

We know we are hopeless, infested with a fatal illness. We know we are drowning in denial and cannot go on much longer. These thoughts bring a level of fear into our life that paralyzes our alcoholic obsession for a short time. But soon we are at it again, using any excuse to tempt fate one more time. Our illness makes us act in crazy ways. The worst thing our illness does is to tell us that it doesn't really matter if we take that first drink. Crazy thoughts and crazy actions—all a part of our disease.

Can I stop believing the lies in my head telling me it's okay to drink and that it will be different next time?

FEBRUARY 5

BILL'S STORY

How dark it is before the dawn! In reality that was the beginning of my last debauch. I was soon to be catapulted into what I like to call the fourth dimension of existence. I was to know happiness, peace, and usefulness, in a way of life that is incredibly more wonderful as time passes.

[Bill's Story p. 8]

CONSIDERATION

No one can ever scare us straight or sober for long. When we are missing our wallet after a blackout, or tending our wounds after a fight, or calling for bail to get out of jail, or begging our spouse to give us just one more chance, or barely surviving a car crash, fear may overcome our drink obsession for a few days or weeks. But in the end, we have to drink, so we do. We forget the consequences of the drink and swear next time will be different. We pledge to muster all our will and control our intake. Our best laid plans work wonderfully up to the point when we take that first drink. Then Katy bar the door and we're off and running, barely noticing that we've lost the race already.

Have I reached my bottom yet?

FEBRUARY 6

BILL'S STORY

My musing was interrupted by the telephone. The cheery voice of an old school friend asked if he might come over. He [Ebby] was sober..... fresh-skinned and glowing....something about his eyes. He was inexplicably different. What had happened? I pushed a drink across the table. He refused it... "Come, what's all this about?" I queried. He looked straight at me. Simply, but smilingly, he said, "I've got religion." I was aghast. So that was it—last summer an alcoholic crackpot; now, I suspected, a little cracked about religion.

[Bill's Story p. 8]

CONSIDERATION

Down deep we hate ourself and our addiction. We hate being a slave to alcohol. We want to control our drinking, at least for a while. We'd love to drink like other people, who can start and stop whenever they choose. We search for a solution to our problem. Maybe a different job, or more money, or a different town, or a new spouse, or a bigger house, or meditation, or self-help books, or a psychiatrist's couch will do the trick. Or maybe the church or synagogue can fix me. Something I can control is bound to work, I just know it.

How many times and in how many ways have I unsuccessfully tried to fix myself?

FEBRUARY 7

BILL'S STORY

In a matter of fact way he told how two men...had told [him] of a simple religious idea and a practical program of action....It worked! He had come to pass his experience along to me—if I cared to have it. I was shocked, but interested...I had to be, for I was hopeless.

[Bill's Story p. 9]

CONSIDERATION

When we cannot stop drinking by ourselves we receive lots of advice. Most of our friends and family tell us to shape up, grow up, pull ourselves up by our bootstraps and just try harder. Lack of willpower, they say, is our problem. Or maybe lack of moral values, or perhaps a lack of faith. Some suggest that we return to the church, repent our sins and pray for salvation. When we hear religion and prayer might stop the drink, biblical visions of priests and ministers and rabbis and choirs and angels and Heaven and Hell flash through our mind, followed by the thought that religion will never work because it never worked before. But somehow, if we just lean forward and really put our back into it, we can surely figure out a way to fix our problem ourself.

Am I at least willing to sit still and listen, as Bill did for Ebby, even if it is with disbelief or scorn, as I'm being told how others found a way out?

FEBRUARY 8

BILL'S STORY

I had always believed in a Power greater than myself. I had often pondered these things. I was not an atheist. Few people really are, for that means blind faith in the strange proposition that this universe originated in a cipher and aimlessly rushes nowhere....I simply had to believe in a Spirit of the Universe, who knew neither time nor limitation. But that was as far as I had gone. With ministers, and the world's religions, I parted right there. When they talked of a God personal to me, who was love, superhuman strength and direction, I became irritated and my mind snapped shut against such a theory.

[Bill's Story p. 10]

CONSIDERATION

Most of us enter A.A. with some type of preconceived belief about God or a Higher Power. Traditional Christian, Jewish, Muslim, Hindu and other religious groups outline for their followers specific doctrines of their order. Some in the Fellowship believe in a universal spirit, but not in an interventional executor called God. They believe life events are random, unplanned, unpredictable and uncontrollable, conforming to the laws of science and nature. Others liken our lives as being as insignificant as a grain of sand along the endless beach of time. Some feel we are simply creations of stardust left over from supernovas after our universe exploded following the Big Bang. Yet no religious or spiritual philosophy precludes the universal human bond we have with one another based on love, compassion, tolerance and kindness. Few debate not trying to do the next right thing or the Golden Rule, treating others as we would like to be treated, as a time-honored approach to everyday living.

Do I understand I can live by the principles of A.A. regardless of how others define God or their Higher Power?

FEBRUARY 9

BILL'S STORY

But my friend sat before me, and he made the point-blank declaration that God had done for him what he could not do for himself. His human will had failed. Doctors had pronounced him incurable. Society was about to lock him up. Like myself, he had admitted complete defeat. Then he had, in effect, been raised from the dead, suddenly taken from the scrap heap to a level of life better than the best he had ever known!

[Bill's Story p. 11]

CONSIDERATION

That remarkable meeting in 1934 between Bill Wilson and his alcoholic boyhood friend Ebby Thacher celebrated the fact that one of them had undergone a profound life changing experience. Ebby's religious conversion into sobriety occurred after he admitted defeat, asked for and accepted help, and became willing to take whatever actions were required to heal. Ebby's psychic change required that he replace his old way of life with an entirely new one. In doing so, he was reborn into a completely new way of living. Any of us can change our life just as Ebby did, if we are brave enough to take a chance and do the work required to recover.

Am I willing to do the work required for a new and better life?

FEBRUARY 10

BILL'S STORY

Had this power originated in him? Obviously it had not. There had been no more power in him than there was in me at that minute; and this was none at all.

[Bill's Story p. 11]

CONSIDERATION

How was Ebby transformed from a hopeless drunk into a sober member of society? What did he do to bring on his religious conversion? How could it have happened? Where did he discover the power to change his life? Bill suspected that religion had a role, since Ebby said that God had done for him what he was unable to do for himself. But Ebby also spoke of a practical program of action he embraced during his journey into recovery. That program was created by the Christian based, non-denominational Oxford Group movement, which encouraged members to lead a spiritual life under God's guidance and carry that message to others. Ebby stopped drinking by doing the work and taking the actions suggested by the Oxford Group, which resulted in his transformation into sobriety.

Am I willing to admit I am powerless over my drinking, and am I willing to do the work required to change?

FEBRUARY 11

BILL'S STORY

Never mind the musty past; here sat a miracle directly across the kitchen table. He shouted great tidings. I saw that my friend was much more than inwardly reorganized. He was on different footing. His roots grasped a new soil.

[Bill's Story p. 11]

CONSIDERATION

When we come into A.A., we soon notice that those around us are not feeling and behaving as we do. Once consumed by their addiction, A.A. members are now free of drink and happy to be alive. Many have reunited with spouses and family, reclaimed their jobs, have a place to live and their children no longer run from them in terror. Something remarkable has transformed those A.A. fellows from a life doomed to a certain death, to a life full of hope and spiritual prosperity.

Do I seek the spiritual transformation that I see in others in A.A.?

FEBRUARY 12

BILL'S STORY

Despite the living example of my friend there remained in me the vestiges of my old prejudice. The word God still aroused a certain antipathy. When the thought was expressed that there might be a God personal to me this feeling was intensified. I didn't like the idea. I could go for such conceptions as Creative Intelligence, Universal Mind or Spirit of Nature but I resisted the thought of a Czar of the Heavens, however loving His sway might be. I have since talked with scores of men who felt the same way.

[Bill's Story p. 12]

CONSIDERATION

Our book states that about half of those who came into A.A. did not believe in God. For us freethinkers, our lack of belief in God is not based on apathy, contempt, prejudice or malice. We simply do not believe in God. It's that simple and it's no big deal. This does not mean we believe in nothing beyond ourselves. Almost all atheists or agnostics have a sustained, robust belief in a greater good and some type of loving, affirmative spiritual power in the universe. Though we may not believe in a personal, life-controlling and directing God, most of us passionately believe in some type of positive spiritual force, energy, power, principles and purpose in this world. The alcoholic's difficulty is that we do not easily accept that we can, and must, learn to harness our spiritual energy in addition to our human will to solve our problem.

Am I willing to examine my own spiritual beliefs in detail, and be willing to harness them, whatever they may be, to treat my alcoholic illness?

FEBRUARY 13

BILL'S STORY

My friend suggested what then seemed a novel idea. He said, "Why don't you choose your own conception of God?" That statement hit me hard. It melted the icy intellectual mountain in whose shadow I had lived and shivered many years. I stood in the sunlight at last.

[Bill's Story p. 12]

CONSIDERATION

Some say the most important nine words in the Big Book were said by Ebby Thacher in "Bill's Story" when he said to Bill Wilson, "Why don't you choose your own conception of God?" With that short sentence the doors of A.A. opened for all of us. No longer are we required to conform to a particular religious doctrine to be accepted in A.A. We can have one God of many names—God, Allah, Jehovah or Mohammad—or many gods of many names like the Hindu. As atheists we can have no God, and as agnostics we can safely say "we just don't know."

If I'm unclear on who or what my god or Higher Power is, am I willing to start writing down my personal conception of my spiritual beliefs and asking what does my spiritual Force, Power, Principle, Purpose, or Good mean to me, and what spiritual and practical principles can I connect with to find a new way of living?

FEBRUARY 14

BILL'S STORY

It was only a matter of being willing to believe in a power greater than myself. Nothing more was required of me to make my beginning. I saw that growth could start from that point. Upon a foundation of complete willingness I might build what I saw in my friend. Would I have it? Of course I would! Thus was I convinced that God is concerned with us humans when we want Him enough. At long last I saw, I felt, I believed. Scales of pride and prejudice fell from my eyes. A new world came into view.

[Bill's Story p. 12]

CONSIDERATION

Consciously connecting with a spiritual power means that we are no longer self-sufficient, and do not need to rely solely on our own will-power to live our life. We have tried running our life on self-will and failed. If we had succeeded in controlling our drinking and managing our lives by ourselves, we would not be in A.A. or need to change. We hate to admit we need help running our life, and that we cannot do everything by ourself. We feel weak and inadequate. Shame and guilt over our past sordid behavior and our current predicament keeps growing, threatening to overwhelm us. We try all sorts of ways to stop drinking and change our life, without success. Now we are offered a way out.

Am I willing to use something beyond human aid to escape the misery and despair consuming my life?

FEBRUARY 15

BILL'S STORY

At the hospital I was separated from alcohol for the last time. Treatment seemed wise, for I showed signs of delirium tremens.

[Bill's Story p. 13]

CONSIDERATION

Once we decide to stop drinking, how we are going to go about it? Should we ask for help or not? Of course, when considering detoxification we're not thinking too clearly. None of us wants to go through the agony of withdrawal, and no one can predict how we will fare. Will we have a seizure? Will we need medical attention? Should we go to a hospital to detoxify? Can we do this safely at home alone? Often it is best to seek professional support and observation when we decide to really stop drinking, since no one can predict our medical outcome. If professional support is not available, perhaps we should try to find someone sober, experienced, and trustworthy that we can stay with during the withdrawal process. Being alone and isolated for several days is the last, and least attractive option for most people. Regardless of the method we choose, experience has shown that it is imperative after detoxification that we immediately become involved in some type of support program for recovery, such as A.A. If we don't, the temptation to return to the bottle may prove to be too much for us.

When I decide to stop drinking for good, will I try to select the medically safest manner to go through the detoxification process?

FEBRUARY 16

BILL'S STORY

There I humbly offered myself to God, as I then understood Him, to do with me as He would. I placed myself unreservedly under His care and direction. I admitted for the first time that of myself I was nothing; that without Him I was lost. I ruthlessly faced my sins and became willing to have my new-found Friend take them away, root and branch. I have not had a drink since.

[Bill's Story p. 13]

CONSIDERATION

Bill shares the details of the sudden event he had while hospitalized that removed his obsession to drink and set him on a new life path. Labeling his white light, or hot flash episode a spiritual experience rather than a religious conversion, Bill recognized the desperate alcoholic he had become, acquired some humility and realized he could not get sober without some type of help. Self-will and self-reliance were insufficient for his recovery, just as they are for ours. Bill found his own Higher Power, that he called God, just as we will find our own spiritual connection at some point during our journey into sobriety.

Have I come to the point in my drinking where I can be honest and humble enough to ask for spiritual help?

FEBRUARY 17

BILL'S STORY

My schoolmate visited me, and I fully acquainted him with my problems and deficiencies. We made a list of people I had hurt or toward whom I felt resentment. I expressed my entire willingness to approach these individuals, admitting my wrong. Never was I to be critical of them. I was to right all such matters to the utmost of my ability.

[Bill's Story p. 13]

CONSIDERATION

When we drink we know that we harm others with our selfish and self-centered behavior. Whether drunk or sober, many of our actions hurt spouses, family, friends, co-workers and strangers. We insist we are right when we know we are wrong. We belittle our family and friends when we want our way. We lie to our employers and co-workers when we want to drink or are caught drinking in secret. We waste money on liquor meant to support our household. We cheat on those who love us. We constantly blame other people for all our problems and our destructive conduct. King Victim is our name. We accept no responsibility for our actions, and take no responsibility for anything other than serving our own needs. Knowing all this, can we become humble enough to admit our part in our past behavior and offer restitution for our past wrongs?

Am I willing to clean up my past as best I can, by admitting my wrongs and being willing to make them right, knowing I can never change my past, but that I can change my future?

FEBRUARY 18

BILL'S STORY

I was to test my thinking by the new God-consciousness within. Common sense would thus become uncommon sense. I was to sit quietly when in doubt, asking only for direction and strength to meet my problems as He would have me. Never was I to pray for myself, except as my requests bore on my usefulness to others. Then only might I expect to receive. But that would be in great measure.

[Bill's Story p. 13]

CONSIDERATION

Bill Wilson finds spiritual help and guidance through a connection with a God of his understanding. His God-consciousness comes to him after being reunited with the traditional Christian God of his childhood. Bill's God is his Higher Power, but God doesn't need to be our Higher Power. Let no one in A.A. ever state or imply that our personal spiritual power must be God. Let no one in A.A. ever suggest that unless a member believes in Bill Wilson's God, they have not truly grasped or accepted the program, or that they are less than a full member of A.A. Our Higher Power is the spiritual power of our own understanding, not someone else's understanding.

Am I willing to seek a spiritual power of my own understanding, and make an effort to develop a conscious contact with that power, no matter what I decide to call it?

FEBRUARY 19

BILL'S STORY

My friend promised when these things were done I would enter upon a new relationship with my Creator; that I would have the elements of a way of living which answered all my problems. Belief in the power of God, plus enough willingness, honesty and humility to establish and maintain the new order of things, were the essential requirements.

[Bill's Story p. 13]

CONSIDERATION

Bill Wilson found a power greater than himself to stop drinking and aid him on his journey into sobriety. He adopted God as his power, and most importantly, he stopped being his own god. He relinquished his God-cape. He gave up being the Director of the Universe. Bill understood that his belief in God alone was insufficient to bring about a new way of living. It had to be accompanied by a willingness to change his attitudes and actions, get honest about his past and present life, and become humble enough to remember he needed daily non-human help and guidance.

Am I willing to find a spiritual Higher Power other than myself, and use that power to help me change my attitudes and actions in life to establish a sober way of living?

FEBRUARY 20

BILL'S STORY

Simple, but not easy; a price had to be paid. It meant destruction of self-centeredness. I must turn in all things to the Father of Light who presides over us all.

[Bill's Story p. 14]

CONSIDERATION

Giving up self-will and self-reliance, asking for help and being willing to receive it, changing our attitudes and actions—these suggestions look easy on paper but are often difficult in practice. It requires a radical change in the way we think and act in life. It is easy to say we must change, but how? How can we change years of habit, and our peculiar comfort living a lie and a life that destroys us and all those who love us? What is this power that will facilitate a change in us, and where can we find it? That is what the Big Book is all about. We seek a spiritual power of our own belief and understanding which will motivate, support, guide and direct us with inspiration and strength during our recovery. That power must be one that we can relate to and engage with on a daily basis. The power is ours alone, but it is not us. It can be nameless and unexplainable, and does not need to conform to anyone else's power. It does not matter if we find our spiritual power deep within us or far outside of us, as long as we embrace it as our own, and start to engage with it.

Will I put a spiritual power greater than myself to work for me as I try to change my life?

FEBRUARY 21

BILL'S STORY

These were revolutionary and drastic proposals, but the moment I fully accepted them, the effect was electric. There was a sense of victory, followed by such a peace and serenity as I had never known. There was utter confidence. I felt lifted up, as though the great clean wind of a mountain top blew through and through. God comes to most men gradually, but His impact on me was sudden and profound.

[Bill's Story p. 14]

CONSIDERATION

During his last admission at Towns Hospital in December of 1934, Bill Wilson had his white light, hot flash, religious transformation experience and was immediately rocketed into the God-centered universe he remembered from childhood. Few of us undergo the abrupt personality shift or psychic change that Bill did. For most of us the events that lead to our own change in attitudes and actions come in the form of a very slow not-so-religious spiritual awakening, as outlined the Big Book section "Appendix II—Spiritual Experience." Early in recovery we are impatient for a spiritual awakening, but most of us don't acquire it before completing the 12 Step work. If we honestly follow our Big Book directions, it is rare that we do not eventually perceive some type of change for the better in our thinking and acting. Additional changes over time almost always lead to profound, long lasting spiritual growth in us, whether we recognize it or not.

Am I willing to do all the work required to find and use my spiritual strength and power to acquire a new way of life?

FEBRUARY 22

BILL'S STORY

While I lay in the hospital the thought came that there were thousands of hopeless alcoholics who might be glad to have what had been so freely given me.

[Bill's Story p. 14]

CONSIDERATION

Ebby Thacher's visits with Bill Wilson cost him nothing more than the price of a subway ticket and his time. A few hours of Bill's own time and effort were all that it took for him to embark on a new path in life. Two men, each making an effort and taking the time to share their stories with each other, enabled both to find a way out of their alcoholic affliction. But they did not stop there. Incredibly, they grasped the fact that in order to keep their own sobriety and better life, they had to try to pass on to other alcoholics what they had experienced. This is what makes A.A. unique—the idea that our own sobriety depends upon sharing our journey of recovery with a fellow sufferer.

Will I make the effort to fully work our program of recovery, and am I willing to give my own time to others so that they may have a chance to receive what I was so freely given?

FEBRUARY 23

BILL'S STORY

My friend had emphasized the absolute necessity of demonstrating these principles in all my affairs. Particularly was it imperative to work with others as he had worked with me. Faith without works was dead, he said. And how appallingly true for the alcoholic!

[Bill's Story p. 14]

CONSIDERATION

We find that practicing the principles of the 12 Steps such as honesty, faith, courage, integrity, willingness, humility, forgiveness, justice, perseverance and service, change our lives forever. No longer do we have an obsession to drink. We can look ourselves in the mirror and smile. We lose our resentments and most of our fears. We start to care about our fellows. We draw upon the human power of the Fellowship and our own spiritual power for motivation, strength and direction in our lives. And most importantly, we discover that working with other alcoholics is the keystone in the arch of our own continued sobriety and a new, wonderful way of life. Faith and prayer alone will never sustain anyone; they must be accompanied by a continuous, generous personal sacrifice for another human being.

Am I willing to pass on to other alcoholics what was so freely given to me, and do I comprehend the true meaning of faith without works is dead?

FEBRUARY 24

BILL'S STORY

For if an alcoholic failed to perfect and enlarge his spiritual life through work and self-sacrifice for others, he could not survive the certain trials and low spots ahead. If he did not work, he would surely drink again, and if he drank, he would surely die. Then faith would be dead indeed. With us it is just like that.

[Bill's Story p. 14]

CONSIDERATION

How many times in A.A. do we hear that faith and prayer can keep us sober, and that God will protect us if we accept him into our heart? While this may be true for some in the beginning, our experience has shown that faith alone never works. A.A. is full of priests, ministers and life-long men of God who can attest to this fact. Unless our spiritual life is forged with the selflessness of helping others, nothing will change. Some believe God designs their life-quilt, but they must do the work of stitching. Some believe God designs absolutely nothing, but they still must do the work of stitching to recover.

Have I accepted the fact that no power—human, spiritual or religious—will keep me sober unless accompanied by constructive, self-sacrificial action on my part?

BILL'S STORY

My wife and I abandoned ourselves with enthusiasm to the idea of helping other alcoholics to a solution of their problems. It was fortunate, for my old business associates remained skeptical for a year and a half, during which I found little work. I was not too well at the time, and was plagued by waves of self-pity and resentment. This sometimes nearly drove me back to drink, but I soon found that when all other measures failed, work with another alcoholic would save the day....It is a design for living that works in rough going.

[Bill's Story p. 15]

CONSIDERATION

Over and over again we discover that no matter how despondent, miserable and frustrated we become trying to live life on life's terms, the one thing that always saves the day is reaching out to another alcoholic. When our spiritual connection stalls, when meetings don't inspire, when the Big Book puts us to sleep, when we get frustrated with our A.A. program and the people in it, there is one thing we can do that always works, which is to touch another in the Fellowship. It matters not whether we extend our hand to our sponsor, a newcomer or a stranger; we get relief when we move away from our selfish selves toward another suffering alcoholic.

Can I accept that I have a guaranteed solution for not drinking by simply reaching out to another alcoholic when I think life is not treating me fairly, and the squirrel cage in my head begins spinning at top speed?

FEBRUARY 26

BILL'S STORY

We commenced to make many fast friends and a Fellowship has grown up among us of which it is a wonderful thing to feel a part. The joy of living we really have, even under pressure and difficulty.

[Bill's Story p. 15]

CONSIDERATION

We drink to fit in. We drink for the effect. Today we don't have to drink to fit in, and are able to feel the effect of a new, wonderful way of life. Sometimes family and friends that we drove away return, sometimes they don't. Either way, we are able to live with the consequences caused by our drinking, and be thankful for whatever companionship we have. On good days and hard days, we're equally glad to be alive and eternally grateful for our sobriety.

Am I able to celebrate what I have been given in my new life rather than lament what I have lost?

FEBRUARY 27

BILL'S STORY

We meet frequently so that newcomers may find the Fellowship they seek.

[Bill's Story p. 15]

CONSIDERATION

When we find folks in the Fellowship like us, we are comfortable being around them. Why would we not want more of their company? Sharing similar experiences and learning from each other how we can stop drinking for good and grow in our new life is a wonderful experience. Because of A.A., it is always easy to find fellow alcoholics and spend time with them on a regular basis.

Do I meet frequently with fellow alcoholics, not only for my own benefit but for theirs?

FEBRUARY 28

BILL'S STORY

There is, however, a vast amount of fun about it all. I suppose some would be shocked at our seeming worldliness and levity. But just underneath there is deadly earnestness. Faith has to work twenty-four hours a day in and through us, or we perish.

[Bill's Story p. 16]

CONSIDERATION

When we stop drinking and engage in the Fellowship we learn how to laugh again. We look forward to being with others like us. We know we have a deadly disease, but can rejoice in the knowledge that we have a daily reprieve in a common solution that works through a spiritually inspired change in our attitudes and actions.

Am I enjoying the Fellowship of A.A.?

FEBRUARY 29

BILL'S STORY

Most of us feel we need look no further for Utopia. We have it with us right here and now. Each day my friend's simple talk in our kitchen multiplies itself in a widening circle of peace on earth and good will to men.

[Bill's Story p. 16]

CONSIDERATION

Interestingly, Bill W. originally wrote "Most of us feel we need look no further for Heaven," but it was suggested by the Catholic clergy that reviewed the Big Book he change the word Heaven to Utopia. Utopia by definition is an imagined place or state of being in which everything is perfect or near-perfect. Our newly found sober Utopia is neither imagined nor perfect, but it is a far cry from the hopeless and helpless state that consumed us before we entered A.A. Our Utopia exists with us and within us, allowing us to meet the challenge of living life on life's terms with integrity, dignity and gratitude.

Have I found my own Utopia in sobriety?

MARCH 1

THERE IS A SOLUTION

We, of Alcoholics Anonymous, know thousands of men and women who were once just as hopeless as Bill. Nearly all have recovered. They have solved the drink problem.

[There Is A Solution p. 17]

CONSIDERATION

We never recover from our chronic medical illness of alcoholism, but we can recover from our seemingly hopeless state of mind and body. By connecting with the Fellowship through meetings, home groups, service work with other alcoholics and our sponsor, and by engaging in the A.A. program by completing all the 12 Step work and following the design for living instructions in the Big Book, we not only have solved our drink problem, but we have solved our living problem. We learn how to live sober since we no longer need to live drunk. No longer are we hopeless and helpless in our new life.

Have I recovered in A.A.?

MARCH 2

THERE IS A SOLUTION

The tremendous fact for every one of us is that we have discovered a common solution. We have a way out on which we can absolutely agree, and upon which we can join in brotherly and harmonious action. This is the great news this book carries to those who suffer from alcoholism.

[There Is A Solution p. 17]

CONSIDERATION

Most of us who come into A.A. feel some sort of camaraderie because at one time none of us could control our drinking or manage our lives. Despite that powerful connection, what we have most in common is a shared solution for our alcoholism. It is the solution of the Fellowship and our design for living, consisting of meetings, home groups, sponsorship, service work, the 12 Steps and the Big Book, which binds us together forever. It is that living solution that we share in meetings and with our fellow alcoholics.

Am I willing to focus on the A.A. solution, rather than reliving, regurgitating and complaining about my drinking problems of the past?

MARCH 3

THERE IS A SOLUTION

But the ex-problem drinker who has found this solution, who is properly armed with facts about himself, can generally win the entire confidence of another alcoholic in a few hours. Until such an understanding is reached, little or nothing can be accomplished.

[There Is A Solution p. 18]

CONSIDERATION

Unless we can relate to another alcoholic by recognizing that their story is in some way our story, we often refuse to consider any solution. When we ask ourselves how we are similar, rather than how we are different from the alcoholics around us, we begin to connect with the Fellowship and hope emerges.

Am I willing to take the time to carefully listen to another alcoholic's experience, looking for the similarities rather than the differences in our life stories?

MARCH 4

THERE IS A SOLUTION

None of us makes a sole vocation of this work, nor do we think its effectiveness would be increased if we did. We feel that elimination of our drinking is but a beginning. A much more important demonstration of our principles lies before us in our respective homes, occupations and affairs.

[There Is A Solution p. 19]

CONSIDERATION

When we stop drinking we regain consciousness. Like it or not, we are S-O-B-E-R, and for the first time Son-Of-a-Bitch-Everything's-Real. We wake up to a terrifying brave new world, and have no clue how to live in it. How do we deal with our spouses, children and other family members? How do we handle our damaged relationships at work? Do we even remember if we still have our job or where we work? It seems as though we are hit by a tidal wave of reality as soon as our eyes open in the morning, and it can be a horrifying place to be. If we are able to not drink and stick with A.A., we soon acquire the 12 Step principles and design for living essential for our daily life, such as doing the next right thing, being honest, exercising love and tolerance, and thinking less of ourselves and more about others.

Can I put aside the fear and confusion my sober life brings long enough to grasp the principles and design for living of the A.A. program, that will direct me in my new way of life?

MARCH 5

THERE IS A SOLUTION

We have concluded to publish an anonymous volume setting forth the problem as we see it. We shall bring to the task our combined experience and knowledge. This should suggest a useful program for anyone concerned with a drinking problem.

[There Is A Solution p. 19]

CONSIDERATION

We have before us a time-tested and proven instruction manual for recovery called *Alcoholic Anonymous*. This book is meant to be read and studied rather than debated. It is meant to be discussed with our sponsor and our fellow alcoholics. It is meant to show us a design for living that will remove our obsession to drink, allow us to clean up our past, give us the privilege of mending our ways and the harms we have done to others, provide daily routines and rituals to keep us sane and sober, and introduce us to some type of spiritual power of our own choosing that can give us strength, and help motivate, guide and direct us throughout our new life.

Will I commit to doing the work required to learn how others stayed sober and found a new way of living in A.A.?

MARCH 6

THERE IS A SOLUTION

If you are an alcoholic who wants to get over it, you may already be asking "What do I have to do?" It is the purpose of this book to answer such questions specifically. We shall tell you what we have done.

[There Is A Solution p. 20]

CONSIDERATION

Many of us go through various phases after we have been sufficiently beaten down by alcohol. We finally realize that we can't fix ourselves. We try and try, but no amount of self-will or self-reliance is able to control our drinking. We can't stop, even when we want to stop. Humiliated, embarrassed, exhausted and disgusted, we mumble something like "Maybe I need help," or "I think I gotta get help." This is really Step Zero, the desire to have the desire to stop drinking. Next we become willing to ask for and accept help, which is called surrender. We murmur something like "Help me please." We are now at Step One, and are ready to listen to the A.A. solution.

Have I truly admitted and accepted the fact that I can't get sober on my own, that I need help from another alcoholic to treat my illness, and that I've reached the point where I'm willing to listen to how someone else got sober?

MARCH 7

THERE IS A SOLUTION

But what about the real alcoholic? He may start off as a moderate drinker; he may or may not become a continuous hard drinker; but at some stage of his drinking career he begins to lose all control of his liquor consumption, once he starts to drink.

[There Is A Solution p. 21]

CONSIDERATION

For most of us, the very first time we took a drink of alcohol we could stop when we wanted. We do not exit the womb unable to control our drinking, but we do leave the womb with a perpetually restless, irritable and discontented temperament. We don't like these feelings, and find we can suppress them with alcohol. Alcohol works for a long time, but we soon discover it is harder and harder to cut back or totally stop drinking whenever we want. Despite our best intentions, once we take that first drink it becomes easier to take the second, and the third, and so on. No longer a moderate or hard drinker, we just throw our hands up and resign ourselves to drinking as often and frequently as we must.

Have I lost all capacity to control my drinking after I take that first drink?

MARCH 8

THERE IS A SOLUTION

Here is a fellow who has been puzzling you, especially in his lack of control. He does absurd, incredible, tragic things while drinking. He is a real Dr. Jekyll and Mr. Hyde. He is seldom mildly intoxicated. He is always more or less insanely drunk. His disposition while drinking resembles his normal nature but little. He may be one of the finest fellows in the world. Yet let him drink for a day, and he frequently becomes disgustingly, and even dangerously anti-social.

[There Is A Solution p. 21]

CONSIDERATION

We seldom recognize how destructive we are while drinking. Looking from the inside out through foggy glasses, we cannot see or comprehend our true actions. Others whisper to us how badly we behave while drunk, and we become embarrassed and ashamed. We cannot acknowledge that behavior in ourselves because of our illness, and try to forget it as quickly as possible, usually by drinking more.

When I am told of my behavior during my drinking, do I believe what people say, or do I just pretend things could not have been that bad?

THERE IS A SOLUTION

As matters grow worse, he begins to use a combination of high-powered sedative and liquor to quiet his nerves so he can go to work. Then comes the day when he simply cannot make it and gets drunk all over again. Perhaps he goes to a doctor who gives him morphine or some sedative with which to taper off. Then he begins to appear at hospitals and sanitariums.

[There Is A Solution p. 22]

CONSIDERATION

As our illness progresses and we slide further into hopelessness and despair, some of us use other medications in an effort to postpone the inevitable. Our desperation only accelerates our descent into insanity, institutionalization or death.

Have I reached the end-stage of my anguish and misery yet, knowing full well that I'm living on borrowed time?

MARCH 10

THERE IS A SOLUTION

Why does he behave like this? If hundreds of experiences have shown him that one drink means another debacle with all its attendant suffering and humiliation, why is it he takes that one drink? Why can't he stay on the water wagon?

[There Is A Solution p. 22]

CONSIDERATION

Few among us fail to ask ourselves at some point why we can't control our drinking. Many around us ask us the same question. Why can't he control his drinking like other people can? Most of us, usually in maudlin self-pity, argue with ourselves why we drink and why can't we stop. Our intoxicated musings generate endless, seemingly justifiable reasons. We know we feel dis-ease trying to live life, and suspect the cause may be buried in our genetic makeup, how we were brought up as a child, and the injustice of our present circumstances. So we end up in a perpetual state of restlessness, irritability and discontentedness. Does knowing all this help us stop drinking? Not in the least. The irony is that it doesn't matter why we can't control our drinking, since self-knowledge alone can't help us. What matters is that we focus on how we can stop drinking for good, rather than why we take a drink in the first place.

How many times do I ask myself the pointless question of why can't I stop drinking?

MARCH 11

THERE IS A SOLUTION

What has become of the common sense and will power that he still sometimes displays with respect to other matters? Perhaps there never will be a full answer to these questions. Opinions vary considerably as to why the alcoholic reacts differently from normal people. We are not sure why, once a certain point is reached, little can be done for him. We cannot answer the riddle.

[There Is A Solution p. 22]

CONSIDERATION

Knowing why we cannot drink like others, and why our will power fails to work when we try to stop might make us feel better, but it doesn't solve our problem. Even if we think we know for certain why we cannot stop drinking, it does little good. The fact is that for whatever reason, we alcoholics react differently from normal drinkers. Medical science has many theories to explain this, but it does not help us as we reach for the bottle even when we don't want to.

Am I spending more time trying to discover why I drink, rather than spending time on stopping drinking for good?

MARCH 12

THERE IS A SOLUTION

We are equally positive that once he takes any alcohol whatever into his system, something happens, both in the bodily and mental sense, which makes it virtually impossible for him to stop. The experience of any alcoholic will abundantly confirm this.

[There Is A Solution p. 22]

CONSIDERATION

"The Doctor's Opinion" says that we are bodily, mentally and spiritually different. Those of us who are alcoholic have an obsession of the mind that drives us to drink, and an allergy of the body to alcohol that condemns us to die. Once we take that first drink, craving automatically develops and we cannot control the amount we end up drinking, nor are we able to stop drinking for good, even if we wish to. It's like that old saying, "Man takes a drink, the drink takes a drink, the drink takes the man." Self-knowledge and will power fail us completely. We become frustrated and angry when we are unable to control our drinking, which paradoxically leads to more drinking, just so we can forget we don't have enough will power to control our consumption. This vicious cycle of drinking to forget that we can no longer control our drinking will kill us eventually.

How many times have I had the experience of being unable to stop drinking, or control the amount I drink, after I take that first drink?

MARCH 13

THERE IS A SOLUTION

These observations would be academic and pointless if our friend never took the first drink, thereby setting the terrible cycle in motion. Therefore, the main problem of the alcoholic centers in his mind, rather than in his body.

[There Is A Solution p. 23]

CONSIDERATION

Alcoholics have an above-the-neck problem. We have a thinking problem which perpetuates our drinking problem. We know that if we don't drink, we won't get drunk. Our problem comes after we take that first drink. What drives us to take that first drink is our overwhelming obsession for the expected release from our daily distress, depression and anxiety through alcohol. Our powerful, reptile, survival brain bellows out "I can't take it anymore! Give me a drink!" Our shy, sensible, rational brain pleads "You know bad things happen whenever you drink, so maybe you better not start." Guess who wins out? Unfortunately, longstanding alcoholic drinking has physically distorted our brain chemistry in areas that affect our thinking and decision-making processes. We are no longer able to make logical and informed choices, more so after we pick up that first drink. Our reptile brain continually cries out for us to quiet the perpetual chaos spinning away inside our head. It constantly reminds us that alcohol will bring us ease and comfort, and produces enormous neuro-chemical forces within us to seek immediate relief. The drive for release is on, and is incredibly difficult to resist.

Do I understand that I have an above-the-neck problem?

MARCH 14

THERE IS A SOLUTION

Once in a while he may tell the truth. And the truth, strange to say, is usually that he has no more idea why he took that first drink than you have. Some drinkers have excuses with which they are satisfied part of the time. But in their hearts they really do not know why they do it. Once this malady has a real hold, they are a baffled lot. There is the obsession that somehow, someday, they will beat the game. But they often suspect they are down for the count.

[There Is A Solution p. 23]

CONSIDERATION

We may think we know why we drink but do we really? Many times we have no specific reason that explains why we reach for the bottle. Are we celebrating good times and just want to feel a little better? Are we anxious and depressed, and need a little pick-me-up? Are things going along as usual and we just want them to continue that way? And once we take that first drink and can't stop, don't we always say to ourselves "It will be different next time?"

What does it matter why I take that first drink, since knowing why I drink won't help me stop drinking?

MARCH 15

THERE IS A SOLUTION

At a certain point in the drinking of every alcoholic, he passes into a state where the most powerful desire to stop drinking is of absolutely no avail. This tragic situation has already arrived in practically every case long before it is suspected.

[There Is A Solution p. 24]

CONSIDERATION

We try and try and try, but after a period of time all the will power in the world cannot stop us from drinking. The combined loving power of our spouses, family and friends cannot prevent us from drinking. Doctors' warnings, priests' prayers and employers' threats have no effect. Many of us remember precisely when we crossed the line into the land of no return, and by that time it was too late. Others of us had already arrived at that desolate place, having no idea when or how we got there.

Have I given up trying to control my drinking on my own?

MARCH 16

THERE IS A SOLUTION

The fact is that most alcoholics, for reasons yet obscure, have lost the power of choice in drink. Our so-called will power becomes practically nonexistent. We are unable, at certain times, to bring into our consciousness with sufficient force the memory of the suffering and humiliation of even a week or a month ago. We are without defense against the first drink.

[There Is A Solution p. 24]

CONSIDERATION

Remembering how we behaved and felt in the past when we lost control of our drinking almost never prevents us from picking up that first drink. We typically remember bits and pieces of disagreeable feelings and awkward situations surrounding past escapades, but they come into our consciousness jumbled and ill-defined. Guilt and shame always tag along for the ride. When everyone arrives, we recoil and attempt to blur and bury those fragmented memories. Our powerful obsession to drink takes center stage as our past failures recede into the twilight. Right now, nothing and no one can prevent us from reaching for that bottle.

Am I without defense against the first drink?

MARCH 17

THERE IS A SOLUTION

The almost certain consequences that follow taking even a glass of beer do not crowd into the mind to deter us. If these thoughts occur, they are hazy and readily supplanted with the old threadbare idea that this time we shall handle ourselves like other people. There is a complete failure of the kind of defense that keeps one from putting his hand on a hot stove.

[There Is A Solution p. 24]

CONSIDERATION

Once we take that first drink we fool ourselves into believing we will drink like gentlemen this time. When that doesn't happen, we promise ourselves that next time will be different. Tomorrow will be better. We'll try harder and show the world how we have mastered our drinking. But tomorrow never comes. We get knocked down again and again, struggle to our feet, and get knocked back to the floor for the thousandth time.

What will it take for me to admit complete defeat?

MARCH 18

THERE IS A SOLUTION

When this sort of thinking is fully established in an individual with alcoholic tendencies, he has probably placed himself beyond human aid, and unless locked up, may die or go permanently insane.

[There Is A Solution p. 24]

CONSIDERATION

We deny we can't control our drinking. We delude ourselves that one day we'll be able to drink normally. We don't really understand exactly why we must drink. We don't believe our will power alone won't one day curb our illness. We still believe we are weak and foolish. Yet we drink and drink and drink. We are cornered and see no way out. It drives us crazy, so we drink even more to forget our failures. Soon the sirens of suicide beckon.

Have I reached the end of the line?

MARCH 19

THERE IS A SOLUTION

There is a solution. Almost none of us liked the self-searching, the leveling of our pride, the confession of shortcomings which the process requires for its successful consummation. But we saw that it really worked in others, and we had come to believe in the hopelessness and futility of life as we had been living it.

[There Is A Solution p. 25]

CONSIDERATION

Could there really be a solution to our hopeless state of mind and body? How could that be possible? Part of us breathes a sigh of relief and thinks "Maybe there is hope after all," while the other part says "It can't be true." But when we look into the eyes and listen to the voice of another alcoholic just like us who says "I found it, and so can you," it's hard to deny they may not be right.

Have I become desperate enough to believe I might have a way out?

MARCH 20

THERE IS A SOLUTION

When, therefore, we were approached by those in whom the problem had been solved, there was nothing left for us but to pick up the simple kit of spiritual tools laid at out feet. We have found much of heaven and we have been rocketed into a fourth dimension of existence of which we had not even dreamed.

[There Is A Solution p. 25]

CONSIDERATION

Early on we have no clue what a "kit of spiritual tools" means, nor have we been rocketed anywhere out of our deep abyss of alcoholism. Recovery experiences are shared by those who have successfully gone before us in A.A. They have done the work and unearthed the solution. The tools they use are the power of the Fellowship, consisting of a sponsor and meetings, and the power of our design for living as outlined in the Big Book and 12 Steps. Using our spiritual toolkit, A.A. works and provides us with a new sober reality beyond our wildest imagination.

Do I believe that my life will improve if I do the work required to learn how to find and use the A.A. kit of spiritual tools?

THERE IS A SOLUTION

The great fact is just this, and nothing less: That we have had deep and effective spiritual experiences which have revolutionized our whole attitude toward life, toward our fellows and toward God's universe.

[There Is A Solution p. 25, Appendices p. 563]

CONSIDERATION

We're told that if we do what those in the Fellowship do, we will find a new way of living, free not only of alcohol, but of the forces that drive us to the bottle in the first place. We have the three-fold illness of mind, body and spirit. Stopping drinking releases our body. Changing our way of thinking re-directs our mind in order that we become able to re-direct our actions. A spiritual awakening transforms our attitudes and actions toward ourselves, others and life in general.

Even if I'm not sure exactly what it is, can I be open to the possibility of a spiritual awakening?

MARCH 22

THERE IS A SOLUTION

If you are as seriously alcoholic as we were, we believe there is no middle-of-the-road solution. We were in a position where life was becoming impossible, and if we had passed into the region from which there is no return through human aid, we had but two alternatives: one was to go on to the bitter end, blotting out the consciousness of our intolerable situation as best we could; and the other, to accept spiritual help.

[There Is A Solution p. 25]

CONSIDERATION

Those who are able to admit and accept that they have failed on their own to fix their problem usually reach a point where they realize that something beyond human aid is needed. Neither spouses, parents, siblings, children, family, friends, employers, priests, ministers, judges, nor anyone else has the power to free us from our alcoholic obsession and living problem. We need additional aid, and that aid is spiritual. It is an intangible motivating force that provides the additional boost to get us out of our alcoholic pit.

Even if I'm not sure exactly what spiritual help is, am I willing to give it a try since I have nothing left to lose?

MARCH 23

THERE IS A SOLUTION

Some or our alcoholic readers may think they can do without spiritual help. Let us tell you the rest of the conversation our friend had with his doctor.

[There Is A Solution p. 27]

CONSIDERATION

Being told that we cannot lick our illness all by ourselves, some of us still hear that mendacious voice in the back of our head, purring "You can do it yourself, because you're different. You don't need those sick losers or their stupid spiritual principles. Just try harder and tomorrow will be better."

Can I put aside my fear of failure and risk seeking spiritual help?

MARCH 24

THERE IS A SOLUTION

Here and there, once in a while, alcoholics have had what are called vital spiritual experiences. To me these occurrences are phenomena. They appear to be in the nature of huge emotional displacements and rearrangements.

[There Is A Solution p. 27; Appendices p. 563]

CONSIDERATION

Most of us early in A.A. have no idea what a vital spiritual experience is, but reading "Appendix II—Spiritual Experience" in the Big Book can be helpful. It states that a sudden, abrupt personality change, or spiritual experience causing us to be instantly "God-struck," as described by Bill Wilson, is neither required nor expected. If we can be honest, open and willing, most of us experience a slower "educational variety" change in our reaction to life, kindled by some type of spiritual awakening or unsuspected inner resource. This results in a change in our attitudes and actions, and the recognition that our spiritual power is worth keeping and cultivating. The Big Book calls this "God-consciousness," but we can call it "Spiritual-consciousness" or whatever we want. One thing remains clear: We need to be willing to accept a major adjustment in our manner of thinking and way of acting to get sober, stay sober and find a better way of living.

Even though I may be confused about vital spiritual experiences or spiritual awakenings, am I still willing to keep an open mind?

MARCH 25

THERE IS A SOLUTION

Upon hearing this, our friend was somewhat relieved, for he reflected that, after all, he was a good church member. This hope, however, was destroyed by the doctor's telling him that while his religious convictions were very good, in his case they did not spell the necessary vital spiritual experience.

[There Is A Solution p. 27]

CONSIDERATION

Some assume that if they are devout Christians and church goers, they can just re-double their religious labors and be relieved of their alcoholism. When we see the rooms of A.A. filled with recovering priests, ministers, rabbis, rectors, clerics, and other men of God, we assume they have temporarily misplaced their faith and will soon be back among their flock, clean and sober. Yet the experience of A.A. suggests otherwise.

Do I understand that religious faith and worship alone will never keep me sober?

MARCH 26

THERE IS A SOLUTION

Ideas, emotions, and attitudes which were once the guiding forces of the lives of these men are suddenly cast to one side, and a completely new set of conceptions and motives begin to dominate them.

[There Is A Solution p. 27; Appendices p. 563]

CONSIDERATION

"Appendix II—Spiritual Experience" in the Big Book says not everyone needs to have a sudden and spectacular personality change, or spiritual experience, on the road to recovery. Most of us undergo a spiritual transformation that occurs gradually over time, which is called a spiritual awakening. An awakening comes about by a slow, conscious change in our response and approach to life; a change which we cannot predict or control. We seek and discover whatever it is we have within us that motivates us to connect with, and use, a higher spiritual Power, Purpose, Principle or life force of our own understanding. We give up self-reliance and self-sufficiency, which alone will never keep us sober. We find our own spiritual power, actively participate in the Fellowship, and complete all of the 12 Step work. It is only then that we undergo a psychic change, and discover we have an entirely new set of attitudes and actions to help us get through life.

Am I willing to be honest, open and willing enough to seek a new set of spiritual concepts that will free me from drinking and lead me into a new way of living?

MARCH 27

THERE IS A SOLUTION

A new life has been given us or, if you prefer, "a design for living" that really works.

[There Is A Solution p. 28]

CONSIDERATION

By following the directions in the Big Book, we are introduced to a new plan for living our life. After all, isn't this what we were seeking all along? When we don't know how to live in the world we are given, we find that we can use alcohol to seemingly change our world into a more tolerable place, or just make it disappear altogether. When alcohol stops working, or when we suffer enough adverse consequences, or when we just get beaten down enough, or when we're just sick and tired of being sick and tired, we discover we don't know how to live sober and we don't know how to live drunk. Now we have the opportunity to learn how to live life sober so we don't have to live life drunk, since down deep we really have no desire to spend the rest of our days in misery.

Am I willing to go to any length to acquire the A.A. design for living?

THERE IS A SOLUTION

We have no desire to convince anyone that there is only one way by which faith can be acquired. If what we have learned and felt and seen means anything at all, it means that all of us, whatever our race, creed, or color are the children of a living Creator with whom we may form a relationship upon simple and understandable terms as soon as we are willing and honest enough to try.

[There Is A Solution p. 28]

CONSIDERATION

Faith means complete trust in someone or something. Religious faith means trust in a supreme being defined by a religious group, and their highest power might be called God, or Allah, or Brahman, or Hashem. Spiritual faith means trust in a Higher Power, or spiritual power of our own understanding, which may not be a power defined by any religion. But we find in A.A. that we will discover and use some kind of Higher Power, or Higher Principle, or Higher Purpose, or Higher Force, or belief beyond ourselves and the Fellowship to aid us in recovery. We need to find a motivating force or power with which we can spiritually connect and have a relationship with, and that power can't be of the human variety, meaning it can't be me or you.

Am I willing to seek and define a spiritual power other than myself that I can begin to form a relationship with?

THERE IS A SOLUTION

We think it no concern of ours what religious bodies our members identify themselves with as individuals. This should be an entirely personal affair which each one decides for himself in the light of past associations, or his present choice.

[There Is A Solution p. 28]

CONSIDERATION

Whatever type of spiritual Higher Power we choose to help us find a new way of living is not important as long as we can begin to form some type of spiritual connection with that power. If our Higher Power is God, then the question we might ask ourselves is "How well can I honestly and effectively connect with God, using Him for strength, guidance and direction in my life?" If our Higher Power is the Force of Love and Good in the universe, can I connect with this power? If our Higher Power is a Higher Purpose to do the next right thing, how well can I connect with this power? If our Higher Power embodies the Higher Principles expressed in the 12 Steps, can I connect with this power? If our Higher Power is the power we receive from a Group-Of-Drunks or Good-Orderly-Direction in the A.A. Fellowship, can I connect with that power? And yes, even if our Higher Power is a door knob, which may symbolize our entry into a new way of living, can I connect with that power? How we define our Higher Power is much less important than how effectively we can connect with that spiritual power.

Am I willing to take the time and do the work to find a spiritual power I can connect with, and use that power to motivate and support me in my new life?

MARCH 30

THERE IS A SOLUTION

Further on, clear-cut directions are given showing how we recovered.

[There Is A Solution p. 29]

CONSIDERATION

We are thankful that more will be revealed. Up to this point the solution to our illness of alcoholism, as described in our Big Book, lifts our hopes, but at times appears confusing and overwhelming. Some of the words and meanings may not be familiar to us, which rightly sends us in search of a dictionary. Some of the proposals offered may ring untrue, while others seem contradictory, vague or ambiguous. Having clear-cut directions ahead lessens our anxiety and fear about our ability to recover.

Can I be patient and persistent in my Big Book study to continue working toward the solution?

MARCH 31

THERE IS A SOLUTION

Our hope is that many alcoholic men and women, desperately in need, will see these pages, and we believe that it is only by fully disclosing ourselves and our problems that they will be persuaded to say, "Yes, I am one of them too; I must have this thing."

[There Is A Solution p. 29]

CONSIDERATION

Most of us find that we have the same hope expressed in the pages of this chapter. Somewhat fearful and unsure about what lies on our road ahead, we know with certainty that we are alcoholics, and are similar to those described thus far in so many ways. Hope stirs that our future will be better. Reading the personal stories of recovery in the back of the Big Book provides further reassurance that we are all in this together, and that all of us can recover from our hopeless state of mind and body as we work and walk together toward an unimaginable new way of living.

Do I continue to have hope for my recovery?

APRIL 1

MORE ABOUT ALCOHOLISM

Most of us have been unwilling to admit we were real alcoholics. No person likes to think he is bodily and mentally different from his fellows. Therefore, it is not surprising that our drinking careers have been characterized by countless vain attempts to prove we could drink like other people. The idea that somehow, someday he will control and enjoy his drinking is the great obsession of every abnormal drinker. The persistence of this illusion is astonishing. Many pursue it into the gates of insanity or death.

[More About Alcoholism p. 30]

CONSIDERATION

Why can't we control our drinking like our friends? Are we really that different from everyone else? We secretly hope A.A. will teach us to drink like gentlemen. If we stay dry and attend A.A. for a while, how could a drink or two now and then be a problem? We hope, plot, and pray, bottle in hand, that there must be some way for us to learn how to control our drinking. This delusional way of thinking is the mental insanity of our disease, and unless cast off, it will kill us eventually.

Do I still have some lurking notion that one day I'll be able to drink normally?

APRIL 2

MORE ABOUT ALCOHOLISM

We learned that we had to fully concede to our innermost selves that we were alcoholics. This is the first step in recovery. The delusion that we are like other people, or presently may be, has to be smashed.

[More About Alcoholism p. 30]

CONSIDERATION

Step One says we admitted we were powerless over alcohol—that our lives had become unmanageable. For whatever reason, we are not like the nine out of ten other people in the world who have no problem controlling their drinking. They can stop and start at will. Maybe they do silly, senseless or regrettable things when they get drunk, but they don't live their lives drunk. When they really want to quit drinking for a short time, or a long time, or forever, they can. Quitting for good is not hard for them, yet it is impossible for us.

Can I admit and accept that I am a real alcoholic, and will never be able to drink successfully again?

MORE ABOUT ALCOHOLISM

We alcoholics are men and women who have lost the ability to control our drinking. We know that no real alcoholic ever recovers control. All of us felt at times that we were regaining control, but such intervals— usually brief—were inevitably followed by still less control, which led in time to pitiful and incomprehensible demoralization. We are convinced to a man that alcoholics of our type are in the grip of a progressive illness. Over any considerable period we get worse, never better.

[More About Alcoholism p. 30]

CONSIDERATION

It is the engine on the train that kills us, not the caboose. Step One means we are not powerless until we take that first sip of that first drink. After that, all bets are off. Maybe we can still stop after a few drinks, but we never know for certain ahead of time. If we behave ourselves and are able to manage our affairs after drinking, as time passes we find it becomes more difficult, and then it becomes impossible. The times we can stop drinking, at least for a bit, when we really want to, become fewer and fewer. Eventually we just throw up our hands and surrender to the bottle. Our life is a shambles, but after we take those next few drinks we don't care anymore.

Do I know in both my gut and my head that my alcoholism has progressed to the point of no return, and I need to stop drinking for good?

APRIL 4

MORE ABOUT ALCOHOLISM

We are like men who have lost their legs; they never grow new ones. Neither does there appear to be any kind of treatment which will make alcoholics of our kind like other men. We have tried every imaginable remedy. In some instances there has been brief recovery, followed always by a still worse relapse. Physicians who are familiar with alcoholism agree there is no such thing as making a normal drinker out of an alcoholic. Science may one day accomplish this, but it hasn't done so yet.

[More About Alcoholism p. 30]

CONSIDERATION

Some of us still hold on to the false expectation that tomorrow will be different. If we can just think of some other way to control our drinking that we haven't tried yet, maybe that will work. If we can only find some mechanism to drink normally, at least most of the time, that might be enough to get us through the day. Today science has confirmed what our founders suspected—there is no way to turn a real alcoholic into a normal drinker. We cannot turn pickles back into cucumbers as surely as we cannot grow new legs after we lose them.

Can I accept the fact that I will never, ever, be able to become a normal drinker?

APRIL 5

MORE ABOUT ALCOHOLISM

Despite all we can say, many who are real alcoholics are not going to believe they are in that class. By every form of self-deception and experimentation, they will try to prove themselves exceptions to the rule, therefore nonalcoholic. If anyone who is showing inability to control his drinking can do the right-about-face and drink like a gentleman, our hats are off to him. Heaven knows, we have tried hard enough and long enough to drink like other people!

[More About Alcoholism p. 31]

CONSIDERATION

We spend weeks or months or years or decades trying to prove we can drink normally. Every time we fail, we dig in deeper and proclaim that next time we'll get it right. But we don't. Our repeated failures drive us further into despair and shame, and for many of us, to suicide. We just can't admit we aren't powerful enough on our own to control something as seemingly simple as being able to take a few drinks and stop.

Have I stopped fooling myself that one day I will be able to drink normally?

APRIL 6

MORE ABOUT ALCOHOLISM

We do not like to pronounce any individual as alcoholic, but you can quickly diagnose yourself. Step over to the nearest barroom and try some controlled drinking. Try to drink and stop abruptly. Try it more than once. It will not take long for you to decide, if you are honest with yourself about it. It may be worth a bad case of jitters if you get a full knowledge of your condition.

[More About Alcoholism p. 31]

CONSIDERATION

How many times have we tried the barroom experiment? How many times do we say "I'll just have two drinks and go home?" We drink a double and then say "One more can't hurt; I feel fine." After the next one we start to relax. Things aren't really that bad. We're having a good time. The bar is lively. Let's have another one for the road. But the road never appears. Somehow another drink arrives, so we might as well drink that one too. At the end of the night we stumble once again out the barroom door, swearing to ourselves that this time will be the last.

Have I given up trying to prove to myself that I'm not an alcoholic?

APRIL 7

MORE ABOUT ALCOHOLISM

Though there is no way of proving it, we believe that early in our drinking careers most of us could have stopped drinking. But the difficulty is that few alcoholics have enough desire to stop while there is yet time.

[More About Alcoholism p. 32]

CONSIDERATION

When we take our very first drink of alcohol, whether it's at age eight or eighty, we are able to stop. As we drink more regularly, many of us can still stop whenever we want. Over time, and depending on our makeup, some of us drink for years or decades with no real problem of control, but most of us don't make it that long. All of us, eventually, lose control of our drinking, and by this time it is too late. Early on, we may suspect we are losing control, but we tell ourselves that since we don't know for certain how our drinking will progress, there is no reason to stop drinking now. We feel a little uneasy, but still safe, as we lean over the top of the cliff. But when we fall off, as we are destined to do, it's too late to turn back.

How many times did I consider during my early drinking days that it was time for me to stop drinking for good?

APRIL 8

MORE ABOUT ALCOHOLISM

A man of thirty was doing a great deal of spree drinking....he made up his mind that until he had been successful in business and had retired, he would not touch another drop...he remained bone dry for twenty-five years and retired at the age of fifty-five. Then he fell victim to a belief which practically every alcoholic has that his long period of sobriety and self-discipline had qualified him to drink as other men. Out came his carpet slippers and a bottle. In two months he was in a hospital, puzzled and humiliated.....he attempted to stop altogether and found he could not.....he went to pieces quickly and was dead within four years.

[More About Alcoholism p. 32]

CONSIDERATION

Twenty-five years of abstinence was not long enough for our young foolish friend to overcome an illness he carried all his life. When he pledges to stop drinking early in his career, surely he suspects that something is wrong with him. As a hard drinker, he likely deduces that he is on the road of no return, but convinces himself that he will be able to stop drinking before he evolves into a real alcoholic. Yet in the end, his years of his sobriety do nothing to protect him from the inevitable. He is doomed from the beginning. Time and tide wait for no man.

Am I convinced that no length of sobriety will protect me from my illness once I take up drinking again?

APRIL 9

MORE ABOUT ALCOHOLISM

Most of us have believed that if we remained sober for a long stretch, we could thereafter drink normally. But here is a man who at fifty-five years found he was just where he had left off at thirty. We have seen the truth demonstrated again and again: "Once an alcoholic, always an alcoholic." Commencing to drink after a period of sobriety, we are in a short time as bad as ever. If we are planning to stop drinking, there must be no reservation of any kind, nor any lurking notion that someday we will be immune to alcohol.

[More About Alcoholism p. 33]

CONSIDERATION

We have an illness of mind, body and spirit. When we stop drinking, our body begins to heal, but what about our mind and spirit? Simply not drinking cannot fully heal those two parts of us that have been severely damaged. This is where A.A. can help. The 12 Step program and Fellowship provides a solution to heal all three aspects of our life. Like a three-legged stool, all three legs are needed for us to sit upright. So naturally when we stop drinking and start again, we pick up just where we left off and our stool remains broken.

Am I ready to admit I am a real alcoholic who will never be able to drink successfully for as long as I live?

APRIL 10

MORE ABOUT ALCOHOLISM

As we look back, we feel we had gone on drinking many years beyond the point where we could quit on our will power. If anyone questions whether he has entered this dangerous area, let him try leaving liquor alone for one year. If he is a real alcoholic and very far advanced, there is scant chance of success.

[More About Alcoholism p. 34]

CONSIDERATION

Most of us don't need to try another special experiment to know if we are alcoholic or not. We have road tested ourselves for years, and failed every time, because we can never stop drinking for good. We are alcoholics. Those of us who can stop and start drinking at will, and have no obsession to drink when not drinking, are probably not alcoholic. Those of us who never crave more alcohol after taking our first drink are probably not alcoholic. Only we can determine if we are alcoholic or not, but for most of us, we do not have to debate ourselves for very long to answer that straightforward question.

Do I really need to test myself, once again, to realize I can't control my drinking or my life?

APRIL 11

MORE ABOUT ALCOHOLISM

For those who are unable to drink moderately the question is how to stop altogether. We are assuming, of course, that the reader desires to stop. Whether such a person can quit upon a non-spiritual basis depends upon the extent to which he has already lost the power to choose whether he will drink or not. Many of us felt that we had plenty of character. There was a tremendous urge to cease forever. Yet we found it impossible. This is the baffling feature of alcoholism as we know it—this utter inability to leave it alone, no matter how great the necessity or the wish.

[More About Alcoholism p. 34]

CONSIDERATION

We are strong. We are smart. We are capable. We have shown the world we can do just about anything we set out to do. So why can't we stop drinking? What is the matter with us? We know we need to quit, and we know all we have to do is put down the bottle, but why can't we? Sure, we can stop for a while now and then, but we can't stop for good. This is the mystery of it—we want to quit with all our might, yet we cannot, no matter how hard we try.

Do I really believe that more wishing and hoping and praying will stop my uncontrollable drinking?

APRIL 12

MORE ABOUT ALCOHOLISM

What sort of thinking dominates an alcoholic who repeats time after time the desperate experiment of the first drink? Friends who have reasoned with him after a spree which has brought him to the point of divorce or bankruptcy are mystified when he walks directly into a saloon. Why does he? Of what is he thinking?

[More About Alcoholism p. 35]

CONSIDERATION

Why do we continue to drink when it is so clear to so many around us that we cannot drink normally? How many times do family, friends and even employers, lovingly or not so lovingly, beg us to stop drinking because of how we behave after we drink, and our inability to stop? How many times do we say to them "Yes, I know I have to cut down, and I promise it won't happen again?" Yet it happens again and again and again. We don't understand why we behave the way we do. We really don't know what is wrong with us, but we know something is wrong with us.

Do I really have any idea why I can't stop drinking?

MORE ABOUT ALCOHOLISM

Our first example is a friend we shall call Jim. This man has a charming wife and family. He inherited a lucrative automobile agency. He had a commendable World War record. He is a good salesman. Everybody likes him. He is an intelligent man, normal so far as we can see, except for a nervous disposition. He did no drinking until he was thirty-five. In a few years he became so violent when intoxicated that he had to be committed. On leaving the asylum he came into contact with us.

[More About Alcoholism p. 35]

CONSIDERATION

All of us know and love Jim, the used car salesman. In many ways, we are Jim. We are good people, care for our family and do our job well. Perhaps we served our country in war, and maybe we once owned our own business. Despite our outward appearance of tranquility, wholesomeness and good citizenry, inside we are intensely restless, irritable and discontented. We are not sure why; we seem to have been born that way. We fear drunken events that happened yesterday that we can't remember today. We worry what new disaster tomorrow will bring. The world owes us, and we aren't getting our due, so we ruminate over past injustices, real or imagined. We hold grudges against people, institutions and events that we presume have harmed us in some way. We discover that alcohol eases our anger, fear and pain. Eventually, we discover alcohol turns us into a person we never wanted to be.

Does alcohol turn me into the person I don't want to be?

APRIL 14

MORE ABOUT ALCOHOLISM

We told him what we knew of alcoholism and the answer we had found. He made a beginning. His family was re-assembled, and he began to work as a salesman for the business he had lost through drinking. All went well for a time, but he failed to enlarge his spiritual life. To his consternation, he found himself drunk half a dozen times in rapid succession.

[More About Alcoholism p. 35]

CONSIDERATION

Mind, body and spirit. Alcoholism ultimately destroys all three. Our body consumes alcohol and the allergy flares up, our mind churns through fears, resentments and failed relationships, and our spirit lies bankrupt, broken and dormant. Some days are more manageable than others. Sometimes we are less drunk than at other times, but eventually our life collapses into a cesspool of helpless and hopeless apathy. We stop caring. We make no effort to heal our body, mind or soul. Just give us another drink.

How many times have I tried to start my life over and failed?

APRIL 15

MORE ABOUT ALCOHOLISM

On each of these occasions we worked with him, reviewing carefully what had happened. He agreed he was a real alcoholic and in a serious condition. He knew he faced another trip to the asylum if he kept on. Moreover, he would lose his family for whom he had a deep affection.

[More About Alcoholism p. 36]

CONSIDERATION

Some say that once we admit and accept the fact that we are a real alcoholic, we can get sober and find a new way of living if we embrace the A.A. program and Fellowship, but that we must do it only for ourselves. While this may be theoretically true, many of us who try A.A. for the first time do not do it for ourselves. We do it for the sake of our spouses, children, and family, or perhaps for our employer or the courts. We are ashamed of our illness, but maybe for a moment, we are able to see how our actions affect those we care for or love. Some of us avoid suicide at the last minute by thinking of the hurt it will inflict on our loved ones as we get ready to pull the trigger or jump off a building. So we decide we'll get sober for them instead. It doesn't matter. Whatever gets us through the doors of A.A. is worth holding on to.

If I am not ready to get sober for myself, am I willing to do it for someone I love or care for?

APRIL 16

MORE ABOUT ALCOHOLISM

Yet he got drunk again. We asked him to tell us exactly how it happened. This is his story: "I came to work on Tuesday morning. I remember I felt irritated that I had to be a salesman for a concern I once owned. I had a few words with the brass, but nothing serious."

[More About Alcoholism p. 36]

CONSIDERATION

In this story of Jim the used car salesman, he arrives for work a day late, likely due to yesterday's hangover. He is resentful that he now must be a lowly employee of the company he once owned. He argues with his boss, probably not for the first time. Tired, sick, angry and emotionally fired up, he has already relapsed, so it's no surprise he drinks later on that day.

Am I able to recognize the stinking thinking that precedes my drinking?

APRIL 17

MORE ABOUT ALCOHOLISM

Then I decided to drive to the country and see one of my prospects for a car. On the way I felt hungry so I stopped at a roadside place where they have a bar. I had no intention of drinking. I just thought I would get a sandwich. I also had the notion that I might find a customer for a car at this place, which was familiar for I had been going to it for years. I had eaten there many times during the months I was sober. I sat down at a table and ordered a sandwich and a glass of milk.

[More About Alcoholism p. 36]

CONSIDERATION

Our friend Jim, tired and likely hung over from his long weekend binge, ashamed he has to work for the company he once owned and perpetually angry at his boss, sets out alone to a familiar roadside establishment to get some lunch. What could possibly go wrong? When we feel this way, even when our circumstances aren't exactly like Jim's, do we recognize these clear warning signs of drinking? When we are Hungry, Angry, Lonely and Tired (H-A-L-T), do we understand that this combination of feelings is almost always a guaranteed recipe for relapse?

How many times do I repress any warning signs of relapse, just so I can take that first drink?

APRIL 18

MORE ABOUT ALCOHOLISM

Still no thought of drinking. I ordered another sandwich and decided to have another glass of milk. "Suddenly the thought crossed my mind that if I were to put an ounce of whiskey in my milk it couldn't hurt me on a full stomach. I ordered a whiskey and poured it into the milk. I vaguely sensed I was not being any too smart, but felt reassured as I was taking the whiskey on a full stomach. The experiment went so well that I ordered another whiskey and poured it into more milk. That didn't seem to bother me so I tried another."

[More About Alcoholism p. 36]

CONSIDERATION

How easy it is for us to delude ourselves that we are able to drink normally. We try all sorts of clever ways to drink like gentlemen, and we get so excited when we discover one method we forgot we had already tried. Maybe this one will work, so let's have a go at it. We love trying these new experiments because maybe the next one will be the one that works. What do we have to lose anyway?

Do I still believe my next new experiment to control my drinking has any real chance of success?

APRIL 19

MORE ABOUT ALCOHOLISM

Thus started one more journey to the asylum for Jim. Here was the threat of commitment, the loss of family and position, to say nothing of that intense mental and physical suffering which drinking always caused him. He had much knowledge about himself as an alcoholic. Yet all reasons for not drinking were easily pushed aside in favor of the foolish idea that he could take whiskey if only he mixed it with milk! Whatever the precise definition of the word may be, we call this plain insanity. How can such a lack of proportion, of the ability to think straight, be called anything else?

[More About Alcoholism p. 36]

CONSIDERATION

Jim is headed for the inebriate asylum just like Bill W. was in "Bill's Story." Over time we get to know ourselves very well, and clearly understand on some level why we cannot and should not drink. But we drink anyway. Our thinking is disrupted and we become unable to make any rational decision or take any sensible action concerning alcohol. Insanity is doing the same thing over and over again and expecting different results, and it is a trademark of alcoholics. It is simply part of our illness.

Can I admit and accept that when it comes to false justifications for drinking, my thinking is truly insane?

APRIL 20

MORE ABOUT ALCOHOLISM

In some circumstances we have gone out deliberately to get drunk, feeling ourselves justified by nervousness, anger, worry, depression, jealousy or the like. But even in this type of beginning we are obliged to admit that our justification for a spree was insanely insufficient in the light of what always happened. We now see that when we began to drink deliberately, instead of casually, there was little serious or effective thought during the period of premeditation of what the terrific consequences might be.

[More About Alcoholism p. 37]

CONSIDERATION

No matter how we are feeling—happy, sad, mad or glad—we want to drink. Actually, we must drink, because we are addicted to alcohol. Our brain chemistry has profoundly changed as a result of our disease, and the continuous consumption of alcohol becomes the primary driving force in our life. Whether we choose to admit it or not, or choose to recognize it or not, there is always a momentary period of thinking before drinking. This premeditation period may last only a few seconds, or perhaps we have ruminated for weeks before taking that next drink. Regardless of the length of time we spend deceiving ourselves, we always end up yielding to the drink. Our brains exhausted, many of us simply give up thinking about it and say to ourselves "Let's just get this over with and take the drink." We have once again lost all control despite our best efforts.

Am I powerless over alcohol?

APRIL 21

MORE ABOUT ALCOHOLISM

Our behavior is as absurd and incomprehensible with respect to the first drink as that of an individual with a passion, say, for jay-walking. He gets a thrill out of skipping in front of fast-moving vehicles. He enjoys himself for a few years in spite of friendly warnings.

[More About Alcoholism p. 37]

CONSIDERATION

None of us becomes alcoholic after taking our very first drink in life. We need time, practice and persistence to move from being a moderate drinker, to a hard drinker, to a real alcoholic. Along the way, family or friends may express concern over our behavior during our journey, but no friendly or threatening admonishment slows us down. We start off drinking more for the thrill of it than the need for it. Even when we discover that our first drink always leads to another, and that our drunken actions often result in misadventure or harm, we persist. Each time we avoid catastrophe we are relieved. When something untoward happens, we quickly forget about it the next time we need a drink. Any risk of injury or death from drinking is rapidly overcome by our alcoholic obsession, leading to an overwhelming need for relief and our relentless determination to get it.

Am I still indifferent to the risks to myself and others when I pick up that first drink?

APRIL 22

MORE ABOUT ALCOHOLISM

Luck then deserts him and he is slightly injured several times in succession. You would expect him, if he were normal, to cut it out...He tries every known means to get the jay-walking idea out of his head. He shuts himself up in an asylum, hoping to mend his ways. But the day he comes out he races in front of a fire engine, which breaks his back. Such a man would be crazy, wouldn't he? We, who have been through the wringer, have to admit if we substituted alcoholism for jay-walking, the illustration would fit exactly. However intelligent we may have been in other respects, where alcohol has been involved, we have been strangely insane.

[More About Alcoholism p. 38]

CONSIDERATION

Long before we decide we must stop drinking, most of us are aware of the damage drinking does to ourselves and others. We are ashamed about our behavior when drinking, and feel guilty over the physical and emotional injuries we cause others. Despite these sentiments, we continue to drink because we must. When we see our fellow alcoholics and addicts die from our disease, it does not scare us into sobriety. We think, "That will never happen to me," and reach for the bottle once again. The insanity of this type of stinking thinking is another trademark of our illness.

Do I continue to delude myself that I alone am immune to the tragic outcomes of my fellow alcoholics?

MORE ABOUT ALCOHOLISM

But the actual or potential alcoholic, with hardly any exception, will be absolutely unable to stop drinking on the basis of self-knowledge. This is a point we wish to emphasize and re-emphasize, to smash home upon our alcoholic readers as it has been revealed to us out of bitter experience.

[More About Alcoholism p. 39]

CONSIDERATION

As we mature in our drinking career, most of us eventually come to the realization that once we take that first drink, we can never predict with certainty where we will end up. At times we plan to have two or three drinks with our friends and stop after that. And we do stop. At other times, having made the same resolution, we end up drinking ourselves into an alcoholic stupor. We never know beforehand how things will turn out. Yet knowing that we cannot predict what will happen to us after taking that first drink never stops us, because we always assume that being aware of the risk will be sufficient to prevent the inevitable outcome—this time.

Do I still believe that I can control my drinking based only on self-knowledge?

APRIL 24

MORE ABOUT ALCOHOLISM

Fred is a partner in a well-known accounting firm....a successful business man....Yet, he is alcoholic...We first saw Fred...in a hospital where he had gone to recover from a bad case of jitters. He made up his mind to quit drinking altogether. It never occurred to him that perhaps he could not do so, in spite of his character and standing. Fred would not believe himself an alcoholic, much less accept a spiritual remedy for his problem......He was positive that this humiliating experience, plus the knowledge he had acquired, would keep him sober the rest of his life. Self-knowledge would fix it.

[More About Alcoholism p. 39]

CONSIDERATION

Fred the accountant, like so many of us, suffers a variety of shameful and humiliating consequences after drinking. We know that drinking plays a role in our own misfortunes, but are determined to control ourselves better next time. Even though we understand that our first drink will lead to more drinks, something inside us says "If I just try harder using all the knowledge and will-power that I can muster, things will turn out differently. I won't get drunk next time, now that I know what alcohol can really do to me." Yet, we drink again, and get drunk again and again and again.

How many times do I have to take another first drink to be convinced that I will have no control over the next drink?

APRIL 25

MORE ABOUT ALCOHOLISM

We heard no more of Fred for a while...One day we were told that he was back in the hospital....here was a chap absolutely convinced he had to stop drinking, who had no excuse for drinking, who exhibited splendid judgment and determination in all his other concerns, yet was flat on his back nevertheless....[Later on] It was the end of a perfect day, not a cloud on the horizon. "I went to my hotel and leisurely dressed for dinner. As I crossed the threshold of the dining room, the thought came to mind that it would be nice to have a couple of cocktails with dinner. That was all. Nothing more. I ordered a cocktail and my meal."

[More About Alcoholism p. 41]

CONSIDERATION

Many of us are amazed at how quickly we return to drinking after barely surviving some fiasco caused by our past alcoholic antics. Maybe we end up in a hospital Emergency Room after injuring ourself in a drunken brawl or auto accident. Perhaps we are taken unwillingly to a detoxification or rehabilitation facility by concerned family or friends. Sometimes we get dragged off to a jail cell with no memory of how we got there. Yet as soon as we are free again, we stop at the liquor store or bar, or both, and start drinking again. We don't even think about it, we just order up a drink and go on as if nothing untoward had just happened to us.

Am I convinced that I have a thinking problem that drives my drinking problem?

APRIL 26

MORE ABOUT ALCOHOLISM

As soon as I regained my ability to think, I went carefully over that evening in Washington. Not only had I been off guard, I had made no fight whatever against the first drink. This time I had not thought of the consequences at all. I had commenced to drink as carelessly as though the cocktails were ginger ale….I knew from that moment that I had an alcoholic mind. I saw that will power and self-knowledge would not help in those strange mental blank spots.

[More About Alcoholism p. 41]

CONSIDERATION

Time after time after time, we never give a second thought about taking that first drink. We wish we'd stop and deliberate about taking that first drink, but when the moment arrives it just doesn't seem worth the trouble. We think, "Why should I bother to pause and think the drink through when I know deep down I'll end up getting drunk anyway? Why waste time trying to fight the inevitable? I may as well give in now and get it over with." If we think like this, we are truly alcoholic.

Do I remember exactly when I knew I could no longer control my drinking?

MORE ABOUT ALCOHOLISM

Two of the members of Alcoholics Anonymous came to see me....and then asked me if I thought myself alcoholic and if I were really licked this time....They piled on me heaps of evidence to the effect that an alcoholic mentality, such as I had exhibited....was [a] hopeless condition...This process snuffed out the last flicker of conviction that I could do the job myself.

[More About Alcoholism p. 42]

CONSIDERATION

Many of us remember the first time we spoke with another recovered alcoholic. Although the details of their story may not have been exactly the same as ours, we understood immediately how they thought and felt. At one time they had the same obsession to drink that we had, the craving for more as soon as they took that first drink, and the total inability to control their drinking or their lives after they started to imbibe. They felt the same guilt and shame as we did over their behavior while drinking. They were just as helpless and hopeless as we are now.

Have I been able to relate, on some level, with recovered alcoholics I have met?

APRIL 28

MORE ABOUT ALCOHOLISM

Then they outlined the spiritual answer and program of action which a hundred of them had followed successfully.....the program of action, though entirely sensible, was pretty drastic. It meant I would have to throw several lifelong conceptions out of the window. That was not easy. But the moment I made up my mind to go through with the process, I had the curious feeling that my alcoholic condition was relieved, as in fact it proved to be.

[More About Alcoholism p. 42]

CONSIDERATION

When we hear testimony from real alcoholics, we relate to their stories on some level. Once we connect with them, we feel that we can begin to trust them. As our trust grows, we come to believe that the solution they use for their alcoholism might just work for us. They explain that the A.A. program of action is something called the 12 Steps, and it involves hands on work on our part. The spiritual program of A.A. may not make complete sense to us in the beginning, but at least it doesn't seem too complicated an approach. Of course, since we have never tried these novel methods before, a fair amount of resistance, doubt and fear usually precedes the relief we later attain in the Fellowship.

Despite being unable to predict my outcome, do I have the courage to embark on the spiritual A.A. journey of recovery?

APRIL 29

MORE ABOUT ALCOHOLISM

Quite as important was the discovery that spiritual principles would solve all my problems. I have since been brought into a way of living infinitely more satisfying and, I hope, more useful than the life I lived before. My old manner of life was by no means a bad one, but I would not exchange its best moments for the worst I have now. I would not go back to it even if I could.

[More About Alcoholism p. 43]

CONSIDERATION

Early on in A.A. we don't know much about spiritual principles or the 12 Steps, or how they will solve any of our problems. All we really want to do is stop drinking, at least for a while. We certainly have no idea how the 12 Step program and the Fellowship can guide us into a new way of living. But once we are on the road to recovery, our life does start to change for the better. Little by little, hour by hour, day by day, we discover we are happier and better off clean and sober, despite all of life's vicissitudes that come our way.

Do I believe that I am better off with my new life than I was with my old one?

APRIL 30

MORE ABOUT ALCOHOLISM

Once more: The alcoholic at certain times has no effective mental defense against the first drink. Except in a few cases, neither he nor any other human being can provide such a defense. His defense must come from a Higher Power.

[More About Alcoholism p. 43]

CONSIDERATION

We try for years not to take that first drink, and fail. Spouses, parents, siblings, children, family, friends and others usually support us in our struggle to keep away from that first drink. Employers often pay for our addiction therapy. Priests and ministers gladly pray for our recovery. Rehabilitation centers we visit educate us on our illness. Yet none of the well-intentioned human efforts that we make, or that others make on our behalf can get us sober. No human will power alone is able to relieve our alcoholism, otherwise we'd be sober. Yet miraculously, we later discover that by accepting both human and spiritual aid, we can develop an effective mental defense against that first drink.

Have I admitted and fully accepted to my core the fact that my own will-power alone will not keep me away from that first drink?

MAY 1

WE AGNOSTICS

We hope we have made clear the distinction between the alcoholic and the non-alcoholic. If, when you honestly want to, you find you cannot quit entirely, or if when drinking, you have little control over the amount you take, you are probably alcoholic. If that be the case, you may be suffering from an illness which only a spiritual experience will conquer.

[We Agnostics p. 44]

CONSIDERATION

Some of us may be confused about whether or not we are a real alcoholic, despite years of evidence demonstrating that we are clearly alcoholic. Denying our addiction and pretending we can drink normally, or almost normally, is a common symptom of our illness. If we can't completely stop drinking for as long and as often as we wish, and if we can't control the amount of alcohol we consume every time we drink, we are most certainly alcoholic. If we keep wondering if we are alcoholic, remind ourselves that few normal drinkers ever wonder if they are alcoholic. Once we accept that we have failed to control our drinking by all the ways we have tried in the past, then some radical new approach is needed.

If I am an alcoholic, am I willing to try a different approach to my illness?

WE AGNOSTICS

To one who feels he is an atheist or agnostic such an experience seems impossible, but to continue as he is means disaster, especially if he is an alcoholic of the hopeless variety. To be doomed to an alcoholic death or to live on a spiritual basis are not always easy alternatives to face.

[We Agnostics p. 44]

CONSIDERATION

Our Big Book suggests that to recover from our alcoholic, hopeless state of mind and body, we need to have some type of spiritual experience or awakening. This means our attitudes and actions must change. We need to change how we think and what we do. If we can get sober on our own, or by some other method, then all the best for us. If we cannot, A.A. offers a spiritual solution if we are willing to sample it. Our natural reaction to trying something we don't understand and have never tried before is often negative. "It won't work for me," or "I'm different, not like all you other alcoholics," are common responses. Or maybe, "I'm too far gone," or "How can something I don't understand help me?" Fear of trying something new and unknown may make us hesitant and looking for excuses not to move forward, but down deep we know we are slowly dying and cannot go on much longer, so why not try something that might work for us?

Am I willing to try a new approach to my illness, despite my fears and doubts?

MAY 3

WE AGNOSTICS

If a mere code of morals or a better philosophy of life were sufficient to overcome alcoholism, many of us would have recovered long ago. But we found that such codes and philosophies did not save us, no matter how much we tried. We could wish to be moral, we could wish to be philosophically comforted, in fact, we could will these things with all our might, but the needed power wasn't there. Our human resources, as marshalled by the will, were not sufficient; they failed utterly.

[We Agnostics p. 44]

CONSIDERATION

We hate the fact we cannot not control our drinking by ourselves. We grit our teeth and summon up all our moral values and society standards, but they are of little practical help. Nothing seems to work. Since we can't control our drinking today, we pretend we might be able to control it tomorrow. How many times do we say to ourselves, "Next time will be different?" or "If I just try harder things will change?" Yet all our solitary efforts fail.

Have I ever been able to control my drinking, each and every time, by using my will-power alone?

MAY 4

WE AGNOSTICS

Lack of power, that was our dilemma. We had to find a power by which we could live, and it had to be a Power greater than ourselves. Obviously. But where and how were we to find this Power? Well, that's exactly what this book is about. Its main object is to enable you to find a Power greater than yourself which will solve your problem. That means we have written a book which we believe to be spiritual as well as moral. And it means, of course, that we are going to talk about God.

[We Agnostics p. 45]

CONSIDERATION

In our quiet moments, often after another unwanted or unexpected binge, we find that for a few seconds or a few minutes, we can be honest with ourselves. During these times we know we are licked, and that everything we have done thus far to control our drinking has failed. We also know that if we can't stop drinking for good, we will never be able to live the life we really want to live. Sure, we want to stop drinking, but what we really want is to find a way to fit in and live sober. And we secretly hope that a new way of living will quiet the chaos in our head, just as alcohol had done for us in the beginning. Our Big Book talks of a power greater than ourself that may be able to help us, and they call that power God. But for some of us, God is just an empty name and nothing more.

Do I still believe that I will be able to stop drinking and manage my life without additional help of some kind?

MAY 5

WE AGNOSTICS

Here difficulty arises with agnostics....his face falls when we speak of spiritual matters, especially when we mention God...We know how he feels....Some of us have been violently anti-religious. To others, the word "God" brought up a particular idea of Him with which someone had tried to impress them during childhood. Perhaps we rejected this particular conception because it seemed inadequate. With that rejection we imagined we had abandoned the God idea entirely.

[We Agnostics p. 45]

CONSIDERATION

In Christianity and other monotheistic religions, God is defined as the creator and ruler of the universe and source of all moral authority—the Supreme Being. In non-Christian religions, a god is a superhuman being or spirit worshiped as having power over nature and human fortunes. Atheism is not a disbelief in God or a denial of God; it is a lack of belief in God and gods. An agnostic is a person who claims neither belief nor disbelief in any god. Our book states that a spiritual solution will solve our problem, and in the next sentence starts talking about God, seeming to imply that spirituality requires believing in God. To make matters worse, Bill W. consistently interchanges Higher Power with God throughout all of the Big Book, making little distinction between the two. For most of us who grow up as Christians, the word God brings up memories of the church's commandments we were taught to worship as a child. Some of us retain our original concept of God, while others of us develop a totally different concept, or reject religious teachings entirely. Or maybe we just hadn't thought about God and religion much during our adulthood for whatever reason.

How do I feel when thinking about God?

MAY 6

WE AGNOSTICS

We were bothered with the thought that faith and dependence upon a Power beyond ourselves was somewhat weak, even cowardly....We looked askance at many individuals who claimed to be godly. How could a Supreme Being have anything to do with it all? And who could comprehend a Supreme Being anyhow? Yet, in other moments, we found ourselves thinking, when enchanted by a starlit night, "Who, then, made all this?" There was a feeling of awe and wonder, but it was fleeting and soon lost.

[We Agnostics p. 46]

CONSIDERATION

Although some of us feel that a person's belief in God or a spiritual Higher Power is a sign of weakness, most of us do not. Few judge another's religious beliefs; all we really care about are our own. Most of us go through a period in our life where we reflect on the existence of a god-like power greater than ourselves that may be able to direct and intervene in our lives. Our acceptance or rejection of this type of religious Higher Power is more often than not based on a feeling in our gut rather than some religious teaching or scientific or critical analysis. We either feel a connection with God or we don't. There is no need for us to judge or analyze our feelings; we just accept them. It's that simple.

What exactly are my thoughts and feelings about God?

MAY 7

WE AGNOSTICS

Yes, we of agnostic temperament have had these thoughts and experiences. Let us make haste to reassure you. We found that as soon as we were able to lay aside prejudice and express even a willingness to believe in a Power greater than ourselves, we commenced to get results, even though it was impossible for any of us to fully define or comprehend that Power, which is God.

[We Agnostics p. 46]

CONSIDERATION

In this paragraph Bill W. makes the point-blank declaration that A.A.'s Higher Power is God. We might, or might not, excuse the author by remembering that the Big Book is a historical document as well as an instruction manual, and that most, but not all, early A.A. members did adopt God as their Higher Power. In a general sense, alcoholics who are comfortable with their religious upbringing rarely have any difficulty returning to their previous Christian faith once sober, and using those beliefs to support their new way of living. For those who don't believe in God, or are unsure about the existence of any god, they are not precluded from discovering a spiritual Higher Power of their own understanding. Most atheists and agnostics have extremely strong beliefs about the significance of all living things in the universe, and how they relate to the spiritual and material world. We can appreciate that although God is always a Higher Power, a Higher Power is not always God. The experience of A.A. shows that however we define it, what matters is that we create and retain some type of non-material, spiritual power of our own understanding that we can connect with in order to help us stay sober.

Am I willing to do the work to identify, or create, my own spiritual power that I can use in recovery?

WE AGNOSTICS

Much to our relief, we discovered we did not need to consider another's conception of God. Our own conception, however inadequate, was sufficient to make the approach and to effect a contact with Him. As soon as we admitted the possible existence of a Creative Intelligence, a Spirit of the Universe underlying the totality of things, we began to be possessed of a new sense of power and direction, provided we took other simple steps.

[We Agnostics p. 46]

CONSIDERATION

Although our Big Book freely interchanges the word God with Higher Power, a forgiving reading makes it clear that God and our Higher Power may represent the same thing for some of us, but need not be the same for all of us. We need to discover and learn to connect with some type of spiritual Higher Power, or Higher Force, or Higher Purpose, or Higher Principles by which we can live our lives. The source of that power usually comes from something deep within us, but can easily be adopted from something outside of us. The only requirement is that it cannot be us. We are not God, we cannot be God, and we need to stop playing God. When we find a spiritual power with which we are able to develop a comfortable spiritual connection, one that can motivate us, guide us and give us strength as we move forward in our new way of life, then we will be well on our road to recovery.

Am I willing to examine and work with myself to actively seek some type of non-material spiritual force, purpose, principle or power that I can relate to?

MAY 9

WE AGNOSTICS

We found that God does not make too hard terms with those who seek Him. To us, the Realm of Spirit is broad, roomy, all inclusive; never exclusive or forbidding to those who earnestly seek. It is open, we believe, to all men.

[We Agnostics p. 46]

CONSIDERATION

Spirituality relates to, or affects the human spirit or soul, as opposed to material or physical things. It is a broad concept awash with dozens of definitions and perspectives. In general, it includes a sense of connection to something greater than ourselves, and it typically involves a search for meaning in life. As such, it is a universal human quest—something that touches all of us. People may describe spirituality as sacred or transcendent, or simply a deep sense of aliveness and interconnectedness. It may reflect universal goodness, or whatever force or principles drive us to be a decent person. Religious folks may find that their spiritual life is intricately linked to their association with a church, temple, mosque, or synagogue. Others may pray or find comfort in a direct personal relationship with God, or some other type of Higher Power. Still others seek meaning through inspirational connections to art or nature as a universal creative force. Like our sense of purpose, our personal meaning of spirituality may change throughout our life, adapting to our own experiences and relationships.

Do I believe that spirituality is open to me if I seek it?

MAY 10

WE AGNOSTICS

When, therefore, we speak to you of God, we mean your own conception of God. This applies, too, to other spiritual expressions which you find in this book. Do not let any prejudice you may have against spiritual terms deter you from honestly asking yourself what they mean to you. At the start, this was all we needed to commence spiritual growth, to affect our first conscious relation with God as we understood Him. Afterward, we found ourselves accepting many things which then seemed entirely out of reach. That was growth, but if we wished to grow we had to begin somewhere. So we used our own conception, however limited it was.

[We Agnostics p. 47]

CONSIDERATION

Although most of A.A.'s founders were traditional Christians, not all of them were. Even those that were Christian presumably had to re-examine their relationship with God during sobriety. We must develop and explore our own spiritual side rather than focusing solely on our material needs. Since the spiritual is everything that is not material, we have a broad area to examine, full of possibilities allowing us to define and connect with our own spiritual power. For some of us, our spiritual Higher Power is A.A. itself, perhaps as a Group-Of-Drunks or Good-Orderly-Direction. Or, our spiritual power may reflect the characteristics of our sponsor, or people we admire inside or outside the A.A. program. For others of us, our spiritual power may represent a Higher Purpose in life, much like the Golden Rule—learning how to treat others in the manner we would like to be treated. Perhaps our spiritual power rests on Higher Forces or Higher Principles in life, such as honesty, integrity, goodness, unselfishness, service, tolerance and love.

Have I been able to find my own spiritual power to incorporate into my life?

WE AGNOSTICS

We needed to ask ourselves but one short question. "Do I now believe, or am I even willing to believe, that there is a Power greater than myself?" As soon as a man can say that he does believe, or is willing to believe, we emphatically assure him that he is on his way. It has been repeatedly proven among us that upon this simple cornerstone a wonderfully effective spiritual structure can be built.

[We Agnostics p. 47]

CONSIDERATION

When we come to A.A. we have no idea how to stay sober and find a new way of life. Over time, as we meet more people in the Fellowship, they tell us that they have found God, or some other type of spiritual Higher Power of their own understanding to help them recover. Since they are sober and we are not, A.A. is some type of higher power in and of itself, just as King Alcohol had been our higher power for years. Bill W. had no clear idea how his friend Ebby Thacher had gotten sober when they reunited, but it was clear to him that Ebby was truly sober, and had used something other than his own will power and self-sufficiency to get him there. So for many of us, we can easily recognize that some type of power is working in the Fellowship, because the results are staring us in the face. Perhaps we cannot define or relate to that power yet, but we know it has to exist.

Can I honestly admit to myself that I am not all-powerful, and that I am not God?

MAY 12

WE AGNOSTICS

That was great news to us, for we had assumed we could not make use of spiritual principles unless we accepted many things on faith which seemed difficult to believe. When people presented us with spiritual approaches, how frequently did we all say, "I wish I had what that man has. I'm sure it would work if I could only believe as he believes. But I cannot accept as surely true the many articles of faith which are so plain to him." So it was comforting to learn that we could commence at a simpler level.

[We Agnostics p. 47]

CONSIDERATION

It is natural that early on some of us feel that we must believe exactly what others in the Fellowship believe; otherwise, we will never get sober. We presume we must adopt and accept whatever Higher Power those "who have what we want" have in order to find a new way of living. Since Bill Wilson's Higher Power was God, we might assume that believing in God, or some other traditional, religious god, is required for us to recover. We fear we must force ourselves to believe in something others believe in but we don't, or we will never make it in A.A. Requiring that we conform to the religious beliefs of those who came before us in the Fellowship is implied in this chapter, but it is not true. The simple fact is that we can believe or not believe whatever we want, if it helps us recover.

Do I understand that to have my new life, I do not have to believe in the same God, Higher Power or spiritual power anyone else in A.A. believes in?

MAY 13

WE AGNOSTICS

Faced with alcoholic destruction, we soon became as open minded on spiritual matters as we had tried to be on other questions. In this respect alcohol was a great persuader. It finally beat us into a state of reasonableness. Sometimes this was a tedious process; we hope no one else will be prejudiced for as long as some of us were.

[We Agnostics p. 48]

CONSIDERATION

Most of us spend years trying to get sober on our own, and we fail. All of our efforts, persistent and creative as they are, cannot remove our obsession to drink and the craving for more that always follows that first drink. Every time we square off with our drinking, we get knocked to the floor. We lay there a while, then slowly bend our knees and arms and wobble back up to our feet once more. In no time, we are back on the floor, smacked down by an unwanted higher power far greater than we are—King Alcohol.

How many times must I hit the floor before I stop trying to get up?

MAY 14

WE AGNOSTICS

When, however, the perfectly logical assumption is suggested that underneath the material world and life as we see it, there is an All Powerful, Guiding, Creative Intelligence, right there our perverse streak comes to the surface and we laboriously set out to convince ourselves it isn't so. We read wordy books and indulge in windy arguments, thinking we believe this universe needs no God to explain it. Were our contentions true, it would follow that life originated out of nothing, means nothing, and proceeds nowhere.

[We Agnostics p. 49]

CONSIDERATION

No one knows for certain how we and our world came to be or what it all means, but we each have our own idea. Our opinion may reflect the beliefs of the various religious denominations, or they may not. Perhaps there is an all-powerful, personal god directing our life, or maybe our universe is simply driven by nature, physics and random chance. Either view, or any view in-between, does not preclude us from creating and connecting with some type of spiritual power, or force within or outside of ourself, to aid us during our journey in recovery.

Do I understand that I do not have to decipher how life began or why we are here on Earth in order to develop and relate to a spiritual power of my own understanding?

MAY 15

WE AGNOSTICS

Instead of regarding ourselves as intelligent agents, spearheads of God's ever advancing Creation, we agnostics and atheists chose to believe that our human intelligence was the last word, the alpha and the omega, the beginning and end of all. Rather vain of us, wasn't it?

[We Agnostics p. 49]

CONSIDERATION

We must remember that our Big Book reflects A.A.'s robust preference for God as their Higher Power since most of the early members were white Protestants, and many had participated in the Evangelical Christian Oxford Group movement, from whence A.A. sprang. Most atheists and agnostics, like most Christians, have very strong beliefs about their place in the universe and the reason they exist. Few believe that human intelligence is the final word in life's puzzle. Not believing in God has nothing to do with not believing in living a spiritual way of life. One man's Higher Power may be God, another's may be Mohammad, or Allah, or HaShem, or one of the hundreds of Hindu gods. Others may follow the god-less Buddhist path, or that of Confucius. Some choose to follow no prescribed religious path or set of beliefs. Instead, their Higher Power is not a thing, but an idea—a Higher Force, or Higher Purpose, or a set of Higher Principles. Vanity has nothing to do with what we believe in; it only exists if we declare our own religious or spiritual beliefs as the only correct beliefs.

Do I still mistakenly think my Higher Power must be God in order to get sober?

MAY 16

WE AGNOSTICS

We, who have traveled this dubious path, beg you to lay aside prejudice, even against organized religion. We have learned that whatever the human frailties of various faiths may be, those faiths have given purpose and direction to millions. People of faith have a logical idea of what life is all about. Actually, we used to have no reasonable conception whatever.

[We Agnostics p. 49]

CONSIDERATION

Most atheists and agnostics are people of deep faith, even though their faith may not reflect a belief in God or the doctrines of a specific religion. Faith means having complete trust or confidence in someone or something, and can be religious or spiritual in nature. In reality, religious people have no more idea of what our existence is about than non-religious people. Neither can prove their way is the right way, or the only way. What matters for alcoholics in recovery is that we learn how to develop a closer connection with whatever spiritual force or power we believe in. However we define our beliefs or faith does not release us from alcoholism. It is the depth of our connection with our human and spiritual natures that eventually frees and heals, as long as it is incorporated into selfless, constructive actions for others.

Can I cast aside my prejudice against any form of faith other than my own?

MAY 17

WE AGNOSTICS

In our personal stories you will find a wide variation in the way each teller approaches and conceives of the Power which is greater than himself. Whether we agree with a particular approach or conception seems to make little difference. Experience has taught us that these are matters about which, for our purpose, we need not be worried. They are questions for each individual to settle for himself.

[We Agnostics p. 50]

CONSIDERATION

Dozens of A.A. members share their experiences through the stories in the back of the Big Book. Reading of how the authors come to surrender to their illness, find and join A.A., discover and define their own Higher Power, and begin the road to recovery is a moving event for many of us. We may not relate to the details of each story, or agree with their religious beliefs, but most of us relate to how the writers tell of their descent into despair and the hope they find after coming to A.A. When speaking of their God or Higher Power, it is clear that each author finds one suited to their makeup and needs, and uses that power to motivate them, guide them and give them strength in sobriety.

Have I taken the time to read a few of the stories in the back of the Big Book?

MAY 18

WE AGNOSTICS

On one proposition, however, these men and women are strikingly agreed. Every one of them has gained access to, and believe in, a Power greater than himself. This Power has in each case accomplished the miraculous, the humanly impossible.

[We Agnostics p. 50]

CONSIDERATION

Most in A.A. say that they would not be sober today without the help of God or some type of spiritual force or energy in their lives. Our book suggests that our human power, alone, cannot relieve our alcoholism. This is not surprising. If any of us had found the power to stop our drinking forever, and learned how to live a new life all by ourselves, why would we be in A.A.? We need help and direction. We cannot figure everything out on our own. We learn we need something outside of ourself, or deep down within ourself, to help us treat our illness. We also learn that no God or spiritual power alone is sufficient for our recovery; we must take additional steps and actions to stop drinking completely and start over with our life. Faith, religion and spirituality alone are totally insufficient.

Do I truly believe that some type of spiritual power beyond my own self-will is needed for my sobriety?

WE AGNOSTICS

Here are thousands of men and women, worldly indeed. They flatly declare that since they have come to believe in a Power greater than themselves, to take a certain attitude toward that Power, and to do certain simple things, there has been a revolutionary change in their way of living and thinking. In the face of collapse and despair, in the face of the total failure of their human resources, they found that a new power, peace, happiness, and sense of direction flowed into them.

[We Agnostics p. 50]

CONSIDERATION

It is impossible to deny the success of A.A. for millions of alcoholics. So many men and women, just like us, beaten down by King Alcohol, consumed with the obsession to drink, being totally unable to stop drinking on our own, without any hope for relief and driven to the brink of suicide, gradually find a way out by following the simple instructions of the A.A. program. We learn that we can't lick alcoholism on our own; we don't have the power. We actually need two powers—the power of the Fellowship and a spiritual power of our own creation—that is anything but us. The Fellowship provides us with a community of experience and human support, including a sponsor that will guide us through the Big Book and the 12 Step program of A.A. Our spiritual power, born out of our own understanding and choosing, provides us with whatever spiritual motivation, strength and guidance we need to change our attitudes and actions, to change the way we are living, and to celebrate a new, wonderful way of life.

Am I willing to draw on the two powers I need for recovery—the human and spiritual?

MAY 20

WE AGNOSTICS

When we saw others solve their problems by a simple reliance upon the Spirit of the Universe, we had to stop doubting the power of God. Our ideas did not work. But the God idea did.

[We Agnostics p. 52]

CONSIDERATION

Since most of the first seventy or so members of A.A. were Christian, God and their Higher Power were one and the same, which may explain why The Big Book refers to God over 140 times, but to a Higher Power only twice. In addition, this chapter and most of the Big Book freely interchange the terms God and Higher Power, implying they are the same thing, when they are not. Atheists, agnostics, free-thinkers and other non-believers never call their Higher Power God. Many non-religious members choose to replace the term God with Higher Power, or Higher Force, or Higher Principles, or Spiritual Power, or with the word Good, or some other term which allows them to more directly connect with their unique non-material, spiritual side. Regardless of what we call our spiritual power, few of us can ignore the mental and emotional benefits we receive, provided we are able to form some type of personal connection with our spirituality.

Have I stopped being confused, irritated or intimidated by the word God in the Big Book?

WE AGNOSTICS

We agnostics and atheists were sticking to the idea that self-sufficiency would solve our problems. When others showed us that "God-sufficiency" worked with them, we began to feel like those who had insisted the Wrights would never fly.

[We Agnostics p. 52]

CONSIDERATION

No one who ever participates in A.A. does not, at some point, try to rely solely on their own will power to solve their alcohol problem and better manage their own lives. When this doesn't work, we seek some other solution. Hearing through other alcoholics' experiences that they have recovered using a spiritual solution, we are naturally skeptical. But most of us keep listening and hoping anyway, just as Bill W. did when Ebby T. shared how he recovered in "Bill's Story." When we begin to supplement our human will with our spiritual will, however we define it, so that we are no longer totally self-reliant, we find we can stop drinking and start to live life in a completely new and better way.

When I question the A.A. solution, am I able to continue to listen with an open mind and tolerant attitude?

MAY 22

WE AGNOSTICS

Logic is great stuff. We like it. We still like it. It is not by chance we were given the power to reason, to examine the evidence of our sense, and to draw conclusions. That is one of man's magnificent attributes. We agnostically inclined would not feel satisfied with a proposal which does not lend itself to reasonable approach and interpretation. Hence we are at pains to tell why we think our present faith is reasonable, why we think it more sane and logical to believe than not to believe, why we say our former thinking was soft and mushy when we threw up our hands in doubt and said, "We don't know."

[We Agnostics p. 53]

CONSIDERATION

Denial means I don't have a problem. Delusion means I can fix myself by myself. Defiance means no one is going to tell me what to do. Denial, delusion and defiance; these are three consistent traits of all alcoholics. Such barriers to sobriety and adopting a spiritual power must be eliminated so we can become honest, open and willing enough to accept the A.A. 12 Step solution. We need to find some source of power, other than our own, that will help relieve our alcoholism. For years alcohol was our only source of power to survive life. Alcohol was undeniably our Higher Power because we couldn't stop drinking. King Alcohol, whether we like to admit it or not, drove us to drink even when we didn't want to, directing and ruling our lives and seemingly solving all our problems, at least when we were drunk. Using what little was left of our brains at the time, we tried all sorts of crazy experiments to stop drinking and none of them worked. So we ended up hopeless, helpless, lost, confused, frustrated, angry, anxious, depressed, fearful and suicidal. We had to find some power greater than King Alcohol to live by.

Can I turn off the noise and chaos in my brain long enough to hear the A.A. message?

MAY 23

WE AGNOSTICS

When we became alcoholics, crushed by a self-imposed crises we could not postpone or evade, we had to fearlessly face the proposition that either God is everything or else He is nothing. God either is or He isn't. What was our choice to be?

[We Agnostics p. 53]

CONSIDERATION

Once we progress from being a hard drinker to a real alcoholic, we acquire the illness of alcoholism. Just as a person is not considered to be a diabetic until his system can no longer manage his metabolism of sugar, we develop a medical malady when we can no longer handle alcohol like normal people. Unfortunately for us, there is no medical solution. No pill or surgery can save us. Some other method is required. Although we, like the diabetic, are never cured of our disease, there is life-saving treatment available in A.A. For alcoholics, our long-term treatment is spiritual, not medical. This does not mean we cannot benefit from working with medical professionals, but most find any medical aid must be accompanied by a spiritual approach to our illness. And the foundation of our spiritual approach is a belief in a spiritual power of our own choosing. No one knows for certain whether God is or isn't, so being asked to make that Hobson's choice is pointless, irrelevant and a waste of time. But we do know that the A.A. experience has shown that if we use some type of spiritual power of our own creation and understanding, however we define it, combined with the other action tools of the Fellowship and A.A. program to treat our disease, we can recover.

Am I willing to treat my illness using a spiritual approach?

MAY 24

WE AGNOSTICS

Arrived at this point, we were squarely confronted with the question of faith. We couldn't duck the issue. Some of us had already walked far over the Bridge of Reason toward the desired shore of faith.

[We Agnostics p. 53]

CONSIDERATION

Faith does not mean being religious. Faith simply means believing without needing proof, such as "I have faith my mother will always love me," or "I have faith the sun will rise in the morning." Few of us initially have any faith that we can recover. But when we walk for the first time into the rooms of A.A., there is some type of faith at work even though we may not know it. Somehow we believe that maybe, just maybe, the Fellowship can help us. We hear others speak of how they recovered using a power greater than themselves in addition to their own human power. Over time, we begin to trust those in the Fellowship who say they have recovered by believing that their own conception of a spiritual Higher Power can help them, has helped them, and will continue to help them.

Do I trust those in the Fellowship enough to believe that what they tell me is true?

WE AGNOSTICS

We found, too, that we had been worshippers. What a state of mental goose-flesh that used to bring on! Had we not variously worshipped people, sentiment, things, money, and ourselves? And then, with a better motive, had we not worshipfully beheld the sunset, the sea, or a flower? Who of us had not loved something or somebody? How much did these feelings, these loves, these worships, have to do with pure reason? Little or nothing, we saw at last. Were not these things the tissue out of which our lives were constructed? Did not these feelings, after all, determine the course of our existence? It was impossible to say we had no capacity for faith, or love, or worship. In one form or another we had been living by faith and little else.

[We Agnostics p. 54]

CONSIDERATION

The feelings and emotions we generate from observing the world around us may cause us to reflect on life, death, the universe, and our place in all of it. We form certain opinions, or beliefs, during our musings, and those beliefs tend to change a bit over time. Whether or not our beliefs transform into faith depends on the individual. If we are unsure about our beliefs, they remain beliefs. If we become certain in our beliefs, then we have faith. Faith is our belief that something is true even though we can't prove it. Worship, by definition, involves actively praising a deity, an idol, or a sacred object, and is basically a religious term. Few alcoholics describe themselves as worshippers of alcohol or anything else, whether drunk or sober. We tend instead to obsess, covet and crave, mainly when it comes to our instinctual demands for money, power, property and prestige. These selfish and self-centered character defects often persist long after our last drink.

Am I confusing the conventional rituals of religious worship with having faith in a spiritual power of my own understanding?

MAY 26

WE AGNOSTICS

Imagine life without faith! Were nothing left but pure reason, it wouldn't be life. But we believed in life—of course we did. We could not prove life in the sense that you can prove a straight line is the shortest distance between two points, yet, there it was. Could we still say the whole thing was nothing but a mass of electrons, created out of nothing, meaning nothing, whirling on to a destiny of nothingness? Of course we couldn't.

[We Agnostics p. 54]

CONSIDERATION

Most of us believe in all sorts of things we cannot prove. Science explains how the Earth revolves around the sun, but it is faith that leads us to believe the sun will rise again tomorrow just as it has for as long as we can remember. We believe in life because we are alive, even though we don't understand every aspect of our existence. However, what each of us believes, without proof, about the origins and meaning of life, is as varied as there are people on this Earth. Some of us believe we began as nothing and will end as nothing, as in ashes to ashes and dust to dust. Others believe life has a purpose unique to each of us. Still others believe in God which is personal to their life plans by guiding, directing and actively intervening in their daily activities. Others don't. What our personal beliefs are do not matter in A.A., as long as we are able to believe in something religious or spiritual which we are willing to use to help us along our journey of recovery. We don't have to figure out why we exist or how the world was formed. All we need to do is come to believe in a power of our own choosing that is not us, is greater than we are, and is something we can connect with and use for strength and guidance as we live out our sober days.

Am I able to put my trust in some type of spiritual power of my own choosing?

WE AGNOSTICS

Actually we were fooling ourselves, for deep down in every man, woman, and child, is the fundamental idea of God. It may be obscured by calamity, by pomp, by worship of other things, but in some form or other it is there. For faith in a Power greater than ourselves, and miraculous demonstrations of that power in human lives, are facts as old as man himself. We finally saw that faith in some kind of God was a part of our make-up, just as much as the feeling we have for a friend. Sometimes we had to search fearlessly, but He was there. He was as much a fact as we were. We found the Great Reality deep down within us. In the last analysis it is only there that He may be found. It was so with us.

[We Agnostics p. 55]

CONSIDERATION

Anything that is not material, that cannot be seen, heard, smelled, touched or tasted, is spiritual. The realm of the spiritual includes our beliefs and faith about everything non-material. We cannot directly see or touch love, goodness, honesty, tolerance, sacrifice or compassion, but we can see those spiritual traits displayed through others. We believe in them, and know them in our minds and hearts even though we cannot bottle them up and put them on a shelf. All of us have some type of spiritual force working in our lives, and it often comes from somewhere inside of us. Nothing and no one can impose or force spirituality on us from the outside. What exactly that spirituality looks and feels like is unique to each of us. What we learn to do is to search out our own spiritual nature, whatever that is, and begin to embrace it.

Am I willing to search for, embrace and use my own spirituality in recovery?

MAY 28

WE AGNOSTICS

We can only clear the ground a bit. If our testimony helps sweep away prejudice, enables you to think honestly, encourages you to search diligently within yourself, then, if you wish, you can join us on the Broad Highway. With this attitude you cannot fail. The consciousness of your belief is sure to come to you.

[We Agnostics p. 55]

CONSIDERATION

Our book suggests "seek and ye shall find" in the biblical Christian tradition. How we seek and what we find may or may not have anything to do with any religion or the church of our childhood. There is no requirement in A.A. that our Higher Power be the God that was so familiar to the A.A. founders, or be the Muslim god Allah, or be any of the Hindu gods. Our Higher Power doesn't have to be a god. The spiritual power of our choosing can be an idea or concept, such as a Higher Principle, Higher Force or Higher Purpose in our lives. It could be Goodness, or The Golden Rule. It could be art or music or any creative, expressive force. It could be life itself—all living things. It could be the power represented by the entire A.A. Fellowship. It could be anything we want it to be, as long as we can form a conscious contact with it, and find a way to use it to ultimately help us help others to stay sober.

Am I willing to seek my own non-material Higher Power, or spiritual power, and not be swayed or intimidated by what others in A.A. believe or say on this topic?

MAY 29

WE AGNOSTICS

You will read the experience of a man who thought he was an atheist...a minister's son...he became rebellious at...an overdose of religious education...One night, when confined in a hospital, he was approached by an alcoholic who had known a spiritual experience. Our friend's gorge rose as he bitterly cried out: "If there is a God, He certainly hasn't done anything for me!" But later, alone in his room, he asked himself this question: "Is it possible that all the religious people I have known are wrong?" While pondering the answer he felt as though he lived in hell. Then, like a thunderbolt, a great thought came. It crowded out all else: "Who are you to say there is no God?"

[We Agnostics p. 55]

CONSIDERATION

We can't force, control, or manipulate our feelings or beliefs about God or religion; we just have them. We cannot make ourselves believe something we don't believe in, and no one else can either. None of our beliefs are right or wrong. We can have God or not have God. If we have no god, it does not mean we are not caring, kind, good people, or that we cannot get sober in A.A. No one can prove their religious beliefs are better or more legitimate than our spiritual beliefs. Whatever we feel, after a thoughtful and honest soul searching, is what we are left with. Although we may refine and grow in our beliefs over time, our core faith, or lack of it, in God or religion is unlikely to change. Some of us, like Bill W., may experience an exceptional, sudden, rare, overwhelming white light event which totally redirects our beliefs and faith, but almost none of us do. So we are left with discovering, defining and holding on to whatever spiritual force we choose to walk with us through recovery.

Am I willing to choose my own spiritual power, defined and conceived as I alone am able, and not feel obligated to adopt someone else's choice of God or their Higher Power?

MAY 30

WE AGNOSTICS

This man recounts that he tumbled out of bed to his knees. In a few seconds he was overwhelmed by a conviction of the Presence of God. It poured over and through him with the certainty and majesty of a great tide at flood. The barriers he had built through the years were swept away. He stood in the Presence of Infinite Power and Love. He had stepped from bridge to shore. For the first time, he lived in conscious companionship with his Creator. Thus was our friend's cornerstone fixed in place. No later vicissitude has shaken it. His alcoholic problem was taken away.

[We Agnostics p. 56]

CONSIDERATION

Bill Wilson's sudden white light, or hot flash episode at Towns Hospital in 1934 was strikingly similar to the religious revelation his alcoholic grandfather Willie Wilson had on top of Mt. Aeolus in East Dorset, Vermont. When the Big Book was first published, many alcoholic readers felt they could not get sober without going through the same type of comparable religious conversion that Bill W. and his grandfather had, and as generally described in William James' *Varieties of Religious Experience*. Bill's subsequent Big Book addition of "Appendix II—Spiritual Experience," suggested no such white light episode was required for recovery. "Appendix II" describes the slower spiritual awakening which comes to most of us in the form of a gradual change in our attitudes and actions as we progress through recovery after joining the Fellowship and completing the 12 Steps. Either path leads to the same result—a realization that with help from our fellows and our own spiritual power, however we experience or define it, we can be freed from alcohol and acquire a new way of living.

Have I begun to have that change in attitude and action that defines my spiritual awakening?

MAY 31

WE AGNOSTICS

What is this but a miracle of healing? Yet its elements are simple. Circumstances made him willing to believe. He humbly offered himself to his Maker—then he knew. Even so has God restored us all to our right minds. To this man, the revelation was sudden. Some of us grow into it more slowly. But He has come to all who have honestly sought Him.

[We Agnostics p. 57]

CONSIDERATION

We need two powers for sobriety and a new way of life—human and spiritual. Unless we are able to connect our head and our heart with the human power of the Fellowship and the spiritual power of our own choosing, change will not come easily. Relying solely on our own will power to cast off our alcoholic obsession and behavior does not work very well, as alcoholics have proven to themselves through years of failed effort. We need help, and we need to ask for it and accept it. A.A. provides us that help through the human Fellowship of meetings, home groups, sponsorship and service work. It provides us with a new design for living through directions given in the Big Book and the 12 Steps. If we adopt and practice the spiritual A.A. program, we can recover from that seemingly hopeless state of mind and body that defined our thinking and our drinking. Together, the power of the Fellowship and the spiritual power of our own choosing will lead the way.

Can I embrace all the power of A.A.?

JUNE 1

HOW IT WORKS

Rarely have we seen a person fail who has thoroughly followed our path. Those who do not recover are people who cannot or will not completely give themselves to this simple program, usually men and women who are constitutionally incapable of being honest with themselves. There are such unfortunates. They are not at fault; they seem to have been born that way. They are naturally incapable of grasping and developing a manner of living which demands rigorous honesty. Their chances are less than average. There are those, too, who suffer from grave emotional and mental disorders, but many of them do recover if they have the capacity to be honest.

[How It Works p. 58]

CONSIDERATION

No one really knows why some people are able to recover in A.A. and others are not. There are probably a hundred reasons, and why does not really matter. What matters is the fact that almost anyone can recover using the A.A. program. Being honest with ourselves so we can be honest with others is the principle of the first Step. If we can do this, we have a chance. Shame and fear often prevent us from honestly looking at our past and present behavior. In overcoming these roadblocks, we may not like what we find, but we will have started on the broad highway of recovery. If we are unable or unwilling to take this first Step, for whatever reason, perhaps we will be able to do so in the future, or we may be able to recover from our illness in some other way.

Do I have the capacity and courage to be honest with myself?

JUNE 2

HOW IT WORKS

Our stories disclose in a general way what we used to be like, what happened, and what we are like now. If you have decided you want what we have and are willing to go to any length to get it—then you are ready to take certain steps. At some of these we balked. We thought we could find an easier, softer way. But we could not. With all the earnestness at our command, we beg of you to be fearless and thorough from the very start. Some of us have tried to hold on to our old ideas and the result was nil until we let go absolutely.

[How It Works p. 58]

CONSIDERATION

Our Fellowship is one of personal support, witnessing and sharing. We tell our stories of what we were like, what happened, and how we came to be where we are today. Most of us who recover in A.A. do so by first asking for help and being willing to accept it. We become willing to follow directions and instructions on how to get sober and find a new way of living. That means we must do the work of the 12 Steps, which is A.A.'s program of recovery. Few relish the time, effort and stress of going through the 12 Steps with a sponsor, but our own experiments seeking sobriety have not worked. Successful recovery requires being all in. Sticking our toe in the water doesn't work. We have to jump in the pool, even if we hold our nose while doing so.

Am I willing to go all in with A.A.?

JUNE 3

HOW IT WORKS

Remember that we deal with alcohol—cunning, baffling, powerful! Without help it is too much for us. But there is One who has all power— that One is God. May you find Him now! Half measures availed us nothing. We stood at the turning point. We asked His protection and care with complete abandon. Here are the steps we took, which are suggested as a program of recovery.

[How It Works p. 58]

CONSIDERATION

To embark on recovery takes courage, honesty, humility and commitment. We crack open the door and see a long dark corridor with no light at the end. Strange sounds and smells emerge, and we are scared. No one pushes us into the passageway, but our fellows tell us we will be safe. We are not so sure. It is only through faith—that belief in something we cannot prove—that gives us the courage and strength to take our first step down that dark passageway. Perhaps our faith comes from God, or some other religious or spiritual power of our own understanding. Or maybe our faith comes from the belief that it is simply our only way out, and we sense we have nothing to lose by trying. Perhaps we step forward because our love for another drives us on, or maybe we feel it's just the right thing for us to do at the time. The reason doesn't matter, but the action does.

Using whatever tools I have at this moment, can I muster all my strength and courage to start the 12 Step work of A.A.?

JUNE 4

HOW IT WORKS

Step 1 — We admitted we were powerless over alcohol—that our lives had become unmanageable.

[How It Works p. 59]

HONESTY, ACCEPTANCE, SURRENDER

It is suggested that we take all the 12 Steps of A.A. in order, with a competent and experienced sponsor who has solid sobriety and has already been through the Steps. This approach makes sense, because it is easy to get lost and sidetracked by going it alone. In Step One we get honest and accept the reality of our addiction to alcohol. We obsess over drinking, can't control it once we start, can't stop forever, and our lives are a mess. Surrender follows acceptance. We're being honest. We accept that we're alcoholic. We give up. We accept, and then we surrender. Remember that our addiction is a fact, not an emotion or judgement. It just exists. The fact of our alcoholism has no power in and of itself, but we can give it the power to move us forward, especially if we are drowning in pain and shame. Even though we are powerless over alcohol once we start drinking, we are not powerless over not drinking after we stop. If we can stop long enough to fully engage in A.A., that's a good start on our road to recovery.

Do I have a desire to stop drinking, or at least to change the way I'm feeling and living?

HOW IT WORKS

Step 2 — Came to believe that a Power greater than ourselves could restore us to sanity.

Step 3 — Made a decision to turn our will and our lives over to the care of God as we understood him.

[How It Works p. 58]

GOD, HIGHER POWER, FAITH & BELIEF

Once we admit and accept that we have an addiction to alcohol and a desire to stop drinking, or at least to stop the pain and insanity related to our drinking, we find we need help from the Fellowship and some type of spiritual power of our own creation to recover. We are unable to recover on our own, otherwise we would have done so by now. No one who loves us has been able to get us sober. Like it or not, we need spiritual help in addition to human help. This is a tall order. We are being asked to accept human aid from other alcoholics, and spiritual aid from whatever spiritual power we can muster. We find we have little difficulty accepting help from our fellows, but we may not be sure how to accept spiritual help, or what that even means. Never give up. Most of us, when working with a capable, experienced, open-minded sponsor who has common sense, start learning about the spiritual side of ourselves as we take our first steps, even if we don't completely understand how it all works.

Am I willing to put aside my doubts and fears long enough to examine my own understanding of a spiritual Higher Power?

JUNE 6

HOW IT WORKS

Step 4 — Made a searching and fearless moral inventory of ourselves.

Step 5 — Admitted to God, to ourselves, and to another human being the exact nature of our wrongs.

Step 6 — Were entirely ready to have God remove all these defects of character.

Step 7 — Humbly asked Him to remove our shortcomings.

[How It Works p. 59]

INVENTORY, CONFESSION & HUMILITY

Putting pen to paper in Step Four is the first tangible product of our 12 Step work, and easily ties into our upcoming Step Eight amends list. There is no reason to postpone, evade or fear the writing process, since it liberates us from the secrets and demons of our past. It allows us to free ourselves, finally and forever, from years of pent up lies, guilt, shame and buried emotions. Our moral inventory defines what is right and what is wrong in our past behavior, and unless we are severely mentally ill, we know the difference between right and wrong. So there is no legitimate reason we cannot honestly and objectively review our past actions, especially as they relate to our resentments, fears, sex relations and people we have harmed. After writing our grudge list, we discover that our role in them is driven by several common character defects: selfishness, dishonesty, resentment and fear. We always play a major part in our selfish and self-centered shortcomings, and those are what block us from enjoying a better life. So we ask for Fellowship and spiritual help to become willing to address our defects, mend our ways, and do our human part in making a conscious effort to change our attitudes and actions toward our fellows. Our Step Four work is critical to our sobriety and gaining a new life, and experience has shown it cannot be successfully avoided.

Can I put aside all my excuses for not doing a moral inventory and get to work?

JUNE 7

HOW IT WORKS

Step 8 — Made a list of all persons we had harmed, and became willing to make amends to them all.

Step 9 — Made direct amends to such people wherever possible, except when to do so would injure them or others.

[How It Works p. 59]

RESTITUTION

Our self-examination in Step Four and sharing in Step Five prepares us for the actions required in Steps Eight and Nine. Once we have completed our homework for Step Four, it is a relief to be able to share it with a trusted sponsor or safe person of our choice who is experienced with the A.A. recovery process. Our sponsor's review of our inventory enables us to recognize parts of ourself previously hidden or suppressed. Sharing our past often relieves much of the shame and guilt over our past conduct. However, talking about our wrongs of the past is not enough. If we want a new way of life, we must take specific action, as best we can, to make restitution for our destructive past behavior and most importantly, to mend our ways, or change our behavior, going forward. A good sponsor can help us here too, by guiding us through the privilege of making amends to those we have harmed. For many of us, as we make our amends, we feel relieved of the obsession to drink and a great weight is lifted from our shoulders. Self-esteem and dignity begin to return. We start to fit in and feel more a part of the human race.

Can I face the temporary anxiety, fear and pain of offering restitution in order to move forward into a new way of life?

JUNE 8

HOW IT WORKS

Step 10 — Continued to take personal inventory and when we were wrong promptly admitted it.

Step 11 — Sought through prayer and meditation to improve our conscious contact with God as we understood him, praying only for knowledge of His will for us and the power to carry that out.

Step 12 — Having had a spiritual awakening as the result of these steps, we tried to carry this message to alcoholics, and to practice these principles in all our affairs.

[How It Works p. 59]

MAINTENANCE, CONTINUANCE & SERVICE

The last three Steps build on the previous nine Steps. If we do an honest, thorough and complete job the first time on Steps One through Nine, there is usually no reason to formally repeat our initial work, other than during our annual or semi-annual house cleanings. The last three Steps provide a guide to daily living that incorporates the principles of all the Steps. Daily spot-check inventories, easy to remember, quick to do, and uncomplicated in format, allow us to review our recent behavior. A more in-depth inventory before retiring provides a mechanism to examine our entire day, allowing us to plan any simple corrective action the following day that may be needed, including amends and further addressing our ever present shortcomings. Creating, and actually performing some type of repetitive daily spiritual prayer and meditation ritual is critical to stay on the beam, and keeps us connected to whatever spiritual power we have decided to use. Trying to carry the message keeps us connected with other alcoholics in the Fellowship, and practicing all the 12 Step principles involves doing our very best to do the next right thing with the spiritual tools we are given this day.

Am I able to live in the present of this present day, using the tools of the program to the best of my ability, for just these twenty-four hours?

JUNE 9

HOW IT WORKS

Many of us exclaimed, "What an order! I can't go through with it." Do not be discouraged. No one among us has been able to maintain anything like perfect adherence to these principles. We are not saints. The point is, that we are willing to grow along spiritual lines. The principles we have set down are guides to progress. We claim spiritual progress rather than spiritual perfection.

[How It Works p. 60]

CONSIDERATION

Progress over perfection. Growth over stagnation. Advancement over retreat. This is the spiritual road we seek. Our Big Book does not identify a specific principle for each of the 12 Steps, but one common list is: Honesty, Hope, Faith, Courage, Integrity, Willingness, Humility, Forgiveness, Justice, Perseverance, Spiritual Awakening and Service. Having had a spiritual awakening, meaning the change in our attitudes and actions that occurs as we complete the 12 Steps, we find that practicing all the 12 Step A.A. principles each day as best we can with the tools we are given is not too difficult, even when we don't want to do it or don't do it perfectly.

Is my life better having worked through all the 12 Steps and started practicing their principles?

JUNE 10

HOW IT WORKS

Our description of the alcoholic, the chapter to the agnostic, and our personal adventures before and after make clear three pertinent ideas: (a) That we were alcoholic and could not manage our own lives. (b) That probably no human power could have relieved our alcoholism. (c) That God could and would if He were sought.

[How It Works p. 60]

CONSIDERATION

We are reminded once again, for today and tomorrow, we need two types of power in our recovery—human and spiritual. It is fairly easy to find the human power contained in the Fellowship, since we have a sponsor and know we can always find alcoholics at meetings and in the A.A. community. Finding our spiritual power somewhere outside of us or deep within us often takes more work, reflection, ritual and practice. But once we discover these two powers and learn how to consciously connect with them on a daily basis, we have received the keys to the kingdom.

Have I absorbed the dual power of A.A. to maintain my sobriety and new way of life?

HOW IT WORKS

Being convinced, we were at Step Three, which is that we decided to turn our will and our life over to God as we understood Him. Just what do we mean by that, and just what do we do?

[How It Works p. 60]

CONSIDERATION

Many of us struggle with Step Three. What exactly does it mean to turn our will and lives over to some God, Higher Power, or spiritual power? How can we do this, whether we want to or not? Step Three sounds like another type of surrender, coming on the heels of our surrender to our powerlessness over alcohol. How can we possibly trust anyone or anything with our life, much less with our will, whatever that is? Many of us are taught to be self-sufficient and self-reliant, never asking or relying upon anyone or anything to help us through life. Asking for help, much less accepting it, is perceived as a sign of weakness, making us vulnerable to manipulation and emotional blackmail by the very people we depend on. If we can't survive by our own means, we are a failure and undeserving of the respect of others. How can we ever let go of self-reliance and self-sufficiency?

Can I put aside contempt prior to investigation before completely rejecting Step Three?

JUNE 12

HOW IT WORKS

The first requirement is that we be convinced that any life run on self-will can hardly be a success. On that basis we are almost always in collision with something or somebody, even though our motives are good. Most people try to live by self-propulsion. Each person is like an actor who wants to run the whole show; is forever trying to arrange the lights, the ballet, the scenery and the rest of the players in his own way. If his arrangements would only stay put, if only people would do as he wished, the show would be great. Everybody, including himself, would be pleased. Life would be wonderful. In trying to make these arrangements our actor may sometimes be quite virtuous. He may be kind, considerate, patient, generous; even modest and self-sacrificing. On the other hand, he may be mean, egotistical, selfish and dishonest. But, as with most humans, he is more likely to have varied traits.

[How It Works p. 60]

CONSIDERATION

One thing is certain, and that is all of us want others to do our bidding. We would not be human otherwise. We want our own way, all of the time. We easily convince ourselves our motives are pure, that we really do know what is best for our fellows, and that we have only their best interest at heart. Sometimes this is true, but most of the time we're lying or simply deluding ourselves. Regardless, we still want our own way, and no one can convince us otherwise.

Am I human enough to admit that I'm inherently selfish and self-centered?

JUNE 13

HOW IT WORKS

What usually happens? The show doesn't come off very well. He begins to think life doesn't treat him right. He decides to exert himself more. He becomes, on the next occasion, still more demanding or gracious, as the case may be. Still the play does not suit him. Admitting he may be somewhat at fault, he is sure that other people are more to blame. He becomes angry, indignant, self-pitying. What is his basic trouble? Is he not really a self-seeker even when trying to be kind? Is he not a victim of the delusion that he can wrest satisfaction and happiness out of this world if he only manages well? Is it not evident to all the rest of the players that these are the things he wants? And do not his actions make each of them wish to retaliate, snatching all they can get out of the show? Is he not, even in his best moments, a producer of confusion rather than harmony?

[How It Works p. 61]

CONSIDERATION

It is natural to try, to some extent, to force others to do what we want them to do. Why would we not try to mold and manipulate others to our wishes? It's part of our makeup. How long we persist with our futile efforts and how forcefully we apply pressure to those around us reflects the level of our desperation. When we ask and plead and cry and scream and tempt and scold and threaten and abandon; how often does that work? If and when we get our way, are the methods we use worth the results we receive? How often do our rantings instill resentment and bitterness in those we attack? How much destruction are we willing to inflict on others just to satisfy our frail ego?

How successful am I when I try to force others to do my bidding?

JUNE 14

HOW IT WORKS

Our actor is self-centered—ego-centric, as people like to call it nowadays. He is like the retired business man who lolls in the Florida sunshine in the winter complaining of the sad state of the nation; the minister who sighs over the sins of the twentieth century; politicians and reformers who are sure all would be Utopia if the rest of the world would only behave; the outlaw safe cracker who thinks society has wronged him; and the alcoholic who has lost all and is locked up. Whatever our protestations, are not most of us concerned with ourselves, our resentments, or our self-pity? Selfishness—self-centeredness! That, we think, is the root of our troubles. Driven by a hundred forms of fear, self-delusion, self-seeking, and self-pity, we step on the toes of our fellows and they retaliate. Sometimes they hurt us, seemingly without provocation, but we invariably find that at some time in the past we have made decisions based on self which later placed us in a position to be hurt.

[How It Works p. 61]

CONSIDERATION

Since selfishness and self-centeredness is the root of our troubles, it is easy to see why resentment is our number one offender. When the world refuses to comply with our demands and pushes back harder the more we fight to get our own way, it is like being stuck in quicksand—the more we struggle the more we sink. Since all of us want our own way, how can any one of us get it since we all want different things? What a dilemma. We keep trying to control our fellows, just as we tried to control our drinking, and always end up with the same result. So we wallow in that maudlin martyrdom of justifiable self-pity, deluding ourselves that we have been unfairly wronged. Our role reverts to playing the victim of an unfair and unjust life, loathe to admit that we are the author of all of our problems.

Am I still playing the victim?

HOW IT WORKS

So our troubles, we think, are basically of our own making. They arise out of ourselves, and the alcoholic is an extreme example of self-will run riot, though he usually doesn't think so. Above everything, we alcoholics must be rid of this selfishness. We must, or it kills us! God makes that possible. And there often seems no way of entirely getting rid of self without His aid. Many of us had moral and philosophical convictions galore, but we could not live up to them even though we would have liked to. Neither could we reduce our self-centeredness much by wishing or trying on our own power. We had to have God's help.

[How It Works p. 62]

CONSIDERATION

When we admit and accept our part in our self-imposed misery and stop playing the victim role, only then can we can begin to change. We start by changing our attitude toward life and the people about us, and in doing so we begin to change our actions. Sometimes, by simply changing our actions we change our attitude, which is why one hears "Fake it till you make it" in A.A. Whichever comes first, we can become less selfish if we become willing to try. For most of us, this requires a conscious effort that does not come easily or naturally. Most of us need both human and spiritual aid to help us become motivated and willing to change our behavior. Some of us make daily lists of people we should call or that we may be able to help in order to remind us that we are not the center of the universe or its director. At the end of the day, it is only our actions that define us, not our dreams, pleas, promises, desires or wishes.

Can I get out of myself long enough to do something for someone else today?

JUNE 16

HOW IT WORKS

This is the how and the why of it. First of all, we had to quit playing God. It didn't work. Next, we decided that hereafter in this drama of life, God was going to be our Director. He is the Principal; we are His agents. He is the Father, and we are His children. Most good ideas are simple, and this concept was the keystone of the new and triumphant arch through which we passed to freedom. When we sincerely took such a position, all sorts of remarkable things followed. We had a new Employer. Being all powerful, He provided what we needed, if we kept close to Him and performed His work well. Established on such a footing we became less and less interested in ourselves, our little plans and designs. More and more we became interested in seeing what we could contribute to life. As we felt new power flow in, as we enjoyed peace of mind, as we discovered we could face life successfully, as we became conscious of His presence, we began to lose our fear of today, tomorrow or the hereafter. We were reborn.

[How It Works p. 62]

CONSIDERATION

Down deep, most of us would love to be the Director of the Universe. We really don't want to be God in the Christian sense because that entails way too much work and responsibility. We just want to get our own way all the time without suffering any delay or consequence. Playing God is a lot of work, and we grow tired and frustrated when things don't go our way. So we start to let go. Over time we find that the less we try to control others, to force them to do our bidding, the easier our life becomes. Our change in attitude and action from one of God to not-God is a spiritual awakening. We begin to rely more on the spiritual principles of the 12 Steps rather than on our own ego and selfishness to direct our lives. Our old ways slip away, allowing our new self to emerge as naturally as the caterpillar is reborn into a beautiful butterfly.

Is life better for me now that I've stopped playing God?

HOW IT WORKS

We were now at Step Three. Many of us said to our Maker, as we understood him: "God, I offer myself to Thee—to build with me and to do with me as Thou wilt. Relieve me of the bondage of self, that I may better do Thy will. Take away my difficulties, that victory over them may bear witness to those I would help of Thy Power, Thy Love, and Thy Way of life. May I do Thy will always!"

[How It Works p. 63]

CONSIDERATION

This Third Step prayer suggests we turn our will and our lives over to the care of our spiritual power, or the God of our understanding. What many of us need to turn over is the erroneous idea that we are totally self-sufficient and self-reliant in this world. We need help from our fellow human companions and whatever spiritual source of strength and direction we can muster. Human aid alone is not enough, just as spiritual aid alone is not enough for us to find that new way of life. Paradoxically, we find that the more we let go of our bondage to self, our selfish and self-centered demands in life, the more we experience a new found peace and serenity. When we reach out to another alcoholic, or any other person in need, we end up thinking of ourselves less, and inexplicably, feeling better about ourselves and our place in this universe.

Am I willing to be guided by my spiritual principles so that I may better serve myself and my fellows?

JUNE 18

HOW IT WORKS

Next we launched out on a course of vigorous action, the first step of which is a personal housecleaning, which many of us had never attempted. Though our decision was a vital and crucial step, it could have little permanent effect unless at once followed by a strenuous effort to face, and to be rid of, the things in ourselves which had been blocking us. Our liquor was but a symptom. So we had to get down to causes and conditions. Therefore, we started upon a personal inventory. This was Step Four....We took stock honestly. First, we searched out the flaws in our make-up which caused our failure. Being convinced that self, manifested in various ways, was what had defeated us, we considered its common manifestations.

[How It Works p. 63]

CONSIDERATION

In Step Four we crack open our Pandora's Box. After we sort through the God language of Steps Two and Three, it is suggested that we immediately start working on Step Four. In addition, our Step Three decision to use our human and spiritual powers to help us create a new life is pointless unless we identify and remove any barriers to getting us where we need to go. That is why we do a searching and fearless moral inventory. We examine the rights and wrongs of our past behavior. We discover what part of ourself was affected by our feelings and actions, and identify our specific role in our past conduct. Our inventory exercise is not meant to explain to us why we drink, but what exactly is blocking us from living a life of sobriety. Our inventory shows us how our past consumes our lives today. The inventory instructions are not written as suggestions. Taking a detailed, personal, in-depth moral inventory is the best way to face our past and come to terms with it so we can let it go. Only by doing so can we begin to move forward into a new and better way of living.

Do I have the courage and commitment to honestly complete my moral inventory?

JUNE 19

HOW IT WORKS

Resentment is the number one offender.....From it stem all forms of spiritual disease, for we have been not only mentally and physically ill, we have been spiritually sick....In dealing with resentments, we set them on paper. We listed people, institutions or principles with whom we were angry. We asked ourselves why we were angry. In most cases it was found that our self-esteem, our pocketbooks, our ambitions, our personal relationships (including sex), were hurt or threatened.....Was it our self-esteem, our security, our ambitions, our personal, or sex relations, which had been interfered with?

[How It Works p. 64]

CONSIDERATION

Some of us confuse resentment and anger. They are not the same. Anger is that immediate reaction of displeasure when something we don't like happens to us, and usually goes away in a short time. Resentment is anger that turns personal, bitter and persistent. If we carry the anger and replay the event in our head long enough, it will become a resentment. We get angry if we accidentally hit our thumb with a hammer, but we don't resent the hammer. If someone else deliberately hits us with a hammer, our anger may well turn into a resentment. Many of us do not realize the breadth and depth of our resentments, especially early in A.A. We imagine we rarely carry a grudge, and if we do, it is soon forgotten after drinking. Sure, we get angry once in a while, but who doesn't? Yet after putting pen to paper, most of us are amazed how many resentments we have. Our list just goes on and on. We resent people, institutions and principles that threaten our instincts of self-esteem, financial and emotional security, ambitions and relationships. Those instincts are the part of our makeup which forms the core of our being, and when they are interfered with, we don't know what else to do other than to drink.

Am I ready to start the real work of Step Four?

JUNE 20

HOW IT WORKS

We went back through our lives. Nothing counted but thoroughness and honesty. When we were finished we considered it carefully. The first thing apparent was that this world and its people were often quite wrong. To conclude that others were wrong was as far as most of us ever got. The usual outcome was that people continued to wrong us and we stayed sore. Sometimes it was remorse and then we were sore at ourselves. But the more we fought and tried to have our own way, the worse matters got. As in war, the victor only seemed to win. Our moments of triumph were short-lived.

[How It Works p. 65]

CONSIDERATION

We are told that we can recover from a seemingly hopeless state of mind and body if we are capable of being honest with ourselves. Step Four tests our commitment. How badly do we want to recover? How far are we willing to go? As we write down our grudge list we begin to recognize a pattern. People are usually our number one resentment, often starting with our spouses, partners, parents, siblings, children, family, friends and employers. Next might come institutions such as the church, the legal system, politics or government. Finally, we may resent certain principles related to God, Heaven, Hell, right and wrong, or good and evil. We fight with those we resent because we want them to do what we want them to do, but they rarely do. So we keep trying, because we want to win the battle. We want to fight, be right and prove them wrong. Pride drives us onward, and our persistent anger fuels our ever growing resentments. In the long run, we never win these battles.

Am I ready to stop trying to prove I'm always right?

JUNE 21

HOW IT WORKS

It is plain that a life which includes deep resentment leads only to futility and unhappiness. To the precise extent that we permit these, do we squander the hours that might have been worthwhile? But with the alcoholic, whose hope is the maintenance and growth of a spiritual experience, this business of resentment is infinitely grave. We found that it is fatal. For when harboring such feeling we shut ourselves off from the sunlight of the Spirit. The insanity of alcohol returns and we drink again. And with us, to drink is to die. If we were to live, we had to be free of anger. The grouch and the brainstorm were not for us. They may be the dubious luxury of normal men, but for alcoholics these things are poison.

[How It Works p. 66]

CONSIDERATION

In this short section on resentment we notice the ominous words "grave, fatal, poison and die." Some of us might add suicide or homicide to the list. Most of us know living in resentment brings us nothing but misery, which is yet another reason we drink. We are warned that resentments will consume us if left unchecked. Not only will resentments kill us, but we will never recover from our alcoholic illness without eliminating them. We will never have a spiritual awakening, a change in attitude and action, while perpetually replaying over and over in our head the perceived wrongs done to us by others.

Am I convinced that I can no longer live with any of my resentments?

JUNE 22

HOW IT WORKS

This was our course: We realized that the people who wronged us were perhaps spiritually sick. Though we did not like their symptoms and the way these disturbed us, they, like ourselves, were sick too. We asked God to help us show them the same tolerance, pity, and patience that we would cheerfully grant a sick friend. When a person offended we said to ourselves, "This is a sick man. How can I be helpful to him? God save me from being angry. Thy will be done."

[How It Works p. 66]

CONSIDERATION

Forgiveness is a very tall order, which requires a radical shift in our attitude, especially when some of our resentments are truly justified. How can we forgive and wish well those who have wronged and harmed us, especially when we had only a minor part in past incidents? How can we forgive something done to us as a young child when we had no role whatsoever in the event? Some say our role in any resentment we still carry is the fact that we are still carrying it. But it doesn't matter how justified our resentments are; if we continue to hold on to them today, then that's our role and our part. It may be a Catch-22, but if ignored, our resentments are still real and will kill us eventually after we return to drinking. So why not let them go? Why not use our spiritual strength to help us forgive both friend and enemy, for they are surely sick people like us, and will always have their own burdens to bear. Forgiveness cannot change our past, but it can transform our future.

Am I willing to ask for spiritual help to forgive others?

JUNE 23

HOW IT WORKS

Referring to our list again. Putting out of our minds the wrongs others had done, we resolutely looked for our own mistakes. Where had we been selfish, dishonest, self-seeking and frightened? Though a situation had not been entirely our fault, we tried to disregard the other person involved entirely. Where were we to blame? The inventory was ours, not the other man's. When we saw our faults we listed them. We placed them before us in black and white. We admitted our wrongs honestly and were willing to set these matters straight.

[How It Works p. 67]

CONSIDERATION

Selfishness, dishonesty, resentment and fear. These are character defects that flow from our instincts of self-esteem, pocketbook, ambition and personal relationships. With resentments, we seek out our part in them no matter how small. Where and how have we been wrong in our behavior, regardless of someone else's behavior? Taking our own inventory rather than the other person's is not easy, especially since we are asked to admit where we were wrong, and be willing to make amends for those wrongs. This is a very tall order, and requires a level of humility most of us have never before encountered.

Am I willing to make restitution for the wrongs and harms I have done to others?

JUNE 24

HOW IT WORKS

Notice that the word "fear" is bracketed alongside the difficulties with Mr. Brown, Mrs. Jones, the employer, and the wife. This short word somehow touches about every aspect of our lives. It was an evil and corroding thread; the fabric of our existence was shot through with it. It set in motion trains of circumstances which brought us misfortune we felt we didn't deserve. But did not we, ourselves, set the ball rolling? Sometimes we think fear ought to be classed with stealing. It seems to cause more trouble.

[How It Works p. 67]

CONSIDERATION

Most of us insist we are fearless. We fear nothing, especially after drinking. When we stop drinking, we aren't so sure anymore. We remain restless and uneasy once sober, but aren't sure exactly why. Slowly we realize that we are afraid. It's hard to put a label on it, but we don't know how to fit in with those around us. Our fear takes off. Now sober, maybe we'll somehow let our family down. We're not making enough money. We aren't smart enough, or pretty enough, or clever enough, or good enough. People laugh at us behind our back, and still don't want to be around us even when we're sober. Maybe they will find out what we did yesterday and our secrets will be discovered. Damaging conduct from our past will catch up with us. And then there is the mystery of tomorrow. Who knows what disasters that will bring? How will we ever cope? Will my spouse leave me? Will I get fired? Will one of my children die? Will I die? We are devoured by fear, for alcoholism is a relentless, exhausting, fear-based disease.

How much of my life does fear consume?

JUNE 25

HOW IT WORKS

We reviewed our fears thoroughly. We put them on paper, even though we had no resentment in connection with them. We asked ourselves why we had them. Wasn't it because self-reliance failed us? Self-reliance was good as far as it went, but it didn't go far enough. Some of us once had great self-confidence, but it didn't fully solve the fear problem, or any other. When it made us cocky, it was worse.

[How It Works p. 68]

CONSIDERATION

After a while, we discover that we can no longer drink our fears away. Without our bottle, we are engulfed by fear. Being sober, we can't bury our fears or effectively wish them away. Fear is like our addiction to drink; it consumes our lives, even when we don't recognize or admit it. But we find that putting our fears on paper and discussing them with another alcoholic is a vital step toward obtaining relief. Next we realize that just like our alcoholic obsession, we are going to need spiritual help to have our fears removed. We have to stop being self-sufficient and playing God again, and use our spiritual power for spiritual aid. We might ask ourselves what fears we have right this minute, in this day, and focus on seeking human and spiritual relief for only those specific fears. Some simply say, "Please remove my fear," each and every day as part of their morning quiet time ritual. Tomorrow's fears can be addressed tomorrow.

Am I willing to accept human and spiritual help to address my fear?

HOW IT WORKS

Now about sex. Many of needed an overhauling there. But above all, we tried to be sensible on this question. It's so easy to get way off the track. Here we find human opinions running to extremes—absurd extremes, perhaps. One set of voices cry that sex is a lust of our lower nature, a base necessity of procreation. Then we have the voices who cry for sex and more sex; who bewail the institution of marriage; who think that most of the troubles of the race are traceable to sex causes. They think we do not have enough of it, or that it isn't the right kind. They see its significance everywhere. One school would allow man no flavor for his fare and the other would have us all on a straight pepper diet. We want to stay out of this controversy. We do not want to be the arbiter of anyone's sex conduct. We all have sex problems. We'd hardly be human if we didn't. What can we do about them?

[How It Works p. 68]

CONSIDERATION

Sex is a relationship with benefits. Most of us are totally selfish in all our relationships, and sex is no exception. Whether we are married or not, we always want our own way with our spouse or partner, so when the sexual component emerges, it's often like adding gasoline to a fire. Our thoughts, feelings, emotions and actions are magnified a hundred fold, and we constantly want to control and dominate the sex relationship. An added bonus to completing our sex inventory is that it makes it easier for us to recognize not only how we behave in those relationships, but in all of our other relationships. We can easily ask and apply the same Big Book inventory questions about sex to all our relationships. All of us have sex problems, and we all have relationship problems, sex or no sex. We find that every one of them needs an overhaul.

Will I use the process of reviewing my sex relations to help me examine my non-sexual relationships as well?

JUNE 27

HOW IT WORKS

We reviewed our own conduct over the years past. Where had we been selfish, dishonest, or inconsiderate? Whom had we hurt? Did we unjustifiably arouse jealousy, suspicion or bitterness? Where were we at fault, what should we have done instead? We got this all down on paper and looked at it.

[How It Works p. 69]

CONSIDERATION

Once again putting pen to paper provides us with relief. By examining our role in our relationships, sexual and otherwise, we begin to see how our behavior affects others. As with our resentments, we always have some part in any injury we cause our fellows. We are never blameless. We plot, plan, pretend, lie, manipulate, threaten, plead and cajole others to do our bidding, sexual or otherwise. We may seek different results from different people, but the game is always the same.

Will I thoroughly review my sexual conduct and reflect on how my behavior applies to all my relationships?

HOW IT WORKS

Whatever our ideal turns out to be, we must be willing to grow toward it. We must be willing to make amends where we have done harm, provided that we do not bring about still more harm in so doing. In other words, we treat sex as we would any other problem. In meditation, we ask God what we should do about each specific matter. The right answer will come, if we want it.

[How It Works p. 69]

CONSIDERATION

Since we harm others in so many of our relationships, sexual or not, we must become willing to make amends during Step Nine if we are to be free of our guilt and shame over past behavior. In Step Four, we simply list and describe our part in our past behavior. How we best deal with our wrongs going forward is part of future Steps.

Can I focus just on my Step Four inventory at this time, and postpone worrying about how I will take corrective action until I get to Steps Eight and Nine?

JUNE 29

HOW IT WORKS

Suppose we fall short of the chosen ideal and stumble? Does this mean we are going to get drunk? Some people tell us so. But this is only a half-truth. It depends on us and on our motives. If we are sorry for what we have done, and have the honest desire to let God take us to better things, we believe we will be forgiven and will have learned our lesson. If we are not sorry, and our conduct continues to harm others, we are quite sure to drink. We are not theorizing. These are facts out of our experience.

[How It Works p. 70]

CONSIDERATION

As we continue our inventory we begin to discover and uncover our character defects and their instinctive roots. Naming and claiming our defects does not mean they will disappear. Far from it. But we start to recognize that since we always have a part in our shortcomings, we must have a part in correcting them. We will never be perfect, but we can improve if our motives are pure and we are willing to do the work to change our behavior. Part of being willing to make restitution as best as we are able allows us to be willing to accept help and direction from all quarters in correcting our defects. Restitution is not simply an amend for past harms, but indicates we are committed to mending our ways by restoring proper conduct going forward.

Am I willing to make right past wrongs and change my behavior going forward to become a better person?

JUNE 30

HOW IT WORKS

If we have been thorough about our personal inventory, we have written down a lot. We have listed and analyzed our resentments. We have begun to comprehend their futility and their fatality. We have commenced to see their terrible destructiveness. We have begun to learn tolerance, patience and good will toward all men, even our enemies, for we look on them as sick people. We have listed the people we have hurt by our conduct, and are willing to straighten out the past if we can.

[How It Works p. 70]

CONSIDERATION

As is often said in these rooms, Step Four is about naming and claiming our character defects so we can dump them in Steps Five through Nine. We uncover, discover and discard our past wrongs and shortcomings through forgiveness and restitution in order that we become able to move forward in our lives without carrying the burden of our past. We drop our rocks of selfishness, dishonesty, resentment and fear so that we can drop those bigger rocks of guilt and shame through making amends and changing our behavior, or mending our ways. After doing so, we can stand tall and look ourselves in the mirror again. This is the beginning of a spiritual awakening.

Have I done as thorough and honest a job with Step Four as I can?

JULY 1

INTO ACTION

Having made our personal inventory, what shall we do about it?....We have admitted certain defects; we have ascertained in a rough way what the trouble is; we have put our finger on the weak times in our personal inventory. Now these are about to be cast out. This requires action on our part, which, when completed, will mean that we have admitted to God, to ourselves, and to another human being, the exact nature of our defects. This brings us to the Fifth Step in the program of recovery mentioned in the preceding chapter.

[Into Action p. 72]

CONSIDERATION

In Step Five we share our flaws, frailties, secrets and shortcomings with a sponsor, or a person experienced in the A.A. program. What we are really doing is confessing our faults, or our sins, as some in A.A. call them, to another. Why do that? Despite the saying that a problem shared is a problem halved, the simple explanation is because A.A. experience has shown that if we don't go through this cleansing process, we won't stay sober. We can deny and debate this fact all we want, certain we are the exception, but why bother? What we really want is to be relieved of the years of guilt and shame we accumulated for our past wrongs. We want a new sober life that has real meaning for us, enables us to fit in anywhere and become comfortable in our own skin. To get there requires confronting and removing as best we can any obstacles to a better life that may lie in our path. Common obstacles are our character defects of selfishness, dishonesty, resentment and fear. Some call our obstacles the seven deadly sins of pride, envy, wrath, gluttony, greed, lust and sloth. Regardless, and for reasons unknown, acknowledging out loud to another human being our secrets and faults is the first of several steps to freedom. If restitution and a change in our attitudes and actions follow, we will most assuredly embark on a new and wonderful way of living.

Am I willing to honestly and completely share my past with another human being?

JULY 2

INTO ACTION

In actual practice, we usually find a solitary self-appraisal insufficient. Many of us thought it necessary to go much further. We will be more reconciled to discussing ourselves with another person when we see good reasons why we should do so. The best reason first: If we skip this vital step, we may not overcome drinking. Time after time newcomers have tried to keep to themselves certain facts about their lives. Trying to avoid this humbling experience, they have turned to easier methods. Almost invariably they got drunk.

[Into Action p. 72]

CONSIDERATION

Solitary spiritual or religious confessions are easier for us to do than sitting across a table from another person, looking them in the eye and admitting our faults. It's just human nature. How many times have we twisted or omitted part of the truth during our cerebral ruminations, rationalizing while repenting to ourselves or an imagined god? Even if we believe our spiritual Higher Power is something that knows all about us without having to speak the truth out loud, or knows what we really mean despite our self-deceit and phony justifications, it's never the same as being with a fellow alcoholic who listens to our inventory without judgement, motive or malice. We may fear sharing our truth with another, but most of us find it is the only way to be able to let go of our past, find forgiveness, and begin living a sane, sober and fulfilling life.

Can I put aside my fear, swallow my pride, and completely confess my past and faults to another person?

JULY 3

INTO ACTION

Having persevered with the rest of the program, they wondered why they fell. We think the reason is that they never completed their housecleaning. They took inventory all right, but hung on to some of the worst items in stock. They only thought they had lost their egoism and fear; they only thought they had humbled themselves. But they had not learned enough of humility, fearlessness and honesty, in the sense we find it necessary, until they told someone else all their life story.

[Into Action p. 73]

CONSIDERATION

So many of us flounder and flee when faced with Steps Four and Five. We either don't finish the work of Step Four, or only do it half-way, or leave out vital pieces, or embellish parts of our past so we won't look so bad. In Step Five, we fail to disclose our entire truth, or delude ourselves into thinking that we did, when in reality we did no such thing. We still cling to our ego and vanity, wanting to look good in front of another, or become so overwhelmed by our guilt and shame that we are too frightened to share certain secrets with anyone. We confuse Step Five with humiliation rather than humility and liberation, either through willfulness, ignorance, denial or delusion. Failure to rigorously complete Steps Four and Five is an extremely grave mistake, and usually results in relapse and eventual death. However, if we proceed the best we can, being as honest as we are able, we will be rewarded beyond our wildest imagination.

For just once in my life, can I be totally and completely honest with another human being?

JULY 4

INTO ACTION

More than most people, the alcoholic leads a double life. He is very much the actor. To the outer world he presents his stage character. This is the one he likes his fellows to see. He wants to enjoy a certain reputation, but knows in his heart he doesn't deserve it.

[Into Action p. 73]

CONSIDERATION

In *As You Like It*, Shakespeare said that "All the world's a stage, and all the men and women merely players. They have their exits and their entrances, and one man in his time plays many parts." We all have our stage characters, carefully molded and modeled over time, adjusted for each different person and situation we encounter. Carefree and outgoing for this fellow, severe and serious for this other one. Perhaps kind and loving for a spouse, yet demanding or indifferent toward our children. The masks we place on each of our stage characters require us to remember which one we must use for which person and circumstance. We must remember so many roles and the lies we fabricate to support them that we use up all our booze, energy, effort and dignity to prevent the world from seeing us as we really are.

Can I tell the difference between my true character and all the different ones I show the world?

JULY 5

INTO ACTION

The inconsistency is made worse by the things he does on his sprees. Coming to his senses, he is revolted at certain episodes he vaguely remembers. These memories are a nightmare. He trembles to think someone might have observed him. As far as he can, he pushes these memories far inside himself. He hopes they will never see the light of day. He is under constant fear and tension—that makes for more drinking.

[Into Action p. 73]

CONSIDERATION

Memory loss and blackouts come to most alcoholics eventually because alcohol disrupts our brain's short-term memory circuits. We drink and drink until at some point part of our brain just shuts off. After we regain consciousness and are unable to remember anything clearly, we panic with the fear that we said or did something horrible that we will forever regret. Maybe we ran over someone with our car, so we better take a look to see if our front end is dented. Perhaps we bad-mouthed our boss, our best friend, or someone else we cared about. Did we make inappropriate sexual advances towards someone's wife or girlfriend? Did we strike our spouse or children during an argument? Those fears drive us to drink even more, so once again we can forget our real or imagined past. Life becomes an endless merry-go-round of drinking and forgetting until we end up dead, jailed or insane.

Have I reached the point of having recurring blackouts?

JULY 6

INTO ACTION

We must be entirely honest with somebody if we expect to live long or happily in this world. Rightly and naturally, we think well before we choose the person or persons with whom to take this intimate and confidential step.

[Into Action p. 73]

CONSIDERATION

Most alcoholics take Step Five with their sponsor or some other trusted alcoholic who has ample experience with Step work and has taken the Steps themselves. Some may share Step Five with a priest or minister familiar with the A.A. program. Just as it is unwise for a physician to treat his own family members, it would be unwise to take this Step with a family member or best friend, even if they are in A.A. Ideally, the person we select should feel safe to us and be completely trustworthy. They should also be unrelated to us, experienced in A.A., a good listener, non-judgmental, and have the ability to be objective and ask us thoughtful, insightful questions as we share our inventory. Above all, they should be able to keep the details of what we share in strict confidence, even with their own sponsor.

Have I given sufficient thought about the qualifications of the person I will ask to hear my Fifth Step?

JULY 7

INTO ACTION

Notwithstanding the great necessity for discussing ourselves with someone, it may be one is so situated that there is no suitable person available. If that is so, this step may be postponed, only, however, if we hold ourselves in complete readiness to go through with it at the first opportunity.

[Into Action p. 74]

CONSIDERATION

Some of us delay Step Five because of legitimate reasons. Others delay out of fear or from habitual procrastination. This is a very bad idea, and will prolong the time until we get relief. Why do all the work of writing down a thorough inventory if we are not going to share our efforts with another as soon as we can? What good will delaying the inevitable bring? We know we'll have to do Step Five eventually if we want to stay sober, have a spiritual awakening and find a new way of living, so why not get on with it?

Am I still making up excuses not to do my Fifth Step?

JULY 8

INTO ACTION

When we decide who is to hear our story, we waste no time.....We pocket our pride and go to it, illuminating every twist of character, every dark cranny of the past. Once we have taken this step, withholding nothing, we are delighted. We can look the world in the eye. We can be alone at perfect peace and ease. Our fears fall from us. We begin to feel the nearness of our Creator. We may have had certain spiritual beliefs, but now we begin to have a spiritual experience. The feeling that the drink problem has disappeared will often come strongly. We feel we are on the Broad Highway, walking hand in hand with the Spirit of the Universe.

[Into Action p. 75]

CONSIDERATION

We carry our past around with us like a sack of rocks. Those rocks are really our character defects, or our shortcomings. We discover and name them in Step Four, and uncover them in Step Five when we share them with another human being. We begin to discard them as we move through the rest of the Steps and out into life as a changed person. We never get rid of all of our defects, nor can we get rid of any one of them completely, but we start making the effort. What possible reason can there be to keep dragging our sack of rocks behind us? Once we share our resentments, fears and damaged relationships, and discuss our role and the shortcomings associated with them, we can begin to straighten up our stooped back, stop mumbling while looking at the ground, and begin to walk tall and proud on that Broad Highway of life. This Step, as with all the Steps, is spiritual in nature, and we begin to rest easier once we complete it.

Do I regret having taken my Fifth Step?

JULY 9

INTO ACTION

Returning home we find a place where we can be quiet for an hour, carefully reviewing what we have done. We thank God from the bottom of our heart that we know Him better. Taking this book down from our shelf we turn to the page which contains the twelve steps. Carefully reading the first five proposals we ask if we have omitted anything, for we are building an arch through which we shall walk a free man at last. Is our work solid so far? Are the stones properly in place? Have we skimped on the cement put into the foundation? Have we tried to make mortar without sand?

[Into Action p. 75]

CONSIDERATION

Immediately after taking Step Five it is suggested we take an hour of quiet time to review what we have just done. We try to relax and reflect on our work to ensure we have been completely honest and thorough in our discussion. If not, we have the opportunity to make additions or corrections by speaking at once with the person who just heard our Fifth Step. This short period of rest and reflection following Step Five should never be omitted or downplayed. It is an essential intermission in the Step process, allowing us to pause and re-group our feelings. Like half-time during a ball game, taking a breather clears the mind and refreshes the spirit.

If I have omitted anything during my Fifth Step, will I immediately call my sponsor and complete Step Five?

JULY 10

INTO ACTION

If we can answer to our satisfaction, we then look at Step Six. We have emphasized willingness as being indispensable. Are we now ready to let God remove from us all the things which we have admitted are objectionable? Can He now take them all—every one? If we still cling to something we will not let go, we ask God to help us be willing.

[Into Action p. 76]

CONSIDERATION

No one can eliminate their defects of character, or anything else in life, by simply wishing or praying them away. God will never take away our defects. No imaginary friend or tooth-fairy will eliminate any shortcomings we place under our pillow at night, expecting them to be magically removed by dawn. Our god or spiritual power may inspire and motivate us to change, but we must do the work. So we ask for the willingness, strength and direction to change our behavior, attitude, and actions. We hear in the rooms, "We let God design the quilt, but we must do the stitching." Nothing and no one has control over the outcome of any person's future, but we understand the connotation behind the expression. Doing the stitching means we take full responsibility for our own actions, and stop behaving in harmful, hurtful and selfish ways. As best we are able, we stop lying, cheating, stealing, living in anger, manipulating others and thinking of ourselves all the time. We pause before acting or speaking, giving us time to decide how best to proceed. Using this approach, we frequently discover that we begin to become less selfish and self-centered, more honest, more compassionate, more tolerant and kinder. We start to behave with integrity and humility, but only if we consciously and deliberately change our behavior, inspired by whatever god, spiritual Power, Force, Purpose or Principles we can muster.

Do I understand that I alone must take personal corrective action to address my character defects?

JULY 11

INTO ACTION

When ready, we say something like this: "My Creator, I am now willing that you should have all of me, good and bad. I pray that you now remove from me every single defect of character which stands in the way of my usefulness to you and my fellows. Grant me strength, as I go out from here, to do your bidding. Amen." We have then completed Step Seven.

[Into Action p. 76]

CONSIDERATION

We assume this Seventh Step Prayer was used by some of our pioneer founders to help them become willing to change their behavior. They asked for removal of whatever shortcomings were blocking them from being useful to God and the people about them. They asked for the strength and direction to do the next right thing. Each of us can develop our own Seventh Step Prayer, such as *"I seek the strength and direction to do the very best I can to do the next right thing with whatever tools I'm able to use today."* Regardless of how we seek spiritual support in addressing our character defects, we have our own role in changing our behavior. If we selfishly neglect our family and friends, we can commit to spending more time with them. If we are a liar, we can pause before speaking and make a conscious effort to tell the truth. If we are a thief, we pause before stealing and make a decision to keep our hands in our pockets. If we are angry or agitated, we pause here too, and decide how best to respond to the situation. Prayer may inspire us, but none of our defects are removed by God or prayer alone. We are totally responsible, and we must do our part if we expect to change.

Do I have a daily routine or ritual to ask for the spiritual support, strength, and guidance to correct my character defects?

JULY 12

INTO ACTION

Now we need more action, without which we find that "Faith without works is dead." Let's look at Steps Eight and Nine. We have a list of all persons we have harmed and to whom we are willing to make amends. We made it when we took inventory. We subjected ourselves to a drastic self-appraisal. Now we go out to our fellows and repair the damage done in the past. We attempt to sweep away the debris which has accumulated out of our effort to live on self-will and run the show ourselves. If we haven't the will to do this, we ask until it comes. Remember it was agreed at the beginning we would go to any lengths for victory over alcohol.

[Into Action p. 76]

CONSIDERATION

"Faith without works is dead" is from the Epistle of James in the New Testament of the Bible. It means that although prayer is part of the Christian faith, prayer alone is inadequate for the truly faithful. Prayer must be followed by personal action and sacrifice. How easy it would be for us to complete our inventory and list the wrongs we did to others in Step Four, confess to another in Step Five, and then take no personal action to rectify the mess we made of our past. It would be much easier to say to ourselves "Let bygones be bygones," or "Let's just go forward from here with our new way of behaving. We'll just make a living amends for the harm we did to others in our past." Experience has shown that if we fail to make all our amends, directly, in person, and face-to-face wherever possible, the shame and guilt of our past remains bottled up. Rejecting any attempt to fully reconcile our past behavior, or making half-hearted attempts, usually results in a return to drinking. Asking for the spiritual strength to surmount our fear of making amends directly to each and every person we have harmed wherever possible, and to give us the courage to get honest and right with the world, is a good start with Step Nine.

Am I really willing to go to any lengths for victory over alcohol?

JULY 13

INTO ACTION

At the moment we are trying to put our lives in order. But this is not an end in itself. Our real purpose is to fit ourselves to be of maximum service to God and the people about us.

[Into Action p. 77]

CONSIDERATION

Some in A.A. say that the phrase, "Our real purpose is to fit ourselves to be of maximum service to God and the people about us," encapsulates our new way of living. It is what we all strive for, in one way or another, at the end of the day. For us, we are here to serve our spiritual values, principles, beliefs and human connections. It does not matter how we view, label, or describe our god, Higher Power, spiritual power or those around us. What does matter is that it's not all about us. We are no longer the center of the world or the Director of the Universe. We remain not-God. We are here to take care of ourselves so that we can help take care of others. How we can best fit ourselves to do that is the question we try to answer each day through our ritual of prayer and meditation. Then we can use the tools we are given this day to try to do the next right thing for ourself and our fellows.

Can I accept that my role in life is to be true to myself, and to do the best I can to help and support those around me?

JULY 14

INTO ACTION

The question of how to approach the man we hated will arise. It may be he has done us more harm than we have done him and, though we may have acquired a better attitude toward him, we are still not too keen about admitting our faults. Nevertheless, with a person we dislike, we take the bit in our teeth. It is harder to go to an enemy than to a friend, but we find it much more beneficial to us. We go to him in a helpful and forgiving spirit, confessing our former ill feeling and expressing our regret.

[Into Action p. 77]

CONSIDERATION

It is hard enough to say to anyone we have harmed, "I was wrong, and how can I make it right?" Admitting we were wrong and offering restitution to someone we dislike, or to someone we feel harmed us more than we harmed them, is especially difficult. But it must be done if we are to move forward in recovery. We often ask our spiritual power to help us become willing to make all our amends, regardless of how we feel about the people or issues involved. We might also want to use our spiritual energy to help us change our attitude about making amends from something we must do, to something we are privileged to do. Saying we are wrong and offering to remedy past wrongs without hesitation and bitterness can release us from the remorse and shame of our past. A sincere desire today to make right whatever we can out of the damage we did up until this point will go a long way in relieving our obsession to drink, and set us squarely on that Broad Highway of recovery.

Am I willing to make a sincere and honest amend to each person I have harmed in the past, whether I like them or not?

JULY 15

INTO ACTION

Under no condition do we criticize such a person or argue. Simply tell him that we will never get over drinking until we have done our utmost to straighten out the past. We are there to sweep off our side of the street, realizing that nothing worthwhile can be accomplished until we do so, never trying to tell him what he should do. His faults are not discussed. We stick to our own. If our manner is calm, frank, and open, we will be gratified with the result.

[Into Action p. 77]

CONSIDERATION

When we took Step Four we took our own inventory, not the other person's. It is not our job to take someone else's inventory, just as it is not our job to make amends for another's actions. It's hard enough to deal with our own garbage, much less another's. It is unnecessary for us to explain exactly, and in great detail, why we are making our amend. No one cares why we are making our amend. All they care about is that we have been willing to admit our wrongs, offer to do something about them, and will try not repeat past mistakes in the future by mending our ways. Making our amends in a calm, honest, polite, straightforward and gracious manner may take much effort, but usually little time. We simply say to that person that we are sorry we hurt them in whatever situation we're discussing, that we were wrong in our behavior, and ask what we can do to make it right. More times than not, our offer will be met with kindness or at least neutrality. If not, we don't withdraw the offer, create a new resentment or drift into self-pity. We simply take comfort in the fact that we have done the right thing and can finally release that piece of our past.

Can I ignore how other people respond to me as I make my amends?

JULY 16

INTO ACTION

Although these reparations take innumerable forms, there are some general principles which we find guiding. Reminding ourselves that we have decided to go to any lengths to find a spiritual experience, we ask that we be given strength and direction to do the right thing, no matter what the personal consequences may be. We may lose our position or reputation or face jail, but we are willing. We have to be. We must not shrink at anything.

[Into Action p. 79]

CONSIDERATION

As we review each of our upcoming amends in consultation with our sponsor, it is easy to become fearful of the outcome. Let's beware our expectations. Even though we know we cannot change our past or return to the way things were, nor do we expect to necessarily become better friends with those we have hurt, most of us have some level of fear about the consequences of our efforts. Confronting an old enemy can be scary and anxiety provoking. How will things turn out? Will I be attacked or humiliated? Will I freeze up and panic? Will I start crying? How can I do this? With our sponsor's help, many of us divide our amends into three sections to lessen our anxiety: those we are willing to do right now, those we are willing to do very soon, and those we dread doing. With the dreaded amends, it may help to write each one down and practice making the amend with our sponsor beforehand to relieve some of our fear. We also try to remember the reason we are making our amends in the first place—we make them to relieve us from the bondage of our past. Only by releasing our past can we move forward in forgiveness and sobriety.

Am I willing to go to any length to make all my amends?

JULY 17

INTO ACTION

The chances are that we have domestic troubles. Perhaps we are mixed up with women in a fashion we wouldn't care to have advertised....A man so involved often feels very remorseful at times, especially if he is married to a loyal and courageous girl who has literally gone through hell for him. Whatever the situation, we usually have to do something about it. If we are sure our wife does not know, should we tell her? Not always, we think. If she knows in a general way that we have been wild, should we tell her in detail? Undoubtedly we should admit our fault....We are sorry for what we have done and, God willing, it shall not be repeated. More than that we cannot do; we have no right to go further. Though there may be justifiable exceptions, and though we wish to lay down no rule of any sort, we have often found this the best course to take.

[Into Action p. 80]

CONSIDERATION

When we reviewed our sex relations in Step Four, some of us faced a past that included adultery or other indiscretions. Perhaps we cheated on our spouse during marriage, or on our partner to whom we were committed. Either way, we betrayed the trust of another, and are now willing to set things right. The degree of detail we choose to share with the person we harmed is up to us after careful reflection and consultation with our sponsor or other trusted advisers in the Fellowship. We must be clear on our motives regardless of our decision, for a careless divulgence could easily be detrimental to all involved.

Have I taken the time and effort to do the work of reviewing all my sexual indiscretions with my sponsor before making any of those amends?

JULY 18

INTO ACTION

Sometimes we hear an alcoholic say that the only thing he needs to do is to keep sober. Certainly he must keep sober, for there will be no home if he doesn't. But he is yet a long way from making good to the wife or parents whom for years he has so shockingly treated. Passing all understanding is the patience mothers and wives have had with alcoholics. Had this not been so, many of us would have no homes today, would perhaps be dead.

[Into Action p. 82]

CONSIDERATION

Simply not drinking is never, ever enough. When we hear the term "dry drunk" in A.A., most of us know exactly what that means. Dry drunks no longer drink, but fail to improve their way of thinking and acting. They may have healed physically, but not mentally or emotionally. They have little or no spiritual foundation, although they often deny this fact. Stinking thinking remains, and they frequently fantasize about drinking. They are not accountable to their fellows nor will they accept the responsibilities that are required for a healthy recovery. They are passive-aggressive, simmering with anger and oozing self-pity. They still play the victim and are unpleasant to be around. Why are they like this? Two common reasons are their failure to be totally honest with themselves and another in Steps Four and Five, and/or failing to complete all their amends in Steps Eight and Nine.

Am I willing to change my actions, or mend my ways, from this point forward?

JULY 19

INTO ACTION

The alcoholic is like a tornado roaring his way through the lives of others. Hearts are broken. Sweet relationships are dead. Affections have been uprooted. Selfish and inconsiderate habits have kept the home in turmoil. We feel a man is unthinking when he says that sobriety is enough. He is like the farmer who came up out of his cyclone cellar to find his home ruined. To his wife, he remarked, "Don't see anything the matter here, Ma, ain't it grand the wind stopped blowin'?"

[Into Action p. 82]

CONSIDERATION

If we're sober the wind has stopped blowing, but the damage we caused remains. Simply not drinking is no way to live, for ourselves or those around us. The path of chaos and destruction we created tearing through other people's lives while drinking cannot be repaired by half measures. Cleaning up the wreckage we caused is the first half of our task, and the second half is changing our behavior, attitudes and actions. Our willingness and ability to change for the better is another spiritual awakening we experience as we move through our Step work. Even if our work is incomplete by Steps Eight and Nine, most of us are well on our way.

Am I able to see the forest for the trees, understanding that simply not drinking is never enough?

JULY 20

INTO ACTION

Yes, there is a long period of reconstruction ahead. We must take the lead. A remorseful mumbling that we are sorry won't fill the bill at all. We ought to sit down with the family and frankly analyze the past as we now see it, being very careful not to criticize them. Their defects may be glaring, but the chances are that our own actions are partly responsible. So we clean house with the family, asking each morning in meditation that our Creator show us the way of patience, tolerance, kindliness and love.

[Into Action p. 83]

CONSIDERATION

During the first part of our amend we may be told directly from the person we had harmed how we can make things right. This could involve creating a payment plan for debts owed, or a return of goods previously stolen. It could involve being asked to spend more time with our spouse or children, if we neglected them in the past. The second part of our amend is making things right by mending our ways. We stop behaving the way we did when we harmed those around us. This is our living amend, and is required for all of our amends. No one wants to listen to another lame apology from an alcoholic who refuses to change. Our promises of future change, never fulfilled in the past, fall on deaf ears. Amends must be spoken, but change must be demonstrated. Our family and friends may start to trust us once they witness a persistent and protracted improvement in our behavior while sober. It may take months or years for those we have harmed to fully trust us, and some may never trust us again despite our new way of living. How others respond to our efforts is unimportant as long as we continue to practice the principles of the 12 Steps. We can't change others, but with our spiritual power and the power of the Fellowship, we can change ourselves for the better.

Am I getting right with my family, friends and those in the world about me?

JULY 21

INTO ACTION

The spiritual life is not a theory. We have to live it. Unless one's family expresses a desire to live upon spiritual principles we think we ought not to urge them. We should not talk incessantly to them about spiritual matters. They will change in time. Our behavior will convince them more than our words. We must remember that ten or twenty years of drunkenness would make a skeptic out of anyone.

[Into Action p. 83]

CONSIDERATION

Time heals most wounds, but not all of them. We ask for patience and tolerance during our new way of living. We focus on changing our own selfish and self-centered way of living and stop trying to change other people. We strive to behave with decency and dignity, each and every day. We continue to try to do the next right thing, even when we are angry or fearful. We stop blaming others for our problems, and accept responsibility for them. We get honest and become reliable and accountable to others. With love, tolerance and humility, we embrace the world around us, and are grateful we are able to be a part of it.

Am I striving to live a spiritual life?

JULY 22

INTO ACTION

There may be some wrongs we can never fully right. We don't worry about them if we can honestly say to ourselves that we would right them if we could. Some people cannot be seen—we send them an honest letter. And there may be a valid reason for postponement in some cases. But we don't delay if it can be avoided. We should be sensible, tactful, considerate and humble without being servile or scraping. As God's people we stand on our feet; we don't crawl before anyone.

[Into Action p. 83]

CONSIDERATION

Not all amends can be made face-to-face, for a variety of reasons. Some people may have died. Others may live far away and are inaccessible. Still others may have vanished completely. None of these situations is a reason not to make our amend. We can write a letter to the unreachable sufferers of our past misconduct, and put down in words what we would say to them in person. We can read our letter to our sponsor, a trusted fellow or someone closely affected by our actions, should that choice be appropriate. The sooner we complete all our amends in the best manner possible, the sooner we will be relieved from the indignity and remorse of our past. Delay and procrastination can be deadly, for if we hesitate too long, we risk drinking again. Done correctly and completely, making amends is an honor and a privilege, never a chore or humiliation.

Am I ready to complete all my amends?

JULY 23

INTO ACTION

If we are painstaking about this phase of our development, we will be amazed before we are half way through. We are going to know a new freedom and a new happiness. We will not regret the past nor wish to shut the door on it. We will comprehend the word serenity and we will know peace. No matter how far down the scale we have gone, we will see how our experience can benefit others. That feeling of uselessness and self-pity will disappear. We will lose interest in selfish things and gain interest in our fellows. Self-seeking will slip away. Our whole attitude and outlook upon life will change. Fear of people and of economic insecurity will leave us. We will intuitively know how to handle situations which used to baffle us. We will suddenly realize that God is doing for us what we could not do for ourselves. Are these extravagant promises? We think not. They are being fulfilled among us—sometimes quickly, sometimes slowly. They will always materialize if we work for them.

[Into Action p. 83]

CONSIDERATION

The Ninth Step promises are just a few of the gifts so freely given to us in A.A. Even though most of us struggle with the work of the Steps to get to his point, we begin to view life in a different way. Some say we have acquired a new pair of glasses, or have turned our glasses around so that we are looking outward toward what we can do for others in life, rather than inward toward ourselves and our selfish interests. We notice we are changing. The committee in our head meets less frequently. Our mental squirrel cage slows down. The perpetual roar of static between our ears subsides. We become less angry and fearful. We are more relaxed. Little things don't bother us as much as they used to. We are less intolerant, judgmental and critical of others. We learn to be grateful. We start to think about how we can help our neighbor before we help ourselves. We begin to care about our fellow man. We have moments of true happiness, fun and joy. Our hope for a better life is renewed.

Have some of these promises started coming true in my life?

INTO ACTION

This thought brings us to Step Ten, which suggests we continue to take personal inventory and continue to set right any new mistakes as we go along. We vigorously commenced this way of living as we cleaned up the past. We have entered the world of the Spirit. Our next function is to grow in understanding and effectiveness. This is not an overnight matter. It should continue for our lifetime. Continue to watch for selfishness, dishonesty, resentment, and fear. When these crop up, we ask God at once to remove them. We discuss them with someone immediately and make amends quickly if we have harmed anyone. Then we resolutely turn our thoughts to someone we can help. Love and tolerance of others is our code.

[Into Action p. 84]

CONSIDERATION

Many refer to A.A.'s Steps Ten through Twelve as maintenance Steps, and some astute members have been reading pages 84 to 88 in the Big Book every day since their very first day in A.A., long before they started their formal Step work. Step Ten, our spot-check inventory, is a condensed Step Four, and gives us rapid fire instructions for living in this day by addressing four of our character defects that always crop up: selfishness, dishonesty, resentment and fear. When these arise, we first seek direction from our spiritual side, or power. Second, we seek human help by sharing our situation with someone who knows us well, such as our sponsor, others in the Fellowship or trusted family or friends. Third, we make an amend if necessary. Fourth, we consider how we may be helpful to someone else. Another acronym that may help us get back on the beam is G-P-S. An electronic GPS unit tells us physically where we are and how to get to where we need to go. Our spiritual G-P-S unit can do the same thing through Gratitude, Prayer and Service. When we quickly review our gratitude list, say the Serenity Prayer or an inspirational motto, think of another person in need that we might help, it is then that we start to grow in understanding and effectiveness.

Do I use Step Ten on a daily basis?

JULY 25

INTO ACTION

And we have ceased fighting anything or anyone—even alcohol. For by this time sanity will have returned. We will seldom be interested in liquor. If tempted, we recoil from it as from a hot flame. We react sanely and normally, and we will find that this has happened automatically. We will see that our new attitude toward liquor has been given us without any thought or effort on our part. It just comes! That is the miracle of it. We are not fighting it, neither are we avoiding temptation. We feel as though we had been placed in a position of neutrality—safe and protected. We have not even sworn off. Instead, the problem has been removed. It does not exist for us. We are neither cocky nor are we afraid. That is our experience. That is how we react so long as we keep in fit spiritual condition.

[Into Action p. 84]

CONSIDERATION

We need the help of our spiritual power, however we define and use it, and the power of the Fellowship to stop drinking and find a new way of life. Coming into A.A., some of us are immediately released from our obsession and preoccupation with drink. Others carry that burden for months or years, despite not drinking and active participation in A.A. At some point, almost all of us discover that our daily obsession to drink has disappeared. We may not know exactly why or how our obsession departed, but we know we did our part by not drinking, attending meetings, getting a sponsor, doing all the 12 Step work, practicing spiritual principles and beginning our service work with other alcoholics. If we fully engage in all the Steps, including Steps Ten and Eleven every day, one day at a time, we should remain in a fit spiritual condition.

Am I still fighting alcohol and the world around me?

JULY 26

INTO ACTION

It is easy to let up on the spiritual program of action and rest on our laurels. We are headed for trouble if we do, for alcohol is a subtle foe. We are not cured of alcoholism. What we really have is a daily reprieve contingent on the maintenance of our spiritual condition. Every day is a day when we must carry the vision of God's will into all of our activities. "How can I best serve Thee—Thy will (not mine) be done." These are thoughts which must go with us constantly. We can exercise our will power along this line all we wish. It is the proper use of the will.

[Into Action p. 85]

CONSIDERATION

How often in A.A. do we hear someone say "We have a daily reprieve based on our spiritual condition?" It is easy to misquote this Step Ten sentence. It actually reads "the maintenance" of our spiritual condition. There will always be days that we don't feel fit or spiritual. This is normal, since our spiritual condition usually varies from day to day, sometimes hour to hour or minute to minute. What matters is that we make a constant effort to do the work to sustain a healthy spiritual mindset. This means finding some spiritual ritual, whether through prayer and meditation or other means, which we can use every day, and throughout the day, to consciously connect us with our spiritual side. The spiritual force in our life, whether it is God, some other Higher Power, a Higher Force, a Higher Purpose or Higher Principles, may do no more than remind us that the best thing we can do is to do the next right thing throughout our day, try to think of someone other than ourself, and be grateful for the Fellowship and people in our new life.

What daily routines or rituals do I use to help me maintain my spiritual condition?

JULY 27

INTO ACTION

Step Eleven suggests prayer and meditation.....When we retire at night, we constructively review our day. Were we resentful, selfish, dishonest or afraid? Do we owe an apology? Have we kept something to ourselves which should be discussed with another person at once? Were we kind and loving toward all? What could we have done better? Were we thinking of ourselves most of the time? Or were we thinking of what we could do for others, of what we could pack into the stream of life? But we must be careful not to drift into worry, remorse or morbid reflection, for that would diminish our usefulness to others. After making our review we ask God's forgiveness and inquire what corrective measures should be taken.

[Into Action p. 85]

CONSIDERATION

As we seek a spiritual power of our understanding, it must be some type of spiritual energy that we can consciously relate to and make a connection with. What good is having a spiritual solution that we cannot turn to for help, motivation, strength, direction and support? After we discover a spiritual force or energy that we can be comfortable with, we use some type of repetitive prayer and meditation—asking and listening—as part of our daily maintenance ritual to keep us in the best possible fit spiritual condition. Even we atheists, agnostics or freethinkers, in some manner or fashion, ask and listen for spiritual help and guidance in our life. Prayer and meditation comes in many forms and colors. Seek out what works for you. Being willing to ask for both human and spiritual aid keeps all of us sane, sober and willing to think of someone other than ourselves all the time, and reminds us once again that we are not the Director of the Universe. It anchors us to the foundation of our new way of living.

Do I review my day upon retiring?

INTO ACTION

On awakening let us think about the twenty-four hours ahead. We consider our plans for the day. Before we begin, we ask God to direct our thinking, especially asking that it be divorced from self-pity, dishonest or self-seeking motives. Under these conditions we can employ our mental faculties with assurance, for after all God gave us brains to use. Our thought-life will be placed on a much higher plane when our thinking is cleared of wrong motives.

[Into Action p. 86]

CONSIDERATION

With a little practice, taking a few minutes at the beginning of each day to review our schedule and obligations becomes natural for most of us. What may not come so easily is to include in our morning quiet time a review of our attitude and motives for our upcoming plans or decisions. Will our day consist of primarily self-centered activities? Are we trying to figure out how to manipulate others so they will do our bidding? Are we thinking up excuses to get out of unwanted commitments and obligations? Will we decide to wallow in the maudlin martyrdom of self-pity because life is so hard and unfair? Are we hoping to play the victim today? Or, are we willing to help someone in need today? Will we start our day with an attitude of gratitude, or wallow in anger and melancholy to deal with forthcoming duties and responsibilities? All of us naturally have self-centered thoughts from time to time, but they can be dispelled during our quiet time. And don't forget that we can use our spiritual G-P-S unit to help us get back on the beam when we drift off. Gratitude, Prayer and Service. G-P-S. Be grateful, keep consciously connected with whatever spiritual Force, Power or Principles we have chosen to guide our life, and go out and help someone today.

Do I use a morning ritual to start my day, and realize that my day will be exactly what I choose to make of it?

JULY 29

INTO ACTION

In thinking about our day we may face indecision....Here we ask God for inspiration, an intuitive thought or a decision. We relax and take it easy. We don't struggle....What used to be the hunch or the occasional inspiration gradually becomes a working part of the mind. Being still inexperienced and having just made conscious contact with God, it is not probable that we are going to be inspired at all times. We might pay for this presumption in all sorts of absurd actions and ideas. Nevertheless, we find that our thinking will, as time passes, be more and more on the plane of inspiration. We come to rely upon it.

[Into Action p. 86]

CONSIDERATION

When we plan our day we can't ensure the outcome of our day. Perhaps things will turn out as hoped, perhaps not. Our day may go smoothly, with no rough spots, or it may degenerate into a scary, chaotic mess that throws us off track. When this happens, especially if we are taken by surprise, we reflexively go into fight or flight mode. Our hackles are up, engine at full throttle, and we get that rush of adrenaline we know and love so well. When this happens, if we immediately reach for a spiritual solution rather than a chemical solution, we stay centered on our road of recovery. The first thing we are taught to do is to pause when agitated, because this provides us a little time to catch our breath and consider what action to take, rather than wildly shooting from the hip before we aim. If we relax and don't panic, we arrive at a better decision much easier. As needed, we can draw on our spiritual power and the power of the Fellowship for help. All this takes practice, often requiring an intense conscious effort. But through repetition, repetition, repetition, we find over time that our days flow easier and we are much less anxious and distressed living life on life's terms.

Can I pause and calm down long enough to ask for spiritual and Fellowship guidance when things aren't going my way?

JULY 30

INTO ACTION

We usually conclude the period of meditation with a prayer that we be shown all through the day what our next step is to be, that we be given whatever we need to take care of such problems. We ask especially for freedom from self-will, and are careful to make no request for ourselves only. We may ask for ourselves, however, if others will be helped. We are careful never to pray for our own selfish ends. Many of us have wasted a lot of time doing that and it doesn't work. You can easily see why. If circumstances warrant, we ask our wives or friends to join us in morning meditation. If we belong to a religious denomination which requires a definite morning devotion, we attend to that also. If not members of religious bodies, we sometimes select and memorize a few set prayers which emphasize the principles we have been discussing. There are many helpful books also. Suggestions about these may be obtained from one's priest, minister, or rabbi. Be quick to see where religious people are right. Make use of what they offer.

[Into Action p. 87]

CONSIDERATION

Many of us end our morning quiet time by asking for spiritual aid and guidance throughout the day. This is called prayer. To have the wisdom and courage to do the next right thing, as best we know it and are able to do it, is what many of us request. We want to be able to act with kindness, decency and dignity throughout our day, and down deep we know how to do this. But will we be willing? Can we embrace the selfless principles expressed through the St. Francis prayer and Golden Rule, and not just pay lip service to them? Can we think of others during the day and how we can best be helpful to them? Most of us find that taking a few minutes each morning to reflect on these questions is time well spent.

Do I ask each day to be relieved of the bondage of self and be willing to do the next right thing by following the 12 Step principles, so that I can be of service to those about me?

JULY 31

INTO ACTION

As we go through the day we pause, when agitated or doubtful, and ask for the right thought or action. We constantly remind ourselves we are no longer running the show, humbly saying to ourselves many times each day "Thy will be done." We are then in much less danger of excitement, fear, anger, worry, self-pity, or foolish decisions. We become much more efficient. We do not tire so easily, for we are not burning up energy foolishly as we did when we were trying to arrange life to suit ourselves. It works—it really does.

[Into Action p. 87]

CONSIDERATION

Since we know that we will forever be restless, irritable and discontented, it is natural to try to run the show. We quickly learn that it takes an enormous amount of effort and energy to try to force everyone else to do our bidding. All day long we lie, scheme, threaten, plead, bargain and manipulate others to our will as best we can. We may succeed at first, but in the end we fail completely. Taking revenge on ourselves, we meet with the committee in our head, fire up our squirrel cage, crank up the static noise, become more and more agitated, and end up drinking because nothing has turned out exactly the way we had hoped or planned. On the other hand, if we adopt a spiritual approach to the stress and strain of daily life and accept that we can control nothing but our own actions, somehow we become more at ease. A degree of peace and serenity enters our lives, and we aren't exhausted all the time trying to get our own way.

Have I given up my role of being the Director of the Universe?

AUGUST 1

WORKING WITH OTHERS

Practical experience shows that nothing will so much insure immunity from drinking as intensive work with other alcoholics. It works when other activities fail. This is our twelfth suggestion: carry this message to other alcoholics! You can help when no one else can. You can secure their confidence when others fail. Remember they are very ill.

[Working With Others p. 89]

CONSIDERATION

Our gold standard for ensuring sobriety is intensive work with another alcoholic. Technically, intensive work means sponsorship, which is really no more than an objective business arrangement where one experienced alcoholic takes another alcoholic through all 12 Steps of A.A. However, experience shows that just about any focused, one-on-one encounter with another alcoholic will protect us from drinking when all other activities fail. For the alcoholic who feels like they are drifting off the beam despite prayer and meditation, attending meetings, chatting with their sponsor and support group, doing a spot-check inventory and making amends if needed, any alcoholic can almost always get back on track by directly lending a hand to a fellow alcoholic. Nothing brings us back to the power and favor of A.A. more than sitting down beside a newcomer, Big Book in hand, sharing our experience with the program of A.A. At that moment we are as one, bound to each other through a common solution, both of us seeking to maintain our sobriety and serenity.

Do I realize my ace in the hole in sobriety is working directly with another alcoholic?

AUGUST 2

WORKING WITH OTHERS

Life will take on new meaning. To watch people recover, to see them help others, to watch loneliness vanish, to see a Fellowship grow up about you, to have a host of friends—this is an experience you must not miss. We know you will not want to miss it. Frequent contact with newcomers and with each other is the bright spot of our lives.

[Working With Others p. 89]

CONSIDERATION

It is difficult to describe the immense joy and pleasure we receive as we witness a fellow alcoholic glowing and growing in the Fellowship. Although we may have gone through a similar transformation ourself, the impact is often greater when we see it in others. We feel a strange mix of happiness and gratitude both for ourselves and our fellow at the same time, for each of us has survived a deadly illness, and are travelling the magnificent road of recovery together.

Do I spend enough time working with newcomers?

WORKING WITH OTHERS

When you discover a prospect for Alcoholics Anonymous, find out all you can about him. If he does not want to stop drinking, don't waste time trying to persuade him. You may spoil a later opportunity. This advice is given for his family also. They should be patient, realizing they are dealing with a sick person.

[Working With Others p. 90]

CONSIDERATION

When we are drinking no one can persuade us to stop until we are good and ready. We cannot be coaxed, cajoled or coerced into sobriety by well-meaning spouses, parents, siblings, children, relatives, friends, or employers. Neither the church nor the courts can get us sober. No one in the A.A. Fellowship can get us sober. No carrot or stick works on us until we reach that jumping off place and whisper "Help me."

Am I wasting my time trying to force someone into sobriety who isn't ready, when there are so many other forlorn sufferers out there willing to accept my help?

AUGUST 4

WORKING WITH OTHERS

If there is any indication that he wants to stop, have a good talk with the person most interested in him—usually his wife. Get an idea of his behavior, his problems, his background, the seriousness of his condition, and his religious leanings. You need this information to put yourself in his place, to see how you would like him to approach you if the tables were turned. Sometimes it is wise to wait till he goes on a binge.

[Working With Others p. 90]

CONSIDERATION

At times we don't really know if we want to stop drinking or not. Our minds are so muddled by alcohol that one moment we say we want to stop, and the next moment we are drinking again. Trying to find out more from the family of an alcoholic who may be on the verge of quitting cannot hurt, but this will have little effect on the alcoholic himself. Many approach an alcoholic by offering assistance saying something like "Whenever you're ready to stop drinking for good I'm here for you—just let me know." Once they are ready, and you have gained their trust as a fellow alcoholic, odds are they will be happy to listen to you and share their own story.

Will I continue to extend my hand to my fellow alcoholic, even if they do not accept it right away?

AUGUST 5

WORKING WITH OTHERS

Don't deal with him when he is very drunk, unless he is ugly and the family needs your help. Wait for the end of the spree, or at least for a lucid interval. Then let his family or a friend ask him if he wants to quit for good and if he would go to any extreme to do so. If he says yes, then his attention should be drawn to you as a person who has recovered....If he does not want to see you, never force yourself upon him.

[Working With Others p. 90]

CONSIDERATION

Most of us, as we approach the end of the line and know in our hearts we cannot go on much longer, are willing to listen to another alcoholic. Even if we think we are different than everyone else, or that we may be able to drink normally one day, or that there is no way out for us, speaking with someone who knows who we are as an alcoholic is often a relief. Should our alcoholic friend not want to speak with us, we do not take it personally, but make it clear to them that we are ready to talk whenever they are.

Have I ever been successful forcing myself on another alcoholic?

AUGUST 6

WORKING WITH OTHERS

See your man alone, if possible. At first engage in general conversation. After a while, turn the talk to some phase of drinking. Tell him enough about your drinking habits, symptoms, and experiences to encourage him to speak of himself. If he wishes to talk, let him do so. You will thus get a better idea of how you ought to proceed. If he is not communicative, give him a sketch of your drinking career up to the time you quit. But say nothing, for the moment, of how that was accomplished. If he is in a serious mood dwell on the troubles liquor has caused you, being careful not to moralize or lecture. If his mood is light, tell him humorous stories of your escapades. Get him to tell some of his.

[Working With Others p. 91]

CONSIDERATION

Rarely does it take long for one alcoholic to recognize and connect with another alcoholic. We easily recognize each other, sometimes without words being spoken, whether passed out in run-down barrooms or suited up in fancy corporate boardrooms. Objectively discussing our drinking addiction and the hopelessness of our illness often puts the newcomer at ease, and they start to trust that we know what we are talking about. Once they recognize that we have stood in their shoes, they may become more willing to listen to the solution we found for our alcoholism. Some say the only time to share your drunk-a-log is when trying to connect one-on-one with a newcomer. Otherwise, those experienced in the Fellowship spend the majority of their time sharing the solution, since we all know how to drink unsuccessfully.

Am I willing to honestly share my story with another alcoholic to gain their trust?

AUGUST 7

WORKING WITH OTHERS

When he sees you know all about the drinking game, commence to describe yourself as an alcoholic. Tell him how baffled you were, how you finally learned that you were sick. Give him an account of the struggles you made to stop. Show him the mental twist which leads to the first drink of a spree. We suggest you do this as we have done it in the chapter on alcoholism. If he is alcoholic, he will understand you at once. He will match your mental inconsistencies with some of his own.

[Working With Others p. 91]

CONSIDERATION

We alcoholics have a thinking problem, not a drinking problem. We have an above-the-neck problem. Most of us cannot understand why we used to be able to control our drinking and then suddenly, it seems, we couldn't. We think we have a will-power problem, not a chemical brain illness, as we know today. Our mental twist says to us that this time it will be different with our drinking. This time we'll be able to control ourselves. Or maybe we reach the point where we really don't want to take that first drink, but are so deep into our addiction that we have no mental or physical choice. We must take a drink to stop the overwhelming obsession, shaking, vomiting and subsequent craving. Many of us are blackout drinkers, on that endless merry-go-round of coming to and then drinking ourselves into unconsciousness, over and over and over. Few real alcoholics fail to relate to these personal stories.

Have I ever had any real difficulty connecting with another alcoholic?

AUGUST 8

WORKING WITH OTHERS

If you are satisfied that he is a real alcoholic, begin to dwell on the hopeless feature of the malady. Show him, from your own experience, how the queer mental condition surrounding that first drink prevents normal functioning of the will power. Don't, at this stage, refer to this book, unless he has seen it and wishes to discuss it. And be careful not to brand him as an alcoholic. Let him draw his own conclusion. If he sticks to the idea that he can still control his drinking, tell him that possibly he can—if he is not too alcoholic. But insist that if he is severely afflicted, there may be little chance he can recover by himself.

[Working With Others p. 92]

CONSIDERATION

As a real alcoholic, making that diagnosis in others does no one any good. Each drinker must come to their own conclusion. But as our alcoholic friend hears our story and shares their story, it usually doesn't take too long before they know if they are alcoholic or not. What surprises so many of us in the beginning is the realization that we are medically sick people, not morally weak people. Our brain chemistry has become so hopelessly deranged over time that no amount of will-power or additional alcohol can return our mind to a healthy state. It is like trying to lower our blood sugar as a diabetic by sheer force of will, or irrationally eating more sweets. It can't be done. As sick individuals, we learn that we have a progressive illness which will eventually kill us. But we also learn there is a treatment for our illness that works for most alcoholics if they make a concerted effort to get well, and are willing to follow directions. So the message we both hear and absorb is that as a real alcoholic we are doomed if left on our own, but there is hope for us if we are willing to stop drinking and accept help.

Do I know that I cannot recover from my alcoholism without help?

AUGUST 9

WORKING WITH OTHERS

Continue to speak of alcoholism as an illness, a fatal malady. Talk about the conditions of body and mind which accompany it. Keep his attention focused mainly on your personal experience. Explain that many are doomed who never realize their predicament. Doctors are rightly loath to tell alcoholic patients the whole story unless it will serve some good purpose.

[Working With Others p. 92]

CONSIDERATION

So many of us think we are weak-willed, bad people, who somehow have not yet found a way to control our drinking. We know we do things while drinking that we barely remember and later regret, but for some reason we don't connect our drinking with the results of our inebriated behavior. Little do we know we have a legitimate medical illness, which if not treated, will put us in our grave. Over time our brain chemistry on alcohol changes to the point where we are truly unable to stop drinking without some type of help, which can include formal medical assistance. Our brain's neuro-chemical damage cannot be undone by self-will alone, but can be treated by abstinence and time. This allows our brain chemicals to settle down and us to heal. Emotionally and physically, we need the help of a spiritual power, the Fellowship, and sometimes help from other support systems. Complete physical recovery may take years, but most of us do end up fully recovering if we remain sober, continue to accept help and follow A.A. suggestions.

When I begin working with another alcoholic do I always remember to start off by describing my alcoholism as a hopeless medical illness?

AUGUST 10

WORKING WITH OTHERS

Tell him exactly what happened to you. Stress the spiritual feature freely. If the man be agnostic or atheist, make it emphatic that he does not have to agree with your conception of God. He can choose any conception he likes, provided it makes sense to him. The main thing is that he be willing to believe in a power greater than himself and that he live by spiritual principles.

[Working With Others p. 92]

CONSIDERATION

When we are introduced to A.A., most of us want to know how to stop drinking and feel better, at least for a little while, so we can get our bearings and perhaps take care of some unsettled family, employment or legal troubles that resulted from our drunken escapades. We are not interested in hearing fancy lectures since we don't like being told what to do, but we will usually listen to someone's personal story as they describe their journey from a hopeless state of mind and body into the new freedom of recovery. Learning that we have a three-fold disease of mind, body and spirit, which requires a three-fold solution, is our beginning. Our body is damaged, but usually can recover if we completely stop drinking and allow it time to heal. Our mind is damaged because we have that peculiar mental twist way of thinking which results in continually justifying and acting out on our emotional impulses and obsession to drink. Our spirit is damaged because we have not found a non-human, spiritual energy we can connect with to help us get through life on life's terms. Time and abstinence will heal the body if not too badly damaged, and will also help heal the mind, allowing our brain chemistry to return to baseline which helps clarify our thinking. Time, abstinence and working A.A.'s 12 Steps will lead us to a spiritual awakening resulting in a change in our attitudes and actions, allowing us to adopt a new design for living.

Do I accept the fact that I have a three-fold disease, treatable with a three-fold solution?

AUGUST 11

WORKING WITH OTHERS

Your prospect may belong to a religious denomination......But he well [may] be curious to learn why his own convictions have not worked and why yours seem to work so well. He may be an example of the truth that faith alone is insufficient. To be vital, faith must be accompanied by self-sacrifice and unselfish, constructive action....call to his attention the fact that however deep his faith and knowledge, he could not have applied it or he would not drink. Perhaps your story will help him see where he has failed to practice the very precepts he knows so well.

[Working With Others p. 93]

CONSIDERATION

Most of us readily recognize and accept the fact that our bodies have been physically damaged from years of alcohol abuse, and that we seem to have a peculiar way of thinking and relating to life and the people about us. But many of us get stuck on the spiritual part—the God part. Some of us consider ourselves religious people of faith. We believe in God. We go to church. We put money in the basket. We stay awake during sermons. We pray. We have the preacher over for dinner. But we find our prayers and our faith alone does not relieve our alcoholism. We are disappointed, confused and angry. What's the matter with God? Why won't He help me? So we abandon our faith because we think it's not working. We fail to realize that faith alone, whether religious or spiritual, will never save us from our alcoholism, because faith without works is dead. Unless we use our faith, whether God based or spiritually driven, to support self-sacrifice and unselfish, constructive actions on our part, we will never recover. We may not drink, but will live out our life as an angry, miserable, depressed dry drunk, unable to experience the joy of the best that life has to offer. Faith is more than believing; faith is action.

Do I understand that I cannot recover from alcoholism by God or faith alone?

AUGUST 12

WORKING WITH OTHERS

Outline the program of action, explaining how you made a self-appraisal, how you straightened out your past and why you are now endeavoring to be helpful to him. It is important for him to realize that your attempt to pass this on to him plays a vital part in your recovery. Actually, he may be helping you more than you are helping him. Make it plain he is under no obligation to you, that you hope only that he will try to help other alcoholics when he escapes his own difficulties. Suggest how important it is that he place the welfare of other people ahead of his own. Make it clear that he is not under pressure, that he needn't see you again if he doesn't want to. You should not be offended if he wants to call it off, for he has helped you more than you have helped him.....The more hopeless he feels, the better...he will be more likely to follow your suggestions.

[Working With Others p. 94]

CONSIDERATION

Once again, experience has shown that faith alone will not save us from our alcoholism, because faith without works is dead. For us alcoholics, we must take additional actions before we are able to have a spiritual awakening which shows us how best to live our new life. These other actions are founded on doing all the work of the 12 Steps of A.A. Only by our willingness to clean up our past, embrace whatever spiritual power or energy we can muster while helping others, can we benefit from a full and useful recovery. "Trust God, clean house and help others" is a recurring traditional A.A. motto. Some say "Trust the process, clean house and help others." We learn that it is not only by practicing the principles of the 12 Steps that keeps us sober, but in doing our best to carry the A.A. message of hope and recovery to other alcoholics. If we make no effort to share our spiritual treasures with another, we will lose them.

Do I share with a newcomer the importance of our three-legged stool of recovery—mind, body and spirit?

WORKING WITH OTHERS

Your candidate may give reasons why he need not follow all of the program. He may rebel at the thought of a drastic housecleaning which requires discussion with other people. Do not contradict such views. Tell him you once felt as he does, but you doubt whether you would have made much progress had you not taken action. On your first visit tell him about the Fellowship of Alcoholics Anonymous. If he shows interest, lend him your copy of this book.

[Working With Others p. 94]

CONSIDERATION

Few of us, including the most desperate and willing of us, fail to object to some aspect of A.A. at some point. Maybe we aren't completely certain that we are alcoholic, or feel that our lives aren't totally unmanageable. Maybe we see no point in attending a bunch of A.A. meetings for the rest of our life. Perhaps we don't believe that it unnecessary to adopt the same God or Higher Power that the A.A. founders did to recover. Or we ask why all this emphasis on reviewing our past behavior, confessing to some sponsor that we barely know, and having to make restitution for harms done long ago? Why all this talk about shortcomings and character defects? Do we really need to pray and meditate each day? Must we always seek to help another alcoholic in order to stay sober? When we ask these questions, more often than not we hear the same short, simple answer from the Fellowship—"Well, that's how we stay sober."

Can I trust the experience of sober alcoholics to guide me through the A.A. program?

AUGUST 14

WORKING WITH OTHERS

Unless your friend wants to talk further about himself, do not wear out your welcome. Give him a chance to think it over. If you do stay, let him steer the conversation in any direction he likes. Sometimes a new man is anxious to proceed at once, and you may be tempted to let him do so. This is sometimes a mistake. If he has trouble later, he is likely to say you rushed him. You will be most successful with alcoholics if you do not exhibit any passion for crusade or reform. Never talk down to an alcoholic from any moral or spiritual hilltop; simply lay out the kit of spiritual tools for his inspection. Show him how they worked with you. Offer him friendship and Fellowship. Tell him that if he wants to get well you will do anything to help.

[Working With Others p. 95]

CONSIDERATION

For we whose lives have been transformed through A.A., it is sometimes difficult not to be overly enthusiastic about the program. We are so grateful and happy to have been released from the bondage of addiction and our own self-centered existence that we are determined to save the world. We insist that all alcoholics must have the freedom and peace that we have. We want to shout from the rooftops "Come and get it!" When thinking about carrying the message, we might reflect on what worked best in our own case. Perhaps it was a quiet chat over coffee with a low-key, sober, sincere fellow alcoholic who calmly and objectively told their story of recovery and the program tools that were most useful to them during that process. Maybe it was listening to a fiery, fun-loving, humorous speaker give their formal recovery presentation. Most importantly, we remember that no A.A. member ever judges us, pushes us, or belittles us when we speak. They simply tell their own story and offer to help us if we ask.

Can I share my experience with sensitivity and tact, and always keep my hand and heart prepared to help another alcoholic, if and when they decide they want my help?

AUGUST 15

WORKING WITH OTHERS

If he is not interested in your solution, if he expects you to act only as a banker for his financial difficulties or a nurse for his sprees, you may have to drop him until he changes his mind. This he may do after he gets hurts some more.

[Working With Others p. 95]

CONSIDERATION

We cannot carry the alcoholic, but we can carry the message of hope and recovery in A.A. We may be tempted to rescue the alcoholic from their material shortages, but should instead encourage them to expand their spiritual side. Do not tolerate the alcoholic playing the victim, complaining that only if this or that were going their way they'd be able to get sober. There is no valid excuse for a newcomer or anyone else in A.A. to ever drink again, not follow Big Book directions, miss meetings, ignore their sponsor, refuse to complete their 12 Step work, reject a spiritual power of their understanding, behave in a constantly selfish manner, or fail to help another alcoholic.

Will I support any alcoholic in working the A.A. program, but only if they are serious about their recovery?

AUGUST 16

WORKING WITH OTHERS

If he is sincerely interested and wants to see you again, ask him to read this book in the interval. After doing that, he must decide for himself whether he wants to go on. He should not be pushed or prodded by you, his wife, or his friends. If he is to find God, the desire must come from within. If he thinks he can do the job in some other way, or prefers some other spiritual approach, encourage him to follow his own conscience. We have no monopoly on God; we merely have an approach that worked with us. But point out that we alcoholics have much in common and that you would like, in any case, to be friendly. Let it go at that.

[Working With Others p. 95]

CONSIDERATION

No alcoholic can be bullied into sobriety. Spouses may threaten to leave. Parents, siblings, children, friends and family may threaten estrangement. Employers may threaten termination. Courts may mandate A.A. attendance. None of these coercions are likely to succeed in forcing a sick alcoholic into the willingness to surrender, or ask for and accept help. Support is available from A.A. and many other recovery programs. Some alcoholics have recovered without A.A., and some have actually recovered entirely on their own. Alcoholics don't enter A.A. looking for God; they are looking for relief. Nor does finding God alone result in sobriety, as Dr. Bob's experience can attest. Faith, whether religious or spiritually based, is useless without constructive, selfless action based on the principles of our 12 Step program. The alcoholic must seek both human and spiritual aid if they are to change their life. God alone will not restore the alcoholic, but seeking both a human and spiritual solution will.

Can I refrain from imposing my personal beliefs and will on alcoholics new to A.A.?

WORKING WITH OTHERS

Do not be discouraged if your prospect does not respond at once. Search out another alcoholic and try again. You are sure to find someone desperate enough to accept with eagerness what you offer. We find it a waste of time to keep chasing a man who cannot or will not work with you. If you leave such a person alone, he may soon become convinced that he cannot recover by himself. To spend too much time on any one situation is to deny some other alcoholic an opportunity to live and be happy.

[Working With Others p. 96]

CONSIDERATION

None of us has the power to get anyone sober, just as we don't have the power to make anyone drink or get them drunk. Remember that the alcoholic is a very sick person with a severe medical illness, which deeply distorts their thinking and behavior. If the alcoholic is unable or unwilling to engage in recovery, most of us tell them we will be available to them should they change their mind, and then we seek out the next alcoholic in need. We may feel sadness or regret that we must move on, because we know the pain that alcoholic will continue to carry, but we do so anyway. We harbor no feelings of personal failure, and have no reason to feel guilty, or that we have failed at our task. We don't have the power to save the world, but we can continue to seek out and offer our experience, hope and assistance to the next alcoholic willing to speak with us.

Will I continue to seek out newcomers and try to help them, even if those I've helped in the past have not remained sober?

AUGUST 18

WORKING WITH OTHERS

Suppose now you are making your second visit to a man. He has read this volume and says he is prepared to go through with the Twelve Steps of the program of recovery. Having had the experience yourself, you can give him much practical advice. Let him know you are available if he wishes to make a decision and tell his story, but do not insist upon it if he prefers to consult someone else.

[Working With Others p. 96]

CONSIDERATION

It is hard to believe, but statistically, the vast majority of average alcohol abusers, over time, recover completely on their own, without A.A. or any type of formal rehabilitation therapy. This fact in no way diminishes the importance or power of A.A., or of other recovery programs that have helped heal millions of sufferers. The small percentage of active alcoholics who choose to engage in A.A.'s Fellowship and 12 Step program are often the most severely ill among us, and they are the ones unlikely to get sober without some type of help. Happily, a large percentage of those that fully and deeply participate in the A.A. program and Fellowship, connect with and persevere in A.A., do find sobriety and a better way of living. Studies have shown that the more intensely an alcoholic becomes involved with all aspects of A.A., the more likely they are to recover. That is why they say in A.A. "Stay in the center of the herd." Nonetheless, celebrating the recovery efforts of all our fellow sufferers, regardless of which method they try or choose, is the best way we can support them. Should our new man or woman wish to try out the A.A. solution, we are here for them.

Can I eliminate any prejudice I have about A.A. being the one and only way to recover?

AUGUST 19

WORKING WITH OTHERS

Never avoid these responsibilities, but be sure you are doing the right thing if you assume them. Helping others is the foundation stone of your recovery. A kindly act once in a while isn't enough. You have to act the Good Samaritan every day, if need be. It may mean the loss of many nights' sleep, great interference with your pleasures, interruptions to your business.

[Working With Others p. 97]

CONSIDERATION

When we choose to sponsor another alcoholic, remembering that it is our job and duty to do so, it helps to adopt an attitude of usefulness and purpose. Remembering how we were best helped often guides us on how to help others. Re-reading the Big Book chapter "Working With Others," which outlines how to sponsor alcoholics, is a useful exercise. Remaining objective as we begin our work usually keeps us focused on our sole job of taking the newcomer through the 12 Step program. Obviously, we first qualify our potential sponsee as a real alcoholic, because if they don't have alcohol in their story, then our own experience with alcohol probably won't connect with them. Next, we can discuss with our newcomer what sponsorship means, and the expectation that they agree to follow directions and go to any length to treat their disease. After that, we can begin the 12 Step work. Whether we like the person or not is irrelevant. Becoming friends is unimportant. We consider sponsorship an objective business relationship rather than a social engagement. As such, much time and effort on our part is often required.

Am I willing to work with another alcoholic intensively as a sponsor, which often involves great personal sacrifice on my part?

WORKING WITH OTHERS

Though an alcoholic does not respond, there is no reason why you should neglect his family. You should continue to be friendly to them. The family should be offered your way of life. Should they accept and practice spiritual principles, there is a much better chance that the head of the family will recover. And even though he continues to drink, the family will find life more bearable.

[Working With Others p. 97]

CONSIDERATION

Many sponsors have never met any of their sponsees' families, unless they have been directly approached by an exasperated family member on behalf of the alcoholic. Should this be the case, common sense and the experience of our own sponsor and others in the Fellowship can often give us direction on how best to proceed. We must remember that our primary purpose is to help the still suffering alcoholic, not the family of the alcoholic. This may sound uncaring, but there are many excellent support programs for the family and friends of alcoholics. Al-Anon and Alateen can frequently bring comfort and direction to those that participate, and are highly recommended for suffering family and friends of alcoholics.

Do I understand my primary purpose is to help the alcoholic, regardless of their family situation?

AUGUST 21

WORKING WITH OTHERS

For the type of alcoholic who is able and willing to get well, little charity, in the ordinary sense of the word, is needed or wanted. The men who cry for money and shelter before conquering alcohol, are on the wrong track. Yet we do go to great extremes to provide each other with these very things, when such action is warranted. This may seem inconsistent, but we think it is not.

[Working With Others p. 97]

CONSIDERATION

If we are completely honest with ourselves, and despite advice to the contrary, few of us can say that we never gave an alcoholic a few dollars to tide them over, or helped them find a job, or put them up for a night or two in our basement, or provided a bit more transportation and other services for them than we probably should have. It seems to be in our nature to help out a fellow sufferer in any way we can, in the hope that our actions will encourage them to continue their path to recovery. We may remember some kindness given us when we were still drinking, or after we stopped drinking, and feel as if we must return the favor. Perhaps we are sometimes taken advantage of by the alcoholic's requests, but if we are, we usually don't get too upset over it.

If I am asked to help another alcoholic in a charitable sense, will I pause to consider whether or not the request relates to their spiritual growth, or simply involves a material need?

AUGUST 22

WORKING WITH OTHERS

It is not the matter of giving that is in question, but when and how to give. That often makes the difference between failure and success. The minute we put our work on a service plane, the alcoholic commences to rely upon our assistance rather than upon God. He clamors for this or that, claiming he cannot master alcohol until his material needs are cared for. Nonsense. Some of us have taken very hard knocks to learn this truth: Job or no job—wife or no wife—we simply do not stop drinking so long as we place dependence upon other people ahead of dependence on God. Burn this idea into the consciousness of every man that he can get well regardless of anyone. The only condition is that he trust in God and clean house.

[Working With Others p. 98]

CONSIDERATION

Despite looking like a duck, walking like a duck and quacking like a duck, A.A. is not a religious program. It is a spiritual Fellowship whose purpose is for members to help each other get and stay sober. For religious members, God often becomes that person's Higher Power. Those who cannot connect with God are tasked to find, define, connect with, and use a spiritual Higher Power of their own creation. Even after that is accomplished, fully connecting with the power of the program is not something that comes quickly or easily for most of us. Very few of us have a sudden, hot flash religious or spiritual experience in A.A. Instead, most of us have that slow spiritual awakening which results in a gradual change in our attitudes and actions. This awakening, with a broader and deeper incorporation of a spiritual power of our own understanding into our life, may occur months or even years after completing our Step work. But it will come eventually, if we remain sober, work with other alcoholics and continue to practice the principles of the Steps.

Do I believe that I will always need the power of the Fellowship and some type of spiritual power of my understanding to grow in my recovery?

WORKING WITH OTHERS

Now, the domestic problem: There may be divorce, separation, or just strained relations. When your prospect has made such reparation as he can to his family, and has thoroughly explained to them the new principles by which he is living, he should proceed to put those principles into action at home. That is, if he is lucky enough to have a home. Though his family be at fault in many respects, he should not be concerned about that. He should concentrate on his own spiritual demonstration. Argument and fault-finding are to be avoided like the plague.

[Working With Others p. 98]

CONSIDERATION

Actions always speak louder than words. How many times do we explain to our spouses and family that this time we will behave differently? We swear and pledge that this time we have stopped drinking for good and are ready to get our life back on track. Yet how can we forget or ignore the harms we did to our family and others through our years of drinking? Those injuries do not go away quickly, and we shouldn't expect them to. Only by our actions in sobriety will we begin to regain the trust of our family and fellows, if we are to regain any of their trust at all. Some people will never trust us again, and exclude us from their lives forever. It doesn't matter. If we continue to try our best to do the next right thing and follow the 12 Step principles each day, then we have done right by ourself, our family and our fellows, regardless of anyone else's opinion, response or reaction.

After making amends to my family, have I explained to them that I am doing the best I can to do right by them, using the tools and principles I'm learning in A.A.?

WORKING WITH OTHERS

After they have seen tangible results, the family will perhaps want to go along. These things will come to pass naturally and in good time provided, however, the alcoholic continues to demonstrate that he can be sober, considerate, and helpful, regardless of what anyone says or does. Of course, we all fall much below this standard many times. But we must try to repair the damage immediately lest we pay the penalty by a spree.

[Working With Others p. 99]

CONSIDERATION

If we depend on the reactions of our family and the people about us to maintain our sobriety, we will never stay sober. Who doesn't want praise and congratulations for not drinking? Who doesn't want to be immediately forgiven and fully trusted by family members, despite having spent years tearing down our relationship with them? Why should the family be distressed, we wonder, if we fall short of the mark from time to time, since we're trying as hard as we can? Sometimes the best approach is to spend less time worrying about what our family thinks of us and more time striving to behave in an honest, kind, tolerant and forthright manner toward those we love. When we get off track, it is not too difficult to admit it, make an amend if necessary, and immediately return to doing the right thing without drinking, pouting or developing a resentment.

Can I stop changing my behavior based on how others respond, and simply behave in accordance with the A.A. principles?

AUGUST 25

WORKING WITH OTHERS

If there be divorce or separation, there should be no undue haste for the couple to get together. The man should be sure of his recovery. The wife should fully understand his new way of life. If their old relationship is to be resumed it must be on a better basis, since the former did not work. This means a new attitude and spirit all around. Sometimes it is to the best interests of all concerned that a couple remains apart. Obviously, no rule can be laid down. Let the alcoholic continue his program day by day. When the time for living together has come, it will be apparent to both parties.

[Working With Others p. 99]

CONSIDERATION

When a person maintains sobriety and develops a new way of living, it involves change. In sobriety, we become a different person than we were while drinking. We change mentally, physically and spiritually. Even though some changes may be seen as positive by our spouses, other changes may paradoxically so upset and distort our marriage that for whatever reason it cannot continue despite our best efforts. Habits change, responsibilities and obligations shift, and anxiety often increases as expectations grow in both parties. Adjusting to these changes may be too much for a spouse. If that be the case, it is never a valid excuse for us to give up, drink, criticize or take revenge. Instead, we may want to work on accepting, at least for the time being, that which we cannot change or control.

Can I stop changing my behavior based on how my spouse or partner is responding, and just continue to practice the A.A. principles?

AUGUST 26

WORKING WITH OTHERS

Let no alcoholic say he cannot recover unless he has his family back. This just isn't so. In some cases the wife will never come back for one reason or another. Remind the prospect that his recovery is not dependent upon people. It is dependent upon his relationship with God. We have seen men get well whose families have not returned at all. We have seen others slip when the family came back too soon. Both you and the new man must walk day by day in the path of spiritual progress. If you persist, remarkable things will happen.

[Working With Others p. 99]

CONSIDERATION

Just as we cannot tie our sobriety to recovering our material possessions, we cannot base our sobriety on the return of our relationships. Nothing and no one can make us take that first drink unless we allow it. If we allow it, the reason we give becomes just one more in the long list of excuses we used to give for drinking in the past. Our sobriety is tied not to people or things, but to our spiritual foundation. If we truly believe that our new purpose in life is to live it in a sober, responsible and loving manner, we can draw strength from this objective. Whatever god or spiritual Higher Power, Force, Purpose or Principles we connect with, it will provide us with adequate and continued strength and guidance, if we permit it. Our friends in the Fellowship can provide human encouragement and suggestions, but cannot do the work for us, just as our spiritual foundation alone is no substitute for our measurable and tangible efforts to change.

Will I refuse to allow my sober journey to be dependent upon what other people think, say or how they act?

AUGUST 27

WORKING WITH OTHERS

Assuming we are spiritually fit, we can do all sorts of things alcoholics are not supposed to do. People have said we must not go where liquor is served....Our experience shows that this is not necessarily so. We meet these conditions every day. An alcoholic who cannot meet them still has an alcoholic mind; there is something the matter with his spiritual status....In our belief any scheme of combating alcoholism which proposes to shield the sick man from temptation is doomed to failure. If the alcoholic tries to shield himself he may succeed for a time, but usually winds up with a bigger explosion than ever. We have tried these methods. These attempts to do the impossible have always failed.

[Working With Others p. 100]

CONSIDERATION

Hiding or denying the reality of everyday living will not protect us from alcohol or the temptation to use it. Sticking our head in the sand, pretending that what we can't see doesn't exist, never works. Just as we must look ourselves in the mirror each day, we must look at life in full force each day. If we continually use all the tools of the A.A. program, we usually find that facing life on life's terms is not too difficult. If we have a solid foundation based on the power of the Fellowship and our spiritual convictions, it is unlikely we will be presented with anything that will delude or weaken us to the extent that we succumb to John Barleycorn. Remember that we have a thinking problem, not a drinking problem. The foundation we build and maintain is to help us keep on track with our thinking. If we do that, we won't be drinking.

Am I still tempted to drink whenever I am around alcohol?

AUGUST 28

WORKING WITH OTHERS

So our rule is not to avoid a place where there is drinking, if we have a legitimate reason for being there....Therefore, ask yourself on each occasion, "Have I any good social, business, or personal reason for going to this place? Or am I expecting to steal a little vicarious pleasure from the atmosphere of such places?"...But be sure you are on solid spiritual ground before you start and that your motive in going is thoroughly good. Do not think of what you will get out of the occasion. Think of what you can bring to it. But if you are shaky, you had better work with another alcoholic instead!

[Working With Others p. 101]

CONSIDERATION

How easy it is for us to reminisce about the good old days when we could control our drinking! What fun we had, relaxing and enjoying the company of seemingly loyal friends. We spoke of grand ideas and imaginary accomplishments. We knew we were at our best after a few sips of the bottle. Not all of our past pleasures were delusions, but many of them were. The truth is that we needed alcohol just to survive each day. We used alcohol to cover over yesterday's failures and fight off tomorrow's fears. Alcohol allows us to wear any mask we choose to present to the world, hiding our true nature. After we stop drinking and visit places which serve alcohol, it is often difficult to shut off our muddled memories of grandeur and invincibility. If we can pause before embarking, seek spiritual direction and Fellowship guidance, remind ourselves that our illness drives us to drink even when we are not drinking, review our motives, ensure that we are emotionally fit for the journey—then we can decide whether to proceed or not. If we are not sure, remember that no personal or business venture is worth us taking a drink. If we feel we are spiritually fit, we can console ourselves by concentrating on what we can bring to the occasion rather than what we can get out of it, thereby avoiding the trap of self-pity of not being able to drink like other people.

Do I have a legitimate reason to be around alcohol today?

WORKING WITH OTHERS

Why set with a long face in places where there is drinking, sighing about the good old days? If it is a happy occasion, try to increase the pleasure of those there; if a business occasion, go and attend to your business enthusiastically.

[Working With Others p. 102]

CONSIDERATION

Most of us drink secretly before social or business occasions to loosen up, as they say. Once we get to the party and continue to drink, we usually have a good time, at least for a while. As our illness progresses, we end up drinking more than we should while in public, and frequently behave in a regrettable manner while we are out and about. This leads to increasing apprehension before our next occasion, as our fear over not knowing how well we can maintain our sobriety in public grows. Eventually, after experiencing frequent embarrassing situations or blacking out, we begin to withdraw from outside engagements. We either drink in seedy public places where no one cares about our drunken, blackout prone behavior, or we drink alone. Now that we are sober, we must re-learn how to venture out in public. We may still have a lingering fear of what people will think of us, and that we will somehow make a fool of ourself. That would be especially humiliating for us since we will be sober and remember every detail. If we can change our attitude before such encounters to one of giving rather than taking, our anxiety diminishes. We can start out slowly as we ease back into the outside events life has to offer, beginning with the ones we are obligated to do first, and then adding others as we grow in maturity, confidence, stability and spiritual fortitude.

Am I willing to think of others in social or business situations, and try to increase their pleasure rather than my own?

AUGUST 30

WORKING WITH OTHERS

Your job now is to be at the place where you may be of maximum helpfulness to others, so never hesitate to go anywhere if you can be helpful. You should not hesitate to visit the most sordid spot on earth on such an errand. Keep on the firing line of life with these motives and God will keep you unharmed.

[Working With Others p. 102]

CONSIDERATION

Part of our new way of living, suggested by Step Twelve, involves trying to carry the A.A. message of hope and recovery to the still suffering alcoholic. But this Step also suggests we practice all the A.A. Step principles, such as love, tolerance, kindness and unselfishness, in all our affairs in order to be of maximum service to others, whether they are alcoholic or not. Today, most of us don't need to visit bars to find other alcoholics. Our meeting rooms are filled with newcomers, as are our jails, hospitals, nursing homes, homeless shelters, half-way houses, sober houses, rehabilitation facilities and treatment centers. There is no reason to fear visiting any of these places to carry the A.A. message of recovery. Of course, no one should ignore the realities of life before setting up a meeting with a newcomer, since some locations and situations could be inappropriate or even dangerous. Some of us may go on a Twelfth Step call alone by necessity, but most of us prefer to go in twos or threes for safety reasons and to share more broadly our experiences. Witnessing with others is the foundation of our program, and every reasonable effort should be made to carry out our primary purpose.

Do I believe that reaching out to an alcoholic every day keeps my obsession away?

AUGUST 31

WORKING WITH OTHERS

After all, our problems were of our own making. Bottles were only a symbol. Besides, we have stopped fighting anybody or anything. We have to!

[Working With Others p. 102]

CONSIDERATION

Our first surrender in A.A. is to alcohol. We cannot always control our drinking once we start, and we can't stop for good when we decide to, and our life is a mess. Our second surrender comes shortly after we get sober. We become willing to do the work and follow the suggested 12 Steps of the A.A. program. In doing so, we realize we have to make a third surrender—to life itself. We learn that we can't control anything in life outside of our own hula-hoop. Only our attitudes and actions are subject to our control, so there is no use in continuing the fight. Just as all of our struggles fail to allow us to drink normally, all of our efforts to bend the world to our will fail. We give up our role as Director of the Universe in Steps 2 and 3; we take off our God-cape. We discover that we have a major role in all our problems, past and present, in Steps 4 and 5. We address our shortcomings in Steps 6 and 7. We make restitution for our past wrongs in Steps 8 and 9. In Steps 10, 11 and 12, we discover our new role in life as we learn how to fit ourselves to be of maximum service to our spiritual self and the people about us. By this time we no longer need to fight anything or anyone. We don't even think about it anymore. Liquor is no longer on our list of solutions for our problems in life. What a wonderful way to live!

Have I stopped fighting the world, and everyone and everything in it?

SEPTEMBER 1

TO WIVES

With few exceptions, our book thus far has spoken of men. But what we have said applies quite as much to women. Our activities on behalf of women who drink are on the increase. There is every evidence that women regain their health as readily as men if they try our suggestions. But for every man who drinks others are involved—the wife who trembles in fear of the next debauch; the mother and father who see their son wasting away.

[To Wives p. 104]

CONSIDERATION

Alcoholism is a family disease. Studies say twelve or more family members are directly and significantly affected by the illness of a single alcoholic. Parents, spouses, siblings and children, being the ones usually closest to the alcoholic, are often the most severely damaged by the destruction and chaos the alcoholic creates. The Al-Anon and Alateen Fellowships, whose 12 Steps and program principles are very similar to those of A.A., are available to support families and friends of alcoholics. Even though most people who read the chapter "To Wives" are alcoholics in recovery, we alcoholics often have family or friends trying to get sober that concern us. So we read the words and suggestions in this chapter not only as one who has stood in an alcoholic's shoes, but as one who also cares about all the other struggling alcoholics in our life.

Do I support the participation of my family and friends in our sister Fellowships?

SEPTEMBER 2

TO WIVES

Among us are wives, relatives and friends whose problem has been solved, as well as some who have not yet found a happy solution. We want the wives of Alcoholics Anonymous to address the wives of men who drink too much. What they say will apply to nearly everyone bound by ties of blood or affection to an alcoholic. As wives of Alcoholics Anonymous, we would like you to feel that we understand as perhaps few can. We want to analyze mistakes we have made. We want to leave you with the feeling that no situation is too difficult and no unhappiness too great to be overcome.

[To Wives p. 104]

CONSIDERATION

As alcoholics, we have spent a lifetime thinking mostly of ourselves. As we try to clean up our past and prepare ourselves for our future, part of our responsibility is to support our non-alcoholic family and the friends we harmed as they struggle to recover from the damage we inflicted upon them while drinking. Whether or not we stay sober, there is no reason we cannot encourage those we love and care about to seek practical and spiritual help for themselves. Our job is not to tell others what to do, but part of our own healing involves being supportive, kind, forgiving and thoughtful toward all those around us in any way we can.

Am I willing to put aside any disapproval or resentment of others who try to get help for themselves as I make my own way in A.A.?

SEPTEMBER 3

TO WIVES

We have traveled rocky roads, there is no mistake about that. We have had long rendezvous with hurt pride, frustration, self-pity, misunderstanding and fear. These are not pleasant companions. We have been driven to maudlin sympathy, to bitter resentment. Some of us veered from extreme to extreme, ever hoping that one day our loved ones would be themselves once more.

[To Wives p. 104]

CONSIDERATION

Most of us have alcoholics in our life that we care about. After we get sober and travel down the road of recovery, we become increasingly concerned about our friends and relatives still in the grip of their addiction. We, who have recovered, want to help them in the same way that our loved ones wanted to help us. We know in our head we cannot make them get sober, but in our heart we really wish we could somehow force them into recovery. Even though that approach doesn't work, we still delude ourselves into thinking that because we are alcoholic, we are automatically more qualified to give advice to other alcoholics we know. Not so. All we can do is make suggestions and accept the choices made by others.

Can I remember that I didn't cause the illness of alcoholism in others, that I can't cure it, and that I can't control it?

SEPTEMBER 4

TO WIVES

Our loyalty and the desire that our husbands hold up their heads and be like other men have begotten all sorts of predicaments. We have been unselfish and self-sacrificing. We have told innumerable lies to protect our pride and our husbands' reputations. We have prayed, we have begged, we have been patient. We have struck out viciously. We have run away. We have been hysterical. We have been terror stricken. We have sought sympathy. We have had retaliatory love affairs with other men.

[To Wives p. 105]

CONSIDERATION

Once sober, we behave like anyone else when around other alcoholics that we love. We react in the same manner as the person who has never taken a drink. We try all sorts of ways to help our fellow alcoholic, and when they do not respond according to our plan, we become frustrated and angry. Why can't my spouse sober up like I did? Why can't my children stop using alcohol and drugs? Why can't my best friend stop killing himself with booze? Threatening the alcoholic with divorce or other intimidating schemes may nudge them into treatment or the rooms of A.A. for a short time, but it will do little good if their heart is not in it. Retaliating against the drinker is about as effective as retaliating against someone who has cancer or any other illness; it doesn't work. Remembering our own experience with alcohol addiction, we may choose to use the approach that worked best with us. Rather than using threats, humiliation and reprisal, we can behave toward our addicted loved ones just as we behave towards any newcomer in A.A—with kindness and tolerance as we share our story of hope and recovery.

Can I treat my loved ones in their addiction in the same kindly way that I was treated?

SEPTEMBER 5

TO WIVES

Our homes have been battlegrounds many an evening. In the morning we have kissed and made up. Our friends have counseled chucking the men and we have done so with finality, only to be back in a little while hoping, always hoping. Our men have sworn great solemn oaths that they were through drinking forever. We have believed them when no one else could or would. Then, in days, weeks, or months, a fresh outburst.

[To Wives p. 105]

CONSIDERATION

Having firsthand experience with alcoholism, it would seem logical that we would be more calm and collected when we are around others similarly addicted. Usually we are, but for some strange reason we often lose all semblance of sanity when those others are close friends or family members. Then we react as any normal person would. We want to believe their lies just as they believed ours. We hope tomorrow will somehow be different, and that time will magically heal our spouse, parent, sibling, child, or best friend even though we were never cured by simply wishing, hoping or pretending. We had to take action, and seek ongoing help from others outside the family to treat our alcoholic disease.

Do I understand that just because I share the same illness as those I care about, I am not immune to the effects their illness has on me?

SEPTEMBER 6

TO WIVES

We seldom had friends at our homes, never knowing how or when the men of the house would appear. We could make few social engagements. We came to live almost alone. When we were invited out, our husbands sneaked so many drinks that they spoiled the occasion. If, on the other hand, they took nothing, their self-pity made them killjoys.

[To Wives p. 105]

CONSIDERATION

As alcoholics, we recognize our own behavior in other alcoholics. Now sober, it is easy for us to identify the progression of alcoholism in our spouses, parents, siblings, children and friends. We know why they refuse to answer our calls or texts, won't open the door to us, and won't return our notes or letters. We know all about the need to sneak drinks before going out to dinners and parties, or any other public or private event. We understand why they pout and sulk when they can't drink openly. It hurts us, and we feel helpless. But we can change our attitude and expectations. Just because our alcoholic isolates, it doesn't mean we must isolate. On the contrary, we often find it comforting to be with other sober family and friends. They give us purpose and strength. They can support us as we deal with the everyday problems of life, and can encourage us to be open and honest with our feelings.

Will I resist isolating even though my alcoholic spouse, partner, family member or friend does?

SEPTEMBER 7

TO WIVES

There was never financial security. Positions were always in jeopardy or gone. An armored car could not have brought the pay envelopes home. The checking account melted like snow in June. Sometimes there were other women. How heart-breaking was this discovery; how cruel to be told they understood our men as we did not! The bill collectors, the sheriffs, the angry taxi drivers, the policemen, the bums, the pals, and even the ladies they sometimes brought home—our husbands thought we were so inhospitable. "Joykiller, nag, wet blanket"—that's what they said. Next day they would be themselves again and we would forgive and try to forget.

[To Wives p. 106]

CONSIDERATION

Just because we have sobered up and our spouse hasn't, it doesn't make it any easier to ignore financial matters. If our spouse cannot work, our family income suffers. If our spouse is stealing money from us, we suffer the loss as well. If our spouse is cheating on us, or creating legal problems for the family which cost money to rectify, or is doing all the other things that we did while intoxicated, everyone suffers. We also suffer mentally, physically and spiritually. During these hard times it is critical that we avoid our old habit of denying the reality of our situation and burying our pain and fear deep inside us. We may be better served to immerse ourselves in our own recovery program, using all the recovery tools we can to help us deal with life's trials and troubles.

Am I sticking close to my own recovery program and support group, keeping myself as healthy as possible, so I will have the strength and purpose to help those I love when the time comes?

SEPTEMBER 8

TO WIVES

We have tried to hold the love of our children for their father. We have told small tots that father was sick, which was much nearer the truth than we realized. They struck the children, kicked out door panels, smashed treasured crockery, and ripped the keys out of pianos. In the midst of such pandemonium they may have rushed out threatening to live with the other woman forever. In desperation, we have even got tight ourselves—the drunk to end all drunks. The unexpected result was that our husbands seemed to like it.

[To Wives p. 106]

CONSIDERATION

When we live with another alcoholic we may have unhealthy thoughts. Our own peculiar mental twists that we know so well may return at any time, so we might want to be prepared. When our loved one is drinking, we may think, "What the heck, I'll just have a drink too," or "I'll show them what a real drunk looks like in case they have forgotten." Even though these feelings may surface from our frustration at not being able to control our alcoholic, at the core they are selfish and self-centered. We do not have to act recklessly simply because we are not getting our own way. Being resentful, vindictive or passive-aggressive helps no one. If instead, we re-double our efforts to seek strength and guidance from our spiritual power and the Fellowship, we may find we are much less disturbed and fearful over any given situation. Getting relief from the insanity of the moment comes easier if we focus on just this day, and try not to be consumed by what happened yesterday or what might happen tomorrow.

Can I commit to stay in this day only, asking for help and guidance for just these twenty-four hours?

TO WIVES

Perhaps at this point we got a divorce and took the children home to father and mother. Then we were severely criticized by our husband's parents for desertion. Usually we did not leave. We stayed on and on. We finally sought employment ourselves as destitution faced us and our families.

[To Wives p. 106]

CONSIDERATION

So many of us alcoholics are sensitive, yet short-tempered, all-or-nothing types of people. When we feel threatened, we get defensive and angry, and we want to fix everything right now. When that doesn't work, we decide "We're getting out of here," scoop up the children, file for divorce from our alcoholic spouse, and think "Good luck and good riddance." Ironically, these actions may be totally appropriate for all involved. Or not. If we can pause when agitated and use our A.A. spiritual toolkit, we find we have more options than fight or flight. Asking for spiritual direction during quiet time, speaking with our sponsor and support group, not rushing any critical decision, seeking professional advice if indicated; all these tools are available to us now that we are sober. We may ultimately decide to stay with our suffering spouse a while longer, or decide that a temporary or trial separation is in order. Since no one knows what the future holds, leaving the door open to later reconciliation if the family situation improves may be an option.

Can I accept that one day I may need to leave the alcoholic to ensure my own survival?

SEPTEMBER 10

TO WIVES

Sometimes we sensed dimly that we were dealing with sick men. Had we fully understood the nature of the alcoholic illness, we might have behaved differently. How could men who loved their wives and children be so unthinking, so callous, so cruel?....And even if they did not love their families, how could they be so blind about themselves? What had become of their judgment, their common sense, their will power?....Why was it, when these dangers were pointed out that they agreed, and then got drunk again immediately? These are some of the questions which race through the mind of every woman who has an alcoholic husband.

[To Wives p. 107]

CONSIDERATION

Just because we are recovered alcoholics with a wealth of knowledge and experience under our belts, rarely does it make it any easier to live with another alcoholic. Having an alcoholic spouse, sibling, child or parent under our roof creates a constant daily stress as we strive to help and support the alcoholic, while at the same time protecting our own sanity and sobriety. We alternate between feelings of compassion and anger, beaten down by a desperate situation we cannot control. Our unpredictable and chaotic lives exhaust us, despite support from friends, family and the Fellowship. We are unsure how to draw personal physical and emotional boundaries so that we are not dragged down by our alcoholic sufferer. Tough love may dictate one approach today, but a totally different approach tomorrow. In the end, we learn to live our own life in sobriety, regardless of how the alcoholic lives theirs. We may think at first that this is cruel and unfeeling, but protecting our own sanity and sobriety always comes first.

Can I separate myself from my fellow alcoholic, not letting my own life be consumed by the alcoholic's firestorm?

SEPTEMBER 11

TO WIVES

Try not to condemn your alcoholic husband no matter what he says or does. He is just another very sick, unreasonable person. Treat him, when you can, as though he had pneumonia. When he angers you, remember that he is very ill. There is an important exception to the foregoing. We realize some men are thoroughly bad intentioned, that no amount of patience will make any difference. An alcoholic of this temperament may be quick to use this chapter as a club over your head. Don't let him get away with it.

[To Wives p. 108]

CONSIDERATION

It is often difficult to remember how badly we behaved while in the grips of our alcoholism. Whether drunk or sober, we were emotionally unstable and unavailable. We cared only about ourselves and our bottle. When confronted with a family alcoholic, we react as a non-alcoholic would, lashing out in anger at their continued drunkenness as all memory of our own past struggles mysteriously vanishes. We think that just because we behaved poorly while drinking doesn't excuse anyone else from behaving in the same way we did. Our intolerance may grow out of the fear of losing the one we love, but it is a poor excuse for our actions. Perhaps it is better to treat our alcoholic as the sick person we were. We continue to not drink, maintain our boundaries, use our Fellowship support group, keep our judgmental mouth shut, protect our emotional sobriety and refuse to be consumed by the destruction, deception and turmoil around us.

Do I have the strength to simply walk away from a situation that continually angers or hurts me?

SEPTEMBER 12

TO WIVES

The problem with which you struggle usually falls within one of four categories: One: Your husband may be only a heavy drinker....His drinking may be constant or it may be heavy only on certain occasions.....Some will moderate or stop altogether, and some will not. Two: Your husband is showing lack of control, for he is unable to stay on the water wagon even when he wants to....Three: This husband has gone much further than husband number two.....He may have come to the point where he desperately wants to stop but cannot.....Four: You may have a husband of whom you completely despair. He has been placed in one institution after another. He is violent, or appears definitely insane when drunk.

[To Wives p. 108]

CONSIDERATION

How damaged the alcoholic in our life is depends on how far their illness has progressed. We know alcoholics will certainly get worse over time without human and spiritual help. From our own experience as an alcoholic, we know that no family member or anyone else can stop the alcoholic's descent into isolation and eventual death by means of pleas or threats. This is our reality, and cannot be denied, wished, or dreamed away.

Do I believe alcoholism is a progressive disease that cannot be stopped in others by my own feelings or actions?

SEPTEMBER 13

TO WIVES

The first principle of success is that you should never be angry. Even though your husband becomes unbearable and you have to leave him temporarily, you should, if you can, go without rancor. Patience and good temper are most necessary. Our next thought is that you should never tell him what he must do about his drinking.

[To Wives p. 111]

CONSIDERATION

We alcoholics rarely get sober for anyone else, nor do we get sober because someone tells us to. We may agree to enter a treatment center or attend A.A. meetings after being cajoled or threatened by a spouse, family member, or employer, when in our heart all we want to do is get them off our back. We agree to seek help because we feel we have no other choice at the time, not because we really want to. Perhaps we are under court ordered treatment, but we just count the days until we will be free to drink again. For those of us living with an alcoholic who is destroying our family, why wouldn't we be angry at having our lives uprooted because of someone else's behavior? Being the kind, loving, thoughtful, patient, tolerant spouse does not come easy when our house is on fire. Why should it anyway? Who wouldn't be angry when forced to deal with such overwhelming problems? If we can acknowledge and accept our anger as justified, but not let it grow into resentment and revenge, we will rest easier at night. Accepting our powerlessness over another's behavior will not fix the situation, but it may bring us a bit of serenity, and the energy to fight yet another day.

Can I accept that I am not responsible for my alcoholic's illness, or for their recovery?

SEPTEMBER 14

TO WIVES

Be determined that your husband's drinking is not going to spoil your relations with your children or your friends. They need your companionship and your help. It is possible to have a full and useful life, though your husband continues to drink. We know women who are unafraid, even happy under these conditions. Do not set your heart on reforming your husband. You may be unable to do so, no matter how hard you try.

[To Wives p. 111]

CONSIDERATION

Experience shows that no one can force another to recover. We can be supportive, encouraging and loving, while leaving the alcoholic to suffer the consequences of their illness without interfering. This is called detaching with love. We must attend to our own health and sanity first, followed by the safety and health of our children and other loved ones. To some, this approach may seem cold-hearted. Some call it tough love, or not enabling the alcoholic by rescuing them from the damaging consequences of their behavior. We have found that trying to shield the alcoholic from the destructiveness of their disease accomplishes nothing in the long run. Only when the alcoholic steps into recovery can our family life start to change for the better.

Will I stop trying to rescue the alcoholic in my life?

SEPTEMBER 15

TO WIVES

Your husband may come to appreciate your reasonableness and patience. This may lay the groundwork for a friendly talk about his alcoholic problem. Try to have him bring up the subject himself. Be sure you are not critical during such a discussion. Attempt instead, to put yourself in his place. Let him see that you want to be helpful rather than critical.....Tell him you have been worried...Show him you have confidence in his power to stop or moderate. Say you do not want to be a wet blanket; that you only want him to take care of his health. Thus you may succeed in interesting him in alcoholism.

[To Wives p. 111]

CONSIDERATION

If we look back on our own alcoholic past and what helped us the most to get into recovery, we often remember it was the gentle and persistent support from those we loved. Pleas and threats had little effect. Non-judgmental concern and offers of assistance whenever we became ready often encouraged us to seek and accept help. We had so much shame and guilt at being unable to stop drinking, just knowing that our loved ones still loved us unconditionally, even if they could not live with us at the time, was comforting. Having family that understood our drinking was a medical illness, rather than a moral failure on our part, made us feel like they wanted us to get well as much as we wanted to. Knowing all this may not have propelled us into recovery immediately, but it became a motivating factor when we finally decided to completely surrender and seek help.

Can I be objective with the alcoholic, expressing my concern and love without undertones of resentment or criticism?

TO WIVES

If this kind of approach does not catch your husband's interest, it may be best to drop the subject, but after a friendly talk your husband will usually revive the topic himself. This may take patient waiting, but it will be worth it. Meanwhile you might try to help the wife of another serious drinker. If you act upon these principles, your husband may stop or moderate.

[To Wives p. 112]

CONSIDERATION

As alcoholics we want to help and heal everyone, even though we know we cannot. We naturally care about our own recovery, but we have a special place in our hearts for family and friends who are addicted. Although a spouse or family member's alcoholism distresses us, we become passionate when discussing how we got sober and found a new way of living. We want every alcoholic to have what we have, but often forget how hard we had to work for what we received. We also tend to forget that our success in recovery is founded on acceptance of the first Step of surrender and honesty. Step One implies that we are really getting sober for ourselves and not for someone else, and we are willing to go to any length to stay sober. But at the end of the day, we got sober when the time was right for us, not when it was right for anyone else.

Can I be patient with my fellow alcoholic sufferer, and pledge to support them whenever they are ready?

SEPTEMBER 17

TO WIVES

But after his next binge, ask him if he would really like to get over drinking for good. Do not ask that he do it for you or anyone else. Just would he like to? The chances are he would. Show him your copy of this book and tell him what you have found out about alcoholism. Show him that as alcoholics, the writers of the book understand....The seed has been planted in his mind. He knows that thousands of men, much like himself, have recovered.

[To Wives p. 112]

CONSIDERATION

For those of us living in recovery, it is easy to share our experience, strength and hope with another alcoholic. We try to carry the message as best we can. It is impossible for us to know with certainty how our message will be received, or if it will encourage the alcoholic into taking any action whatsoever. However, we have done our part when we share our story. That is all we can do, other than hope our words will not fall on deaf ears. Whether our fellow responds now, later, or never is not under our control.

Am I willing to share my story of recovery with another alcoholic if asked, despite not knowing what the results will be?

SEPTEMBER 18

TO WIVES

Some men have been so impaired by alcohol that they cannot stop. Sometimes there are cases where alcoholism is complicated by other disorders. A good doctor or psychiatrist can tell you whether these complications are serious. In any event, try to have your husband read this book....If he is already committed to an institution.....we have been working with alcoholics committed to institutions....[and] A.A. has released thousands of alcoholics from asylums and hospitals of every kind. The majority have never returned.

[To Wives p. 114]

CONSIDERATION

Some alcoholics have other medical problems in addition to alcoholism. In most cases the alcoholic can recover if they are able to be honest with themselves and others. Should they have a severe mental illness they can still recover, but may need additional medical treatment in addition to A.A. Just because an alcoholic has been or is hospitalized, or has a mental illness, does not exclude them from recovery or prevent us from reaching out to them. As long as they can be honest, know the difference between right and wrong, and are not a severe sociopath or psychopath, more times than not they will be able to recover if they are willing and able to complete the work of the 12 Step program.

Do I remind myself that no one should be written off without speaking with them about recovery first?

TO WIVES

But sometimes you must start life anew. We know women who have done it. If such women adopt a spiritual way of life their road will be smoother. If your husband is a drinker, you probably worry over what other people are thinking and you hate to meet your friends. You draw more and more into yourself and you think everyone is talking about conditions at your home. You avoid the subject of drinking, even with your own parents. You do not know what to tell your children. When your husband is bad, you become a trembling recluse, wishing the telephone had never been invented.

[To Wives p. 114]

CONSIDERATION

As an alcoholic living with another alcoholic, we cannot tell them what to do or how to get sober. Perhaps we pass along some of our own recovery experience, and if they are living with us they are able to see with their own eyes how we have changed. It may seem strange or even a little embarrassing to admit we are able to stay sober, but that our spouse or partner cannot. We may wonder why we are successful while our loved one still struggles. Discussing our situation in Al-Anon, Alateen or with qualified professionals may ease our anxiety and help us learn how to more constructively share our frustration and feelings with our family and friends.

Can I be sensitive, kind and supporting with my spouse's struggles, just as I was gently supported during my own struggles?

SEPTEMBER 20

TO WIVES

We find that most of this embarrassment is unnecessary....you can quietly let your friends know the nature of his illness....When you have carefully explained to such people that he is a sick person, you will have created a new atmosphere. Barriers which have sprung up between you and your friends will disappear with the growth of sympathetic understanding. You will no longer be self-conscious or feel that you must apologize as though your husband were a weak character. He may be anything but that. Your new courage, good nature and lack of self-consciousness will do wonders for you socially.

[To Wives p. 115]

CONSIDERATION

Sharing our troubles as honestly as possible with others, both inside and outside of A.A., somehow reduces the burden we carry. It is natural for us to want to ignore or hide the truth, or be ashamed of it. There is no reason for this. We, like our spouse or loved one, share an illness we know can destroy our relationship and family unless treated. Each of us progresses through recovery at our own pace, and all we can do is be supportive, tolerant and patient. Trying to bring some humor into our lives and remembering Rule 62—let's not take ourselves too seriously—often helps reduce the tension in most situations.

Am I avoiding my friends, sponsor and Fellowship support group because of shame or anxiety over my spouse's illness?

TO WIVES

The same principle applies in dealing with the children. Unless they actually need protection from their father, it is best not to take sides in any argument he has with them while drinking. Use your energies to promote a better understanding all around. Then that terrible tension which grips the home of every problem drinker will be lessened.

[To Wives p. 115]

CONSIDERATION

Depending on the age of our children, the depth of our discussion of alcoholism with them will vary. One understandable truth in most cases is that Father or Mother is a very sick person. It is not their fault that they are ill, but there are certain things we hope they will do to treat their illness. Protecting the children from physical or emotional harm from the alcoholic is often much more difficult, and requires constant vigilance on our part. Sometimes legal action or a physical move away from the alcoholic must be undertaken. The chaos created by the alcoholic tornado running through our lives is usually unpredictable and uncontrollable. Developing plans ahead of time for those sudden eruptions helps us cope with them when they arise. In desperate cases, planning an escape route and having friends available for shelter on a moment's notice usually gives us comfort as the days progress. Rarely, a restraining order will need to be obtained. Keeping ourselves and our children safe is a top priority.

Have I explained to my children the true nature of our family situation?

SEPTEMBER 22

TO WIVES

Frequently, you have felt obliged to tell your husband's employer and his friends that he was sick, when as a matter of fact he was tight. Avoid answering these inquiries as much as you can. Whenever possible, let your husband explain. Your desire to protect him should not cause you to lie to people when they have a right to know where he is and what he is doing....You may be afraid your husband will lose his position; you are thinking of the disgrace and hard times which will befall you and the children....Should it [fear] happen again, regard it in a different light. Maybe it will prove a blessing! It may convince your husband he wants to stop drinking forever. And now you know that he can stop if he will!

[To Wives p. 115]

CONSIDERATION

When we were drinking, we always hoped that people would make excuses for us when we were drunk. Now, as the sober spouse of an alcoholic, we become skilled in lying for them, even more so if we are ashamed of our spouse's behavior. We don't want anyone to know how bad off they are, and subconsciously may believe their illness is partially our own fault. Over time, we get tired of having to lie, and usually say "I don't know," or stop responding to inquiries all together. Eventually we stop lying to keep their secrets, and soon realize that everyone knew what they were up to despite our fabrications. We find that if we persist in trying to protect our alcoholic spouse from the consequences of their actions, we become more and more angry and withdrawn. If that be our situation, seeking help from Al-Anon or Alateen to learn how to detach from the alcoholic with love is often a life-saver for us, should we choose to seek such help.

Am I still lying to others to protect my alcoholic?

TO WIVES

We have elsewhere remarked how much better life is when lived on a spiritual plane. If God can solve the age-old riddle of alcoholism, He can solve your problems too. We wives found that, like everybody else, we were afflicted with pride, self-pity, vanity and all the things which go to make up the self-centered person; and we were not above selfishness or dishonesty. As our husbands began to apply spiritual principles in their lives, we began to see the desirability of doing so too.

[To Wives p. 116]

CONSIDERATION

We who have found recovery can employ the same principles that provide us with emotional sobriety and a new way of living when we confront any fellow sufferer. Whether that person is a family member or just a close friend, we can use our spiritual toolkit to combat the anger, fear and frustration that we feel not being able to control or cure the alcoholic in our life. It is easy to say we are powerless over the behavior of another person, alcoholic or not, but often difficult to accept that fact deep in our core. Even when we remember that no one could control our own alcoholic addiction at the time, it provides little solace when life gets hectic and out of control. All we can do is use the tools we have: prayer and share, an attitude of gratitude, sticking close to our Fellowship, and staying with the one-day-at-a-time spiritual A.A. approach.

Am I willing to use everything in my spiritual toolkit to bring me some emotional serenity and stability?

TO WIVES

At first, some of us did not believe we needed this help. We thought, on the whole, we were pretty good women, capable of being nicer if our husbands stopped drinking. But it was a silly idea that we were too good to need God. Now we try to put spiritual principles to work in every department of our lives. When we do that, we find it solves our problems too; the ensuing lack of fear, worry and hurt feelings is a wonderful thing. We urge you to try our program, for nothing will be so helpful to your husband as the radically changed attitude toward him which God will show you how to have. Go along with your husband if you possibly can.

[To Wives p. 116]

CONSIDERATION

Over time in A.A. we find that the principles we apply to treat our alcoholism can be applied to every aspect of our life. A.A. does not teach us how to stop drinking, but how to live a full and prosperous sober life. Once upon a time, we didn't know how to live sober and we didn't know how to live drunk. Today, we know how to live sober thanks to the tangible and spiritual tools of the A.A. program. The choice of how we want to live this day is completely up to us. Do I want to live life the way I do now, or the way I used to?

Am I better off with the life I have today, or do I want to return to the lonely subsistence I had before?

SEPTEMBER 25

TO WIVES

If you and your husband find a solution for the pressing problem of drink you are, of course, going to very happy. But all problems will not be solved at once. Seed has started to sprout in a new soil, but growth has only begun. In spite of your new-found happiness, there will be ups and downs. Many of the old problems will still be with you. This is as it should be. The faith and sincerity of both you and your husband will be put to the test. These workouts should be regarded as part of your education, for thus you will be learning to live. You will make mistakes, but if you are in earnest they will not drag you down. Instead, you will capitalize them. A better way of life will emerge when they are overcome.

[To Wives p. 117]

CONSIDERATION

Living life on life's terms is never effortless. We are challenged every day by events we cannot control and often disturb us deeply. Some days are easier than others. Some are wonderful and some are absolutely miserable. But we learn to rejoice and give thanks for the wonderful days, and build up our strength for the rough days sure to come. We seldom give thanks at the time for our difficult days, but when we look back on them at least we know we were able to survive them without drinking. Perhaps that was all we could do at the time— just not drink. Hopefully, we survive each day with some poise and dignity, but if not, we can review our inventory at any time during the day, reflecting on what we might have done differently, and taking any corrective action needed as soon as possible. If we learn something more from our experience, so much the better.

Regardless of the type of day I am having, can I remember the most important thing to do is not pick up a drink, and that I can start my day over at any time?

TO WIVES

Your husband will sometimes be unreasonable and you will want to criticize. Starting from a speck on the domestic horizon, great thunderclouds of dispute may gather. These family dissensions are very dangerous, especially to your husband....Never forget that resentment is a deadly hazard to an alcoholic. We do not mean that you have to agree with you husband whenever there is an honest difference of opinion. Just be careful not to disagree in a resentful or critical spirit.

[To Wives p. 117]

CONSIDERATION

Especially as alcoholics, it is critical for us to understand the difference between anger and resentment, and learn how to prevent anger from metastasizing into resentment. Anger is a strong feeling of annoyance, displeasure, or hostility over how we perceive something that may or may not have actually happened to us. Whether or not our perception is accurate, or reflects the truth, does not prevent our emotional reaction. Anger may be sudden and extreme, but it is temporary and soon passes. Resentment is re-living past anger over and over. It is carrying the bitterness of believing we were wronged by someone or something and re-playing the perceived injury again and again in our minds. Even if we were not really harmed, we may think we were, and that is enough for us to become resentful. As we encounter our fellows, alcoholic or not, we must make a conscious and concerted effort to curtail our impulse to transform our anger into resentment. By speaking with another person to ventilate and validate our feelings, looking closely at our part in the situation, trying to incorporate a bit of humor and common sense in our response, remembering our gratitudes and practicing quick forgiveness, we will usually be able to let go of our anger in short order. If not, we best speak with our sponsor or another alcoholic and try to think of someone we can help.

Do I make every effort to let go of anger as soon as I can?

SEPTEMBER 27

TO WIVES

You and your husband will find that you can dispose of serious problems easier than you can the trivial ones. Next time you and he have a heated discussion, no matter what the subject, it should be the privilege of either to smile and say, "This is getting serious. I'm sorry I got disturbed. Let's talk about it later." If your husband is trying to live on a spiritual basis, he will also be doing everything in his power to avoid disagreement or contention. Your husband knows he owes you more than sobriety. He wants to make good. Yet you must not expect too much. His ways of thinking and doing are the habits of years. Patience, tolerance, understanding and love are the watchwords. Show him these things in yourself and they will be reflected back to you from him. Live and let live is the rule. If you both show a willingness to remedy your own defects, there will be little need to criticize each other.

[To Wives p. 118]

CONSIDERATION

It is nearly impossible for us alcoholics not to take someone else's inventory, especially our spouse's, and even more so when we disagree. Sometimes when we start bickering with someone we start off gently, but by the end we are ranting and raving as we try to win the fight. Regardless of the outcome, we get sore and often want a drink. If we are really sore, we start carrying a resentment, justified of course, against the person involved. We add his or her name to our already long list of people we resent, all for good reason. Those of us with some time in recovery quickly recognize the danger of getting into these types of situations. This does not mean we can't argue or debate our position, but attacking the other person in a hostile, non-spiritual manner often results in us doing more damage to ourselves than to the other person. As is often said in A.A., it is like hitting ourselves on the head with a hammer, hoping the other person will feel our pain.

Do I avoid escalating arguments that may result in resentments, and can I adopt an attitude of love and tolerance towards my alcoholic?

TO WIVES

Another feeling we are very likely to entertain is one of resentment that love and loyalty could not cure our husbands of alcoholism. We do not like the thought that the contents of a book or the work of another alcoholic has accomplished in a few weeks that for which we struggled for years. At such moments we forget that alcoholism is an illness over which we could not possibly have had any power.....When resentful thoughts come, try to pause and count your blessings. After all, your family is reunited, alcohol is no longer a problem and you and your husband are working together toward an undreamed of future.

[To Wives p. 118]

CONSIDERATION

As a recovered alcoholic we know what it feels like not to be able to rescue and transform a fellow alcoholic, whether that alcoholic is our spouse, family member or friend. If someone else is able to help a person dear to us better than we can, we know we should celebrate, but may wonder why we couldn't do it ourselves and someone else could. Perhaps there is something wrong with us. We try to carry the message to the person we love, so why don't they respond to us? If these thoughts intrude, we might take off our God-cape and remember that thankfully, we're no longer running the show. We can stop being jealous, vain and self-centered, express gratitude for the outcome, and enjoy the company of our family on this day as best we are able.

Can I simply rejoice in the improvement of everyone in their program, whether it is A.A. or Al-Anon, regardless of my perceived contribution to their recovery?

SEPTEMBER 29

TO WIVES

Still another difficulty is that you may become jealous of the attention he bestows on other people, especially alcoholics. You have been starving for his companionship, yet he spends long hours helping other men and their families. You feel he should now be yours. The fact is that he should work with other people to maintain his own sobriety....We find it a real mistake to dampen his enthusiasm for alcoholic work......We suggest that you direct some of your thought to the wives of his new alcoholic friends. They need the counsel and love of a woman who has gone through what you have.

[To Wives p. 119]

CONSIDERATION

Just as we as alcoholics find that working with another alcoholic is the very best thing we can do to maintain our own sobriety, so it is with other alcoholics. We may be jealous that we are not the center of attention of our recovering spouse or family member, but envy is our own character defect to address and remove. Being fully supportive of any alcoholic trying to follow the suggestions of our program is our duty as a member of the Fellowship, and paradoxically strengthens the foundation of our own recovery.

Can I temporarily put aside my own needs from my spouse, and reach out to some other alcoholic instead?

SEPTEMBER 30

TO WIVES

We never, never try to arrange a man's life so as to shield him from temptation. The slightest disposition on your part to guide his appointment or his affairs so he will not be tempted will be noticed. Make him feel absolutely free to come and go as he likes. This is important. If he gets drunk, don't blame yourself. God has either removed your husband's liquor problem or He has not. If not, it had better be found out right away. Then you and your husband can get right down to fundamentals. If a repetition is to be prevented, place the problem, along with everything else, in God's hands.

[To Wives p. 120]

CONSIDERATION

Since alcohol was the solution for our problems and not the cause, simply avoiding alcohol is no guarantee we will never drink again. Selfishness and self-centeredness is the root of our troubles, so our solution is to make every effort to overcome that core character defect. We often discover that the more we practice the 12 Step principles of honesty, faith, courage, love, tolerance, kindness and service, the less distressed we become when faced with the temptation to drink. If we relapse frequently, the reason is not because alcohol was available somewhere, but because we either failed to complete all our 12 Step work, failed to work with other alcoholics, failed to fully and deeply engage in the Fellowship, failed to follow our daily rituals to try to maintain our spiritual fitness, or stopped doing all the other things that kept us sober in the first place.

Have I stopped trying to control the alcoholic in my life?

OCTOBER 1

THE FAMILY AFTERWARD

Our women folk have suggested certain attitudes a wife may take with the husband who is recovering. Perhaps they created the impression that he is to be wrapped in cotton wool and placed on a pedestal. Successful readjustment means the opposite. All members of the family should meet upon the common ground of tolerance, understanding and love. This involves a process of deflation. The alcoholic, his wife, his children, his "in-laws," each one is likely to have fixed ideas about the family's attitude towards himself or herself. Each is interested in having his or her wishes respected. We find the more one member of the family demands that the others concede to him, the more resentful they become. This makes for discord and unhappiness.

[The Family Afterward p. 122]

CONSIDERATION

Experience has shown that one of the best yardsticks of how well the alcoholic has recovered can be measured by the quality of his current relationship with his family. All we have to do is ask them. We realize that every family member has their own unique personality and set of burdens to bear. Over time the recently recovered alcoholic develops a new relationship and set of coping skills when dealing with other family members. There is a predictable ebb and flow to family dynamics that is well known to each family member. When an alcoholic in their cups enters this mix, they disrupt the dynamic and chaos ensues. The haphazard destruction and damage caused by the alcoholic frequently generates multiple and various types of resentments in family members. The alcoholic's offences are never forgotten and not always forgiven. So when the alcoholic sobers up and changes their way of living, the family is not sure what to make of it. Are these changes genuine, and how long will they last this time? How do we deal with our pent-up resentments? What is our new family dynamic now that we are presented with a sober alcoholic family member?

What steps can I take to improve my relationship with my family, now that I am sober?

OCTOBER 2

THE FAMILY AFTERWARD

Cessation of drinking is but the first step away from a highly strained, abnormal condition. A doctor said to us, "Years of living with an alcoholic is almost sure to make any wife or child neurotic. The entire family is, to some extent, ill." Let families realize, as they start their journey, that all will not be fair weather. Each in his turn may be footsore and may straggle. There will be alluring shortcuts and by-paths down which they may wander and lose their way.

[The Family Afterward p. 122]

CONSIDERATION

Almost no one can deny that alcoholism is a harsh family illness. Few family members can avoid the devastation the alcoholic renders upon every person in their path. As the alcoholic sobers and heals, one hopes the family does as well. Since each family member has been harmed in unique ways, each will heal, or not, in their own time and manner. The spouse, usually the one most beaten and broken, may recover with the help of Al-Anon or Alateen and the support of their own family and friends. On the other hand, the spouse may already have separated from, or divorced the alcoholic. Even so, he or she will need recovery support. Children of alcoholics are often deeply affected for their entire lives, and many need professional care at some point. How well and how far each family member recovers from having lived with an alcoholic is unpredictable, both in outcome and in time.

Am I willing to do all I can to support the efforts of my family to recover from the damage I caused them?

OCTOBER 3

THE FAMILY AFTERWARD

The family of an alcoholic longs for the return of happiness and security. They remember when father was romantic, thoughtful and successful. Today's life is measured against that of other years and, when it falls short, the family may be unhappy. Family confidence in dad is rising high. The good old days will soon be back, they think. Sometimes they demand that dad bring them back instantly! God, they believe, almost owes this recompense on a long overdue account.

[The Family Afterward p. 123]

CONSIDERATION

We cannot return to the past, nor should we try. Little do we realize that our memories of the good old days are often distorted by how we want to remember those events, rather than how they actually occurred. We massage, trim and embellish our old memories, often subconsciously, because they bring us comfort as we deal with our current problems. If we remain stuck in an imaginary past, we are unable to be fully present in this day, and today is the only day that matters since it is the only day we have. No one owes us anything, but we do owe ourselves the permission to live in this day as fully as we can, free from our mangled past.

Am I living as fully as I can in this day, and not worrying about what tomorrow may bring?

OCTOBER 4

THE FAMILY AFTERWARD

But the head of the house has spent years in pulling down the structures of business, romance, friendship, health—these things are now ruined or damaged. It will take time to clear away the wreck. Though the old buildings will eventually be replaced by finer ones, the new structures will take years to complete. Father knows he is to blame; it may take him many seasons of hard work to be restored financially, but he shouldn't be reproached. Perhaps he will never have much money again. But the wise family will admire him for what he is trying to be, rather than for what he is trying to get.

[The Family Afterward p. 123]

CONSIDERATION

We alcoholics are impatient people. Having gone through the 12 Step work we recognize and admit our role in the damage we caused ourselves and those around us. We attempt to make restitution to those we have harmed, mend our ways, and embark on a new way of living. Our journey is bumpy at times, and we cannot always succeed in repairing all the damage we caused. We may never be able to fully restore our life to what we imagine it should be, and convincing others that we are doing the best we can in this regard is not our job. Our job is to make a daily effort to do the next right thing in all our affairs, and practice all the principles of the 12 Steps as best we are able.

Can I practice kindness, patience and tolerance with all my family members during the long healing process ahead?

OCTOBER 5

THE FAMILY AFTERWARD

Now and then the family will be plagued by specters from the past, for the drinking career of almost every alcoholic has been marked by escapades, funny, humiliating, shameful or tragic. The first impulse will be to bury these skeletons in a dark closet and padlock the door. The family may be possessed by the idea that future happiness can be based only upon forgetfulness of the past. We think that such a view is self-centered and in direct conflict with the new way of living. Henry Ford once made a wise remark to the effect that experience is the thing of supreme value in life. That is true only if one is willing to turn the past to good account. We grow by our willingness to face and rectify errors and convert them into assets. The alcoholic's past thus becomes the principal asset of the family and frequently it is almost the only one!

[The Family Afterward p. 123]

CONSIDERATION

Shutting the door on our past after we have completed our Fifth Step prevents us from using our experience to connect with other alcoholics. How can we share the A.A. solution without discussing our past alcoholic behavior? The same holds true for our interactions with our family. There is no point in re-living the carnage of our past with family members, but true healing requires that all involved acknowledge the past, and that we alcoholics make amends for harms caused by our past conduct as we mend our ways by changing our behavior going forward. Once we have done that, we hope that past events will be forgiven as we proceed with our living amends. What we hope is not that our family will forget the past, but will forgive the past. Perhaps they can also use their own past experience in living with an alcoholic to help others who currently live with an alcoholic.

Can I use my past experiences to help my family and others heal from the damage I caused them?

OCTOBER 6

THE FAMILY AFTERWARD

This painful past may be of infinite value to other families still struggling with their problem. We think each family which has been relieved owes something to those who have not, and when the occasion requires, each member of it should be only too willing to bring former mistakes, no matter how grievous, out of their hiding places. Showing others who suffer how we were given help is the very thing which makes life seem so worthwhile to us now. Cling to the thought that, in God's hands, the dark past is the greatest possession you have—the key to life and happiness for others. With it you can avert death and misery for them.

[The Family Afterward p. 124]

CONSIDERATION

Using our experience as family members of alcoholics to help other family members in similar circumstances is the foundation of the Al-Anon and Alateen programs. Just as alcoholics can help other alcoholics through shared experiences in A.A., recovered alcoholics living with an active alcoholic can help families of alcoholics through their shared experiences in Al-Anon. Alcoholics who participate in both A.A. and Al-Anon are nicknamed "double winners," because they benefit from both Fellowships, and are able to share their experience with alcoholics and non-alcoholics alike.

Am I willing to use my experience, if appropriate, to the fullest extent possible to help the families of alcoholics?

OCTOBER 7

THE FAMILY AFTERWARD

It is possible to dig up past misdeeds so they become a blight, a veritable plague. For example, we know of situations in which the alcoholic or his wife have had love affairs. In the first flush of spiritual experience they forgave each other and drew closer together. The miracle of reconciliation was at hand. Then, under one provocation or another, the aggrieved one would unearth the old affair and angrily cast its ashes about. Husbands and wives have sometimes been obliged to separate for a time until new perspective, new victory over hurt pride could be re-won. In most cases, the alcoholic survived this ordeal without relapse, but not always. So we think that unless some good and useful purpose is to be served, past occurrences should not be discussed.

[The Family Afterward p. 124]

CONSIDERATION

Whether alcoholic or not, we are all normal human beings first. We react in various ways when we are stressed in any relationship. During arguments it is easy for us to use past behavior as ammunition in our current battle. Dragging a past indiscretion out of the closet, bringing up previous lies we were told, rehashing bygone financial failures, and listing harms done to us from years ago does little good other than to fuel the flames of any quarrel. No one wins during these volatile situations. When such events occur, it is often best to curtail the discussion until both parties can calm down.

Do I avoid using past wrongdoings as a weapon when I get angry?

OCTOBER 8

THE FAMILY AFTERWARD

We do talk about each other a great deal, but we almost invariably temper such talk by a spirit of love and tolerance. Another principle we observe carefully is that we do not relate intimate experiences of another person unless we are sure he would approve. We find it better, when possible, to stick to our own stories. A man may criticize or laugh at himself and it will affect others favorably, but criticism or ridicule coming from another often produces the contrary effect. Members of a family should watch such matters carefully, for one careless, inconsiderate remark has been known to raise the very devil. We alcoholics are sensitive people. It takes some of us a long time to outgrow that serious handicap.

[The Family Afterward p. 125]

CONSIDERATION

Gossip and criticism of others, whether initiated by the alcoholic or a family member, can be quite damaging for many reasons. Sharing confidential information about another person, inside or outside the family circle, or in the rooms of A.A., is rarely appropriate. If we do this deliberately, we might want to carefully examine our motives and take immediate corrective action. If we disclose information accidentally, we can make our amend and not make the same mistake again. How sensitive we are to having our own past disclosed by others, deliberately or otherwise, depends on how comfortable we are in our own skin, and how solid our foundation is in the spiritual principles of our program. Some of us care little what others disclose about us, but if we have requested confidentiality over a matter and it has been broken, we can address this indiscretion directly with the person involved. We might also reflect on our role in the matter; perhaps we should not have shared certain information with certain people, or perhaps we should have been less specific in the details.

Do I gossip or violate the confidentiality of others?

OCTOBER 9

THE FAMILY AFTERWARD

Many alcoholics are enthusiasts. They run to extremes. At the beginning of recovery a man will take, as a rule, one of two directions. He may either plunge into a frantic attempt to get on his feet in business, or he may be so enthralled by his new life that he talks or thinks of little else. In either case certain family problems will arise. With these we have had experience galore.

[The Family Afterward p. 125]

CONSIDERATION

Sometimes it seems as if we alcoholics have only one switch—on or off. We're missing the dial that we can use to gradually adjust our responses to our own perceptions, reactions, impulses, emotions and the events swirling inside our head. When our switch is off, we loaf, ignore, deny, procrastinate or postpone decisions or actions. When our switch is on, we power up full throttle and blindly blast off into whatever perceived crisis or situation has attracted our attention. Often we change direction mid-course, depending on what new, shiny item flickers by as we speed along. We stay sober, but create a new kind of chaos in our lives not unlike the bedlam we created while drinking. Learning to slow down, deliberate, consider how our enthusiasm and actions might affect others, and speak with another alcoholic before embarking on an important upcoming task might help us stay on track without disrupting the lives of those around us.

Am I willing to consult with my sponsor and Fellowship support group to guide me in making decisions concerning important family matters if I need assistance in that area?

OCTOBER 10

THE FAMILY AFTERWARD

We think it dangerous if he rushes headlong at his economic problem. The family will be affected also, pleasantly at first, as they feel their money troubles are about to be solved, then not so pleasantly as they find themselves neglected. Dad may be tired at night and preoccupied by day. He may take small interest in the children and may show irritation when reproved for his delinquencies. If not irritable, he may seem dull and boring, not gay and affectionate as the family would like him to be. Mother may complain of inattention. They are all disappointed, and often let him feel it. Beginning with such complaints, a barrier arises. He is straining every nerve to make up for lost time. He is striving to recover fortune and reputation and feels he is doing very well.

[The Family Afterward p. 126]

CONSIDERATION

Although we have completed our 12 Step work, had a spiritual awakening and embarked on a new way of living, many of us have no clue how to live as newly sober adults. We spend our life as little children seeking only self-satisfaction. Although we physically age, our mental age is stuck in adolescent immaturity. Some call us "His Majesty the Baby," because we think the world owes us whatever we want, and when we don't get our way we scream and cry, shaking our tiny little fists in the air like a spoiled two year old child. We can learn much from our fellow alcoholics. How can we best balance our work and our family duties? How can we help other alcoholics without neglecting our spouse, children, family members and friends? How can we improve our mental and spiritual outlook on life? Behaving as a humble and responsible adult, being sensitive to the feelings and concerns of those around us without taking offense or developing resentments, requires instruction, practice and time.

Am I ignoring my family and friends by spending too much time working to make up for lost earnings or trying to improve my status in the community?

OCTOBER 11

THE FAMILY AFTERWARD

Sometimes mother and children don't think so. Having been neglected and misused in the past, they think father owes them more than they are getting....But dad doesn't give freely of himself. Resentment grows. He becomes still less communicative. Sometimes he explodes over a trifle. The family is mystified. They criticize, pointing out how he is falling down on his spiritual program. This sort of thing can be avoided....The family must realize that dad, though marvelously improved, is still convalescing....Let them remember that his drinking wrought all kinds of damage that may take long to repair. If they sense these things, they will not take so seriously his periods of crankiness, depression, or apathy, which will disappear when there is tolerance, love, and spiritual understanding.

[The Family Afterward p. 126]

CONSIDERATION

Most families understand that alcoholism is truly a family illness, since few family members can escape the caustic fallout from the alcoholic they love. But many families are unfamiliar with the recovery process once the alcoholic stops drinking for good. The old alcoholic has been reborn into something unfamiliar, foreign in nature, and occasionally scary. Who is this new person we thought we knew so well? What's going on? How should we deal with them now? Just as the physician cannot tell the patient exactly how long it will take them to heal, few can predict how long and in what manner it will take the newly sober alcoholic to learn how to live in their new environment. This adjustment period, difficult as it may be, is unavoidable for most families, and is often best approached with empathy, love, tolerance and compassion, one hour or one day at a time. As a family resource, members of Al-Anon or Alateen will readily share their experience on how they learned to live with a newly recovered alcoholic who is adapting to a life of sobriety and trying to be a responsible adult.

Can I be patient and tolerant with everyone around me as our family heals?

OCTOBER 12

THE FAMILY AFTERWARD

The head of the house ought to remember that he is mainly to blame for what befell his home. He can scarcely square the account in his lifetime. But he must see the danger of over-concentration on financial success. Although financial recovery is on the way for many of us, we found we could not place money first. For us, material well-being always followed spiritual progress; it never preceded.

[The Family Afterward p. 127]

CONSIDERATION

Some of us use our income as an indicator of our self-worth, and think that the more money we make, the better person we are compared to other people. If we have that sprawling house and fancy car, we can show the world what big shots we have become, and secretly hope others will be impressed and jealous of our good fortune. As we descend into our addiction, money is squandered on alcohol and other selfish activities. We no longer care about outside appearances or even the well-being of our family. Bills are ignored, rent is overdue and credit card balances pile up. Once sober, we panic when we realize how neglectful we have been, and charge full steam ahead to reconcile our debts and show the world we are back on track using money as our proxy. If our sobriety and spiritual growth become secondary to the weight of our material possessions, we are headed for trouble.

Am I putting my material demands before my spiritual growth?

OCTOBER 13

THE FAMILY AFTERWARD

Since the home has suffered more than anything else, it is well that a man exert himself there. He is not likely to get far in any direction if he fails to show unselfishness and love under his own roof. We know there are difficult wives and families, but the man who is getting over alcoholism must remember he did much to make them so. As each member of a resentful family begins to see his shortcomings and admits them to the others, he lays a basis for helpful discussion. These family talks will be constructive if they can be carried on without heated argument, self-pity, self-justification or resentful criticism. Little by little, mother and children will see they ask too much, and father will see he gives too little. Giving, rather than getting, will become the guiding principle.

[The Family Afterward p. 127]

CONSIDERATION

It is difficult enough for the alcoholic to objectively examine their own behavior, take their own inventory and make a decision to change their ways. It is much easier for them to take the inventory of their spouse, children and family members, even with the knowledge that they have a role in their families' dysfunction. And just because the alcoholic is able to use the A.A. program to examine and share their past, make restitution and change their way of life, it doesn't mean that any family member will be eager to go through the same process. Expecting the family to follow the 12 Step path just because the alcoholic chooses to do so is a recipe for failure. Should the family choose to do their own inventory, so much the better, but if they do not, we must put aside any resentment and continue to practice the loving principles of the Steps.

Will I continue to practice the A.A. principles regardless of the behavior of my family, friends and those about me?

OCTOBER 14

THE FAMILY AFTERWARD

Assume on the other hand that father has...a stirring spiritual experience. He is a different man...a religious enthusiast...unable to focus on anything else. As soon as his sobriety begins to be taken as a matter of course, the family may look at their strange new dad with apprehension, then with irritation. There is talk about spiritual matters morning, noon and night....When father takes this tack, the family may react unfavorably. They may be jealous of a God who has stolen dad's affections. While grateful that he drinks no more, they may not like the idea that God has accomplished the miracle where they failed.....They may not see why their love and devotion did not straighten him out. Dad is not so spiritual after all, they say. If he means to right his past wrongs, why all this concern for everyone in the world but his family? What about his talk that God will take care of them? They suspect father is a bit balmy!

[The Family Afterward p. 128]

CONSIDERATION

The changes we undergo during recovery, whether slow or sudden, are usually exciting and relieving. No longer are we obsessed with drink, and are profoundly grateful to have been given the freedom from alcohol and the opportunity for a new life. Some of us experience a pink cloud of contentment, which often dissolves into a more realistic and balanced daily reprieve. These changes may stimulate us to become overly zealous in sharing the details of our spiritual journey. Early in recovery it is easy to cross the line from sharing to preaching. No one objects to an alcoholic celebrating their bounty, but few of us will tolerate for very long any spiritual or religious round-the-clock campaigning, including family members. Hopefully other members of the Fellowship or a sharp-eyed sponsor will intervene with the overly enthusiastic alcoholic before they get out of control, and end up doing more harm than good with their incessant, but sincere, proselytizing.

Am I overwhelming my family with constant talk of A.A.?

OCTOBER 15

THE FAMILY AFTERWARD

He is not so unbalanced as they might think. Many of us have experienced dad's elation. We have indulged in spiritual intoxication. Like a gaunt prospector, belt drawn in over the ounce of food, our pick struck gold. Joy at our release from a lifetime of frustration knew no bounds. Father feels he has struck something better than gold. For a time he may try to hug the new treasure to himself. He may not see at once that he has barely scratched a limitless lode which will pay dividends only if he mines it for the rest of his life and insists on giving away the entire product.

[The Family Afterward p. 128]

CONSIDERATION

Trying to carry the message of recovery to other alcoholics is the foundation of A.A. and our sobriety, assuming we have completed the 12 Steps, had a spiritual awakening resulting in a change in our attitudes and actions, and have a legitimate message to carry. After Bill Wilson had his hot flash event in Towns Hospital in 1934, he became so electrified he ran amuck for six months trying to save other alcoholics by preaching to them of his spontaneous religious transformation into sobriety. He failed every time. His wise physician, Dr. Silkworth, suggested that Bill slow down a bit, and emphasize the hopeless medical aspect of alcoholism before revealing the spiritual solution. Using this more balanced and composed approach, Bill became much more successful in attracting alcoholics into the Fellowship. He was still carrying the message and staying sober, but doing so in a far more effective manner.

Can I temper my excitement over my recovery with a more balanced approach as I share with others the benefits of A.A.?

OCTOBER 16

THE FAMILY AFTERWARD

If the family cooperates, dad will soon see that he is suffering from a distortion of values. He will perceive that his spiritual growth is lopsided, that for an average man like himself, a spiritual life which does not include his family obligations may not be so perfect after all. If the family will appreciate that dad's current behavior is but a phase of his development, all will be well. In the midst of an understanding and sympathetic family, these vagaries of dad's spiritual infancy will quickly disappear.

[The Family Afterward p. 128]

CONSIDERATION

We have no guarantee that just because we are now sober all will be well with our family. Wounds take time to heal, and we have inflicted many of them on those we love. It takes time for us to learn how to balance our family obligations with our A.A. obligations. Receiving advice and guidance from our sponsor and other members of the Fellowship is often indispensable in improving our family relationships. Patience, tolerance and understanding go a long way in dealing with family members who don't yet trust us, and are bewildered about the spiritual changes they see in us. All we can do as newly sober alcoholics is to continue our living amends by trying to abide by the 12 Step principles of the program as best we can. As we work with other alcoholics, we try not to neglect our family responsibilities during the process. Our first priority is our own sobriety of course, but our family is the second priority for most of us. That said, if we fear we are going to drink straightaway, it may be best to work with another alcoholic as soon as possible. Afterwards, we can return to our family, spend quality time with them, and continue our efforts to repair any damage we caused them in the past.

Will I use all the resources available to me to learn how to balance my family life and my A.A. work?

OCTOBER 17

THE FAMILY AFTERWARD

Dad may feel that for years his drinking has placed him on the wrong side of every argument, but that now he has become a superior person with God on his side....Instead of treating the family as he should, he may retreat further into himself and feel he has spiritual justification for so doing....Even if he displays a certain amount of neglect and irresponsibility towards the family, it is well to let him go as far as he likes in helping other alcoholics. During those first days of convalescence, this will do more to insure his sobriety than anything else.

[The Family Afterward p. 129]

CONSIDERATION

Beware using A.A. or God as a weapon. If, when sober, our pride and arrogance return, and we believe that everything we do is justified because we are crusading for A.A. with God at our side, experience has shown that we will be drinking soon. Vanity, conceit and hubris will be our downfall, and they are deadly character defects. We must not delude ourselves into believing that neglecting our worldly responsibilities is acceptable because we have embarked on a greater spiritual calling. Most of us know how far we can push the family to get our way. Few families dismiss the importance of one alcoholic working with another to maintain their own sobriety, especially early on in recovery. But we alcoholics must practice being more sensitive to the needs of our family, even when it conflicts with our own need to work with another in the Fellowship. Seeking advice from our sponsor and other seasoned alcoholics is helpful. However, if we know we are going to drink unless we urgently work with another alcoholic, it is better to place our own sobriety above all else.

Will I refrain from using my new found spirituality and willingness to help other alcoholics as a weapon against my family, but if my sobriety is imminently at risk, will I reach out immediately to another alcoholic, regardless of family consequences?

OCTOBER 18

THE FAMILY AFTERWARD

Those of us who have spent much time in the world of spiritual make-believe have eventually seen the childishness of it. This dream world has been replaced by a great sense of purpose, accompanied by a growing consciousness of the power of God in our lives. We have come to believe He would like us to keep our heads in the clouds with Him, but that our feet ought to be firmly planted on earth. That is where our fellow travelers are, and that is where our work must be done. These are the realities for us. We have found nothing incompatible between a powerful spiritual experience and a life of sane and happy usefulness.

[The Family Afterward p. 130]

CONSIDERATION

If we are willing to make the effort and take direction from a spiritual Higher Power of our understanding and those in the Fellowship who have experience to share, we find that learning to balance our material life with our spiritual life is not all that difficult. By not turning every mole-hill into a mountain, we can, with time and practice, fully incorporate our spiritual life into our normal day-to-day life. We learn to be humble, responsible and accountable. No longer do we consider our A.A. circle separate from our family and work circle. We are no longer living two separate lives, but one merged life where we simply meld our new spiritually based attitudes and actions into our existing world. Our life circles coalesce into one, which is broader than the two are separately. We can be grateful and use the tools we have been given by doing our part, doing the next right thing, and helping those around us, whether they are alcoholics or not.

Since I've been given a set of spiritual tools, am I willing to do my part and use them?

OCTOBER 19

THE FAMILY AFTERWARD

Liquor incapacitated father for so many years that mother became head of the house...By force of circumstances, she was often obliged to treat father as a sick or wayward child....Mother made all the plans and gave the directions. When sober, father usually obeyed. Thus mother, through no fault of her own, became accustomed to wearing the family trousers. Father, coming suddenly to life again, often begins to assert himself. This means trouble, unless the family watches for these tendencies in each other and comes to a friendly agreement about them.

[The Family Afterward p. 130]

CONSIDERATION

Most of us like to think that husband and wife, or mother or father, or spouse or partner, or sometimes an elder child, have equal roles in running the household. In reality, this is rarely true. Usually one or the other takes the lead, and sometimes the lead person changes, depending on the situation. As our alcoholism progresses we become less able to lead at anything, other than finding a ready drink for ourselves. Our self-centeredness makes it easy to abdicate responsibility for family matters, and we are eager to dispose of all obligations both at home and at work. Now sober, guilt and shame over our abandonment of the family drives us to instantly take charge, as part of attempted restitution for past neglect. Unless we proceed carefully with our good intention, anger and resentment may surface in family members as we try to force our will on them. Continuously discussing with our spouse or partner how we can be most helpful as we integrate ourself back into family life may be more effective than just grabbing the reins and taking off. A gentle assimilation into the various family responsibilities may be in order, rather than a forced, rough transition.

Am I willing to work with my spouse and family, seeking their help in directing how I can be most useful to them, as I progress in my recovery?

OCTOBER 20

THE FAMILY AFTERWARD

At the very beginning, the couple ought to frankly face the fact that each will have to yield here and there if the family is going to play an effective part in the new life. Father will necessarily spend much time with other alcoholics, but this activity should be balanced. New acquaintances who know nothing of alcoholism might be made and thoughtful experiences given their needs. The problems of the community might engage attention. Though the family has no religious connections, they may wish to make contact with or take membership in a religious body.

[The Family Afterward p. 131]

CONSIDERATION

How the family learns to adjust to their newly sober alcoholic takes time and a bit of trial and error. We alcoholics might want to go the extra mile to consider another family member's viewpoint when requests and conflicts arise. It can be tempting to use our A.A. work as an excuse to avoid undesirable obligations, responsibilities or interactions with certain family members. This attitude should be avoided, for in doing so, our motive is self-centered and may lead to resentment, and ultimately a return to drinking. If we are as attentive to, and honest with our family as we are with another struggling alcoholic that we wish to help, and if we can fairly balance our time between our family and A.A. work, the odds are that all involved will benefit.

Will I make an extra effort with my family to fully incorporate them into my new life?

OCTOBER 21

THE FAMILY AFTERWARD

We have been speaking to you of serious, sometimes tragic things. We have been dealing with alcohol in its worst aspect. But we aren't a glum lot. If newcomers could see no joy or fun in our existence, they wouldn't want it. We absolutely insist on enjoying life. We try not to indulge in cynicism over the state of the nations, nor do we carry the world's troubles on our shoulders.

[The Family Afterward p. 132]

CONSIDERATION

Early in our drinking careers most of us had fun. Alcohol relaxes our inhibitions, soothes our anxiety, relieves our fears, and makes it easier for us to be around other people. We are not so self-conscious, and feel the ease and comfort of being alive in our own skin. As our illness progresses and we withdraw from society, having fun no longer matters since we are consumed by ensuring we drink enough just to get through the day. After we sober up, recover from a seemingly hopeless state of mind and body, and have a spiritual awakening through the 12 Steps, our lives are totally different. We do not return to the elusive sober life of our past, but find an entirely new design for living. We aren't quite sure how to live our new life other than one day at a time the best we can, using our program principles. Having fun is not something we think much about, because most of us are laboring and learning how to carry on without alcohol. A few of us may still be stuck in survival mode, barely hanging on. Eventually we learn how to have sober fun, which is not the same as drunk fun. When we develop the courage to let our guard down and focus on what we can bring to the party rather than what we can get out of it, many of us are surprised to find that we actually can enjoy ourselves, our situation and the people about us. We may not be certain that we are having fun, but at least it's a start.

Am I willing to make a concerted effort to learn how to bring healthy play and fun into my life?

THE FAMILY AFTERWARD

When we see a man sinking into the mire that is alcoholism, we give him first aid and place what we have at his disposal. For his sake, we do recount and almost relive the horrors of our past. But those of us who have tried to shoulder the entire burden and trouble of others find we are soon overcome by them. So we think cheerfulness and laughter make for usefulness. Outsiders are sometimes shocked when we burst into merriment over a seemingly tragic experience out of the past. But why shouldn't we laugh? We have recovered, and have been given the power to help others.

[The Family Afterward p. 132]

CONSIDERATION

Many in our medical community can attest to the healing power of laughter. As we share our own experiences in A.A. and listen to those of others, sometimes the only choice we have is to either laugh or cry. Almost all of us recognize the depth and severity of our alcoholic illness, as well as the significance of our destructive behavior while drinking. But we can use those past experiences to connect with another alcoholic so they will start to trust us enough to listen to the A.A. solution. Sometimes our escapades were horrendous, sometimes they were not, but somewhere in all our stories a bit of levity can often be found. We tell our fellow newcomer that we are not laughing at them, but are laughing with them, because we have all been there before.

Can I relax enough when working with other alcoholics to include some lighthearted humor in discussing my experiences?

OCTOBER 23

THE FAMILY AFTERWARD

Everybody knows that those in bad health, and those who seldom play, do not laugh much....We are sure God wants us to be happy, joyous, and free. We cannot subscribe to the belief that this life is a vale of tears, though it once was just that for many of us. But it is clear that we made our own misery. God didn't do it. Avoid then, the deliberate manufacture of misery, but if trouble comes, cheerfully capitalize it as an opportunity to demonstrate His omnipotence.

[The Family Afterward p. 132]

CONSIDERATION

Just as we alcoholics must learn how to have fun, we must learn how to play. Play and fun are not the same thing. Fun is a feeling; play is an action. In our past we may never have been given the freedom to play and enjoy its results, much less the opportunity to experience joy or happiness. While drinking we often delude ourselves into thinking we are playing and having fun, when all we are really doing is trying to get drunk enough so we won't care one way or another. Once we enter sobriety, many of us must learn or re-learn how to play and have fun. As adults, it may seem strange to have to learn something that comes naturally to most people in their childhood, but we find the challenge is not too great once we make the effort. Although not all our days will be happy or joyous, we should always be free since we are no longer shackled to our alcoholic addiction. During our hard days, we can still live one day or one hour at a time, adopt an attitude of gratitude, try to think less of ourselves by helping another, and know that in time most of our hardships will pass. Remember that our day is whatever we choose to make of it. It's totally our choice, and we can choose to start our day over again at any time if necessary.

Can I maintain a positive, helpful and grateful attitude regardless of how my day is going?

OCTOBER 24

THE FAMILY AFTERWARD

Now about health: A body badly burned by alcohol does not often recover overnight nor do twisted thinking and depression vanish in a twinkling. We are convinced that a spiritual mode of living is a most powerful health restorative.....But this does not mean that we disregard human health measures. God has abundantly supplied this world with fine doctors, psychologists, and practitioners of various kinds. Do not hesitate to take your health problems to such persons.....One of the many doctors who had the opportunity of reading this book in manuscript form told us that the use of sweets was often helpful, of course depending upon a doctor's advice.

[The Family Afterward p. 133]

CONSIDERATION

In "The Doctor's Opinion," Dr. Silkworth introduces us to the concept of alcoholism as a three-fold disease of mind, body and spirit. Each aspect of our illness requires treatment and healing. Unless we have an obvious and significant medical condition as a result of our drinking, many of us forget, ignore or are unaware of the more subtle physical damage we may have acquired while drinking. When we withdraw from society as our drinking progresses, we often retreat from seeking medical attention for our ailments. Sometimes this is out of fear of being discovered to be an alcoholic by our physician, or perhaps we prefer to spend our money on drink rather than our health, or maybe we just don't care anymore. Regardless of our reasons, as newly sober individuals we might consider getting a medical checkup from our physician or visit a counselor if needed, in order to determine if any additional treatment for the physical or mental part of our illness might be beneficial.

Am I willing to put aside my fear and at least obtain a routine medical checkup?

OCTOBER 25

THE FAMILY AFTERWARD

Couples are occasionally dismayed to find that when drinking is stopped the man tends to be impotent....Some of us had this experience, only to enjoy, in a few months, a finer intimacy than ever. There should be no hesitancy in consulting a doctor or psychologist if the condition persists. We do not know of many cases where this difficulty lasted long.

[The Family Afterward p. 134]

CONSIDERATION

Some joke that sex is little more than a relationship with benefits. However, most of us wish for a sustained, honest and healthy sexual relationship with someone we love or care about. Alcohol is actually a depressant drug, rarely enhancing our sexual performance, even when we swear otherwise. As our drinking increases, our sexual activity usually decreases, occasionally coming to a complete stop as liquor fully consumes our life. If we are still having sex, many of us cannot engage without a drink. Some of us cheat on our spouse or partner if we have them, and those of us that have no attachment often use sex randomly and selfishly to gratify our impulsive needs. In the beginning we think that alcohol makes us more potent, when it actually has the opposite effect. What alcohol really does is to make us feel more bold and aggressive during the hunt, but frequently lets us down after the capture. For most of us, unless we pay for sex, we must first establish some kind of interactive, personal relationship before we engage, even if it lasts only a few minutes. Since few of us have any real idea how to have an honest and sincere sexual relationship, current efforts might be directed toward improving the non-sexual aspect of our relationship first. As we make progress in that area, most of us find little difficulty progressing into more intimate areas, and sexual performance rarely suffers for long.

Will I work on improving my personal relationship with my spouse or partner before expanding my sexual relationship?

OCTOBER 26

THE FAMILY AFTERWARD

The alcoholic may find it hard to re-establish friendly relations with his children. Their young minds were impressionable while he was drinking. Without saying so, they may cordially hate him for what he has done to them and to their mother. The children are sometimes dominated by a pathetic hardness and cynicism. They cannot seem to forgive and forget. This may hang on for months, long after their mother has accepted dad's new way of living and thinking.

[The Family Afterward p. 134]

CONSIDERATION

Depending on the age of the children, the alcoholic in the family may damage their lives for years or a lifetime. Some children never fully recover from the harms done to them, even after the alcoholic has stopped drinking. Despite the support of Al-Anon and Alateen, children may require professional therapy. If we are honest with our children about the extent of our disease and demonstrate that we have changed by our actions rather than by our words, our children may slowly begin to trust us once again. The longer we remain sober and practice responsible, accountable, compassionate parenting, the better the odds that our children will return to the family fold. On occasion, despite our best efforts, some of our children will never end up trusting us, and will never forgive our past behavior. Should this occur, it is best we accept this sad situation without resentment or judgement, remembering we had a major role in our family's dysfunction and destruction.

Can I accept the fact that some of my family members, including my children, may never welcome me back, even as I remain sober?

OCTOBER 27

THE FAMILY AFTERWARD

In time they will see that he is a new man and in their own way they will let him know it. When this happens, they can be invited to join in morning meditation and then they can take part in the daily discussion without rancor or bias. From that point on, progress will be rapid. Marvelous results often follow such a reunion.

[The Family Afterward p. 134]

CONSIDERATION

If our children start to trust us again based on our actions over time, there is a chance that the parent-child relationship will improve. The extent and timing of any improvement is unpredictable, and may never occur. This should not prevent us from continuing on our path of sobriety and spiritual growth. Unresolved anger and resentment at family members for not accepting us as sober adults is best avoided, since it may lead to our drinking once again. Trying to force family members to adopt the recovery habits of our new way of life is just one more way we try to play the director, attempting to control the behavior of others since we think we know their best interest, and playing God should be avoided at all costs. Our family members will follow their own path in life, and we can support their journey without judging or directing that journey. If the family decides, on their own, to take part in any spiritual rituals we may offer, we can easily welcome them and partake of any benefit that may result.

Will I avoid attempting to force my new way of living on others, including my family members?

OCTOBER 28

THE FAMILY AFTERWARD

Whether the family goes on a spiritual basis or not, the alcoholic member has to if he would recover. The others must be convinced of his new status beyond the shadow of a doubt. Seeing is believing to most families who have lived with a drinker.

[The Family Afterward p. 134]

CONSIDERATION

We alcoholics must constantly remind ourselves we are not running the show. Despite our best intentions, we have no right or duty to impose our will on others. The family must find their own way. We can choose to be loving, kind, tolerant, non-judgmental and gentle as we support their personal journey. Our task is to remain sober, moderate our shortcomings, practice the 12 Step principles, do the next right thing and help others. As we improve our own lives, we cannot help but improve the lives of our family members. The final outcome of our efforts is not under our control, but hopefully our domestic situation will improve over time.

Am I committed to living my life on a spiritual basis, and not interfering in the lives of others, including my family members?

OCTOBER 29

THE FAMILY AFTERWARD

We have three little mottoes which are apropos. First Things First.

[The Family Afterward p. 135]

CONSIDERATION

A motto represents a guiding principle. A slogan is simply a memorable phrase, often used in advertising, such as "This is your brain on drugs," or "Things go better with Coke," or "A diamond is forever." When we see that our first guiding principle is "First Things First," most of us agree that our own sobriety must come first. For without sobriety, all bets are off and nothing else matters. A corollary to this motto suggests we might remember and prioritize what keeps us sober in the first place. If we stop practicing the daily activities we learn in A.A. to try to maintain our sobriety, if we neglect and slowly eliminate the habits and rituals we have acquired that keep our spiritual foundation firm, then we may begin to drift off that Broad Highway that leads to a better life.

Am I placing not drinking as my first thing first?

OCTOBER 30

THE FAMILY AFTERWARD

We have three little mottoes which are apropos. Live and Let Live.

[The Family Afterward p. 135]

CONSIDERATION

Once we stop drinking and allow the A.A. program to teach us how to live a new, sober life, we find we no longer need to control the world. We abandon our need to be Director of the Universe, which includes being the director of other people's lives. We find we have our hands full coping with our own life, with little time, temperament or competence left over to manage the lives of our fellows. At first we are distressed over our lack of power to mold people to our own way of thinking and behaving, but as time passes we discover that our life is a lot easier not having to manage the lives of so many others. No longer are our days occupied taking the inventory of our family and friends. We learn how to live and let live. We have more time and strength to improve our own relationship with the people and world about us. We can grow spiritually and focus on our real purpose of fitting ourselves to be of maximum service to our spiritual principles and the people in our life.

Have I stopped trying to control the lives of others?

OCTOBER 31

THE FAMILY AFTERWARD

We have three little mottoes which are apropos. Easy Does It.

[The Family Afterward p. 135]

CONSIDERATION

When we were drinking we roared through people's lives like a tornado, leaving behind a trail of debris and devastation we never imagined possible. Once sober, we become more like a steam engine, slowly huffing, puffing, belching and billowing smoke and fumes as we rumble through life. The frenzied lives we created and embraced while drinking have been reduced to a more structured lifestyle devoted to sobriety and service work. Yet we find we cannot completely eliminate all of our irritability, restlessness and discontentment with the world around us. This is because we were born a quart low with some of our brain chemicals, aggravating our divine dissatisfaction with life, and that will never change. So like Bill Wilson, we will carry some degree of smoldering unrest within us for the rest of our lives. The committee in our head will never completely disband, but we don't have to meet as frequently, so we are no longer totally ruled by our emotions. "Easy does it" reminds us that if we persistently try to relax and take it easy during our day, especially when faced with indecision or irritation, our day usually ends up more manageable, and we remain fairly content. Repeating the Serenity Prayer, taking time to meditate, inviting some humor into our life, and abiding by Rule 62—not taking ourselves too seriously—often helps in these areas.

Am I making an effort to slow down and take it easy during my day?

NOVEMBER 1

TO EMPLOYERS

Among many employers nowadays, we think of one member who has spent much of his life in the world of big business. He has hired and fired hundreds of men. He knows the alcoholic as the employer sees him. His present views ought to prove exceptionally useful to business men everywhere.

[To Employers p. 136]

CONSIDERATION

Alcoholics are frequently exceptional in business, driven and motivated to succeed, and are often recognized as leaders in their field. Many alcoholic men and women are persistent, effective and highly intelligent workaholics. As a normal part of business activities, at least in days past, alcohol played a significant social and professional role. It was a common denominator that often brought buyer and seller together to do their business. For most of society, this was business as usual. However, once a real alcoholic enters the mix, innumerable complications arise.

Have I ever been able to successfully keep my alcoholic illness separate from my work environment?

NOVEMBER 2

TO EMPLOYERS

I was at one time assistant manager of a corporation department employing sixty-six hundred men. One day my secretary came in saying Mr. B. insisted on speaking with me. I told her to say that I was not interested. I had warned him several times that he had but one more chance. Not long afterward he had called me from Hartford on two successive days, so drunk he could hardly speak. I told him he was through—finally and forever.

[To Employers p. 136]

CONSIDERATION

Despite our best efforts at hiding our alcoholism from our bosses, co-workers or employees, most of us eventually slip up. We make an inappropriate comment to our boss during a holiday party, or we stagger and stumble into an employee as we cross the room holding our fifth drink in our hand. Maybe we become too friendly with a member of the opposite sex who works with us. Or perhaps our illness has progressed to the point where we secretly drink while at work, which makes getting through the day a lot more complicated. Over time, hiding our drinking from fellow employees and customers becomes more of a challenge than performing the job we are actually hired to do, and we have the constant fear that we are not acting sober enough to fool the people around us. When we look back on our actions, we become anxious that someone may have noticed how intoxicated we were and how poorly we behaved. We hope we have done nothing so grave that we will be fired over it, but are never certain.

Do I have to drink to work?

NOVEMBER 3

TO EMPLOYERS

My secretary returned to say that it was not Mr. B on the phone; it was Mr. B's brother, and he wished to give me a message. I still expected a plea for clemency, but these words came through the receiver: "I just wanted to tell you Paul jumped from a hotel window in Hartford last Saturday. He left us a note saying you were the best boss he ever had, and that you were not to blame in any way." Another time, as I opened a letter which lay on my desk, a newspaper clipping fell out. It was the obituary of one of the best salesmen I ever had. After two weeks of drinking, he had placed his toe on the trigger of a loaded shotgun—the barrel was in his mouth. I had discharged him for drinking six weeks before.

[To Employers p. 136]

CONSIDERATION

Almost no one in A.A. has not met a fellow member who has not contemplated or attempted suicide. Many of us seriously considered suicide ourselves. We reach the end of the line. We see no way out. We can't stop drinking and don't know what to do. Our spouses, family and friends cannot convince us to seek or accept help. Priests, physicians and counselors cannot stop the progression of our illness. Our obsession to drink surpasses all rational thought and consumes every waking moment. The uproar in our head clamors for attention, filling us with remorse and shame over past wrongs, and igniting fear over what might happen tomorrow. We are dying a slow death, and just want everything to be quiet and peaceful, whether for that moment or an eternity.

How many times have I thought about killing myself during my illness?

NOVEMBER 4

TO EMPLOYERS

Still another experience: A woman's voice came faintly over long distance from Virginia. She wanted to know if her husband's company insurance was still in force. Four days before he had hanged himself in his woodshed. I had been obliged to discharge him for drinking, though he was brilliant, alert, and one of the best organizers I have ever known.

[To Employers p. 136]

CONSIDERATION

Some of us shoot ourselves, some use the hangman's noose, some jump from high places, some tie a plastic bag over their head, some overdose on medication. When the pain of alcoholism is too much for us because we must drink despite not wanting to, all we seek in the end is for the chatter and static in our head to quiet down. We want relief from the insanity of not being able to live sober or live drunk. We are not so much depressed as we are desperate. Just give us something to stop the madness. So often at funerals of alcoholics we hear, "Well, at least he's at peace now."

Do I still have suicidal thoughts?

NOVEMBER 5

TO EMPLOYERS

Here were three exceptional men lost to this world because I did not understand alcoholism as I do now. What irony—I became an alcoholic myself! And but for the intervention of an understanding person, I might have followed in their footsteps. My downfall cost the business community unknown thousands of dollars, for it takes real money to train a man for an executive position. This kind of waste goes on unabated. We think the business fabric is shot through with a situation which might be helped by better understanding all around.

[To Employers p. 137]

CONSIDERATION

Most of us value life over money. The loss of a tortured alcoholic to suicide, drunken accidents, car crashes, liver failure or anything else caused by drinking is always a sad affair. Death destroys not only the individual but devastates their family and friends. Spouses lose their partner, children lose a parent, a sister loses her brother, a best friend loses a lifelong mate, and a community loses a valued citizen. As a business person, the loss of a capable alcoholic employee always affects the bottom line. There is the cost to hire and train the person, costs to support them in their position, and the cost of having to replace them. There is also the emotional cost of grief to the organization when a popular, fellow employee is no longer present.

Have I lost someone close to me in the workplace or community from alcoholism?

NOVEMBER 6

TO EMPLOYERS

Here, for instance, is a typical example: An officer of one of the largest banking institutions in America knows I no longer drink. One day he told me about an executive of the same bank who, from his description, was undoubtedly alcoholic. This seemed to me like an opportunity to be helpful, so I spent two hours talking about alcoholism, the malady, and described the symptoms and results as well as I could. His comment was, "Very interesting. But I'm sure this man is done drinking. He has just returned from a three-months' leave of absence, has taken a cure, looks fine, and to clinch the matter, the board of directors told him this was his last chance."

[To Employers p. 138]

CONSIDERATION

For those of us who have been discovered drinking on the job, or whose behavior at work makes it apparent we have a drinking problem, we may not be fired immediately. These days most large companies have special programs to assist alcoholics in getting help for their illness, but there is no guarantee of continued employment if the alcoholic is unable to recover. One thing for certain is that the threat from our employer of losing our job if we continue drinking cannot, alone, make us stop. Nothing an employer does or threatens to do can force us to permanently quit drinking if we are not ready.

How many times have I been told I would be fired unless I quit drinking?

NOVEMBER 7

TO EMPLOYERS

The only answer I could make was that if the man followed the usual pattern, he would go on a bigger bust than ever. I felt this was inevitable and wondered if the bank was doing the man an injustice. Why not bring him into contact with some of our alcoholic crowd? He might have a chance. I pointed out that I had had nothing to drink whatever for three years, and this in the face of difficulties that would have made nine out of ten men drink their heads off. Why not at least afford him an opportunity to hear my story? "Oh no," said my friend, "this chap is either through with liquor, or he is minus a job. If he has your will power and guts, he will make the grade."

[To Employers p. 138]

CONSIDERATION

Even in this modern day and age, where it has been clearly demonstrated that alcoholism is a chronic medical illness, so many people, deep in their hearts, still believe it is caused by an individual's weak will and personal moral failure. Despite confirmation from the medical community that addiction is a legitimate and treatable chronic lifetime disease, there are a surprisingly large number of professionals and laypersons alike who don't believe it. Many people still suspect immersion in religion and greater moral will-power is all that is needed to overcome our deadly illness, and no facts or evidence will convince them otherwise.

Do I truly believe alcoholism is a treatable medical illness?

NOVEMBER 8

TO EMPLOYERS

I wanted to throw up my hands in discouragement, for I saw that I had failed to help my banker friend understand. He simply could not believe that his brother-executive suffered from a serious illness.

[To Employers p. 138]

CONSIDERATION

Those of us who know that alcoholism is an illness often find it difficult to convince others of this fact. In our modern society there is overwhelming evidence that social drinking is not an illness, but when someone has reached the point of not being able to control their drinking despite their deepest desire and best efforts, they are medically sick. The chemicals in their brain have become severely rearranged and don't work normally. Will-power alone cannot repair this type of progressive neurological damage. Continued drinking will eventually kill the alcoholic, one way or another, unless complete abstinence and effective lifetime treatment is sought and initiated.

Do I believe untreated alcoholism is a fatal illness?

NOVEMBER 9

TO EMPLOYERS

Presently the man did slip and was fired. Following his discharge, we contacted him. Without much ado, he accepted the principles and procedure that had helped us. He is undoubtedly on the road to recovery. To me, this incident illustrates lack of understanding as to what really ails the alcoholic, and lack of knowledge as to what part employers might profitably take in salvaging their sick employees. If you desire to help it might be well to disregard your own drinking, or lack of it. Whether you are a hard drinker, a moderate drinker or a teetotaler, you may have some pretty strong opinions, perhaps prejudices.

[To Employers p. 139]

CONSIDERATION

Although we may not have thought so at the time, losing our job may have been the best wake-up call ever. When we lose our job, it is harder for us to ignore the detrimental consequences of our drinking. We naturally want to blame others for being fired, such as our fellow co-workers, subordinates or superiors. As a last resort, we easily delude ourselves by saying "I was going to quit anyway." Then we try to convince ourselves that we are better off without our job, since everyone knows we were over-qualified and under-paid for it, and deserved something better. Not having a steady income disturbs us, but we are sure we can find a more prestigious and higher paying position once we put our mind to it. Later on we think "Maybe I should start looking for a new job, but let's have a drink now, and I'll deal with the problem tomorrow."

How many jobs have I lost due to my drinking?

NOVEMBER 10

TO EMPLOYERS

Those who drink moderately may be more annoyed with an alcoholic than a total abstainer would be. Drinking occasionally, and understanding your own reactions, it is possible for you to become quite sure of many things which, so far as the alcoholic is concerned, are not always so. As a moderate drinker, you can take your liquor or leave it alone. Whenever you want to, you control your drinking. Of an evening, you can go on a mild bender, get up in the morning, shake your head and go to business. To you, liquor is no real problem. You cannot see why it should be to anyone else, save the spineless and stupid. When dealing with an alcoholic, there may be a natural annoyance that a man could be so weak, stupid and irresponsible. Even when you understand the malady better, you may feel this feeling rising.

[To Employers p. 139]

CONSIDERATION

How many times have we sober, sincere and compassionate alcoholics looked at one of our fellow newcomers or chronic relapsers and thought to ourselves, "What an idiot. What's the matter with that fellow? It's clear to everyone he's an alcoholic and he knows it too, so why doesn't he accept help? Why doesn't he shape up and get on with the program? Why does he still think he can control his drinking and lick this thing by himself, when it's so obvious he can't?" Of course when we reflect on our own journey into recovery, if we are honest, we know we behaved just as our friend did. We denied our addiction, deluded ourselves into thinking we could solve our problem without any help, and became defiant when anyone else suggested using the A.A. program for relief. When we recognize we reacted just like the fellow we are criticizing, we can chuckle to ourselves, put aside our reflexive judgment and disapproval, and offer a helping hand instead.

Do I treat the alcoholic newcomer with dignity and respect?

NOVEMBER 11

TO EMPLOYERS

If you concede that your employee is ill, can he be forgiven for what he has done in the past? Can his past absurdities be forgotten? Can it be appreciated that he has been a victim of crooked thinking, directly caused by the action of alcohol on his brain?

[To Employers p. 140]

CONSIDERATION

If we are a sole employer and decision maker, and we have a solid foundation in A.A., we should have little difficulty dealing with an alcoholic employee. But if we are not completely in charge, we still may be in a position of influence or authority in our company. If this be the case, we have the added duty to help and support our organization in their efforts to help its alcoholic employees. In these enlightened times most large companies have formal Employee Assistance Programs to help those with addiction, and they are structured to take a medical approach with the employee. However, there are many small mom-and-pop businesses with few employees and no formal structure to deal with the alcoholic. Perhaps it is in these types of establishments where we can be most useful. If permitted, we should not shy away from sharing our knowledge that alcoholism is a medical illness and treatment is available for the alcoholic. We should never allow fear to prevent us from trying to help another alcoholic. If we are concerned about our own anonymity, we can still carry the message to company owners and staff in ways which will not expose us. By sharing general suggestions based on well-known approaches to treating alcoholism such as participation in A.A., and sharing our experience about other alcoholics we know who have recovered, we may be able to make a difference in the less sophisticated workplace.

Am I willing to confidentially share my knowledge and experience about alcoholism and A.A. with my employer if appropriate?

NOVEMBER 12

TO EMPLOYERS

Your man has probably been trying to conceal a number of scrapes, perhaps pretty messy ones. They may be disgusting. You may be at a loss to understand how such a seemingly above-board chap could be so involved. But these scrapes can generally be charged, no matter how bad, to the abnormal action of alcohol on his mind. When drinking, or getting over a bout, an alcoholic, sometimes the model of honesty when normal, will do incredible things. Afterward, his revulsion will be terrible. Nearly always, these antics indicate nothing more than temporary conditions.

[To Employers p. 140]

CONSIDERATION

As an employed alcoholic, we know how insanely we can act while drinking on the company clock. How many times are we on the road, away from family and out of sight of our boss, when the worst events occur? If we are lucky, no one finds out about them, and any damage we cause is not so severe that we can't hide it, or lie our way out of it. Eventually, reality catches up with us and we are exposed as an employee with a serious drinking problem who can no longer be trusted to represent the business. At this point we are usually offered one of two choices: seek treatment for our alcoholism or be fired. The choice is usually up to us.

Have I ever behaved inappropriately when under the influence while working for my company?

NOVEMBER 13

TO EMPLOYERS

This is not to say that all alcoholics are honest and upright when not drinking. Of course that isn't so, and such people may often impose on you. Seeing your attempt to understand and help, some men will try to take advantage of your kindness. If you are sure your man does not want to stop, he may as well be discharged, the sooner the better. You are not doing him a favor by keeping him on. Firing such an individual may prove a blessing to him. It may be just the jolt he needs. I know, in my own particular case, that nothing my company could have done would have stopped me for, so long as I was able to hold my position, I could not possibly realize how serious my situation was. Had they fired me first, and had they then taken steps to see that I was presented with the solution contained in this book, I might have returned to them six months later, a well man.

[To Employers p. 141]

CONSIDERATION

One advantage we have as recovered alcoholics in the workplace is that we know how other alcoholics think and act. Rarely are they able to fool us with their endless lies, promises to quit, and tearful pleas to be given just one more chance. Since we usually know when another alcoholic is deceiving us, we can usually distinguish between an employee's sincere desire to stop drinking and seek out a solution for their illness, compared to an employee who is just trying to pull the wool over our eyes by telling us nothing more than what they think we want to hear in order to save their job. If we are unsure what to do when faced with an employee we are uncertain about, offering them a leave of absence for treatment may provide enough time for us to come to a fair and balanced decision based on their behavior after they return to work.

Am I willing to give an alcoholic employee the benefit of the doubt if I am unsure how to proceed?

NOVEMBER 14

TO EMPLOYERS

But there are many men who want to stop, and with them you can go far. Your understanding treatment of their cases will pay dividends. Perhaps you have such a man in mind. He wants to quit drinking and you want to help him, even if it be only a matter of good business. You now know more about alcoholism. You can see that he is mentally and physically sick. You are willing to overlook his past performances. Suppose an approach is made something like this: State that you know about his drinking, and that it must stop. You might say you appreciate his abilities, would like to keep him, but cannot if he continues to drink. A firm attitude at this point has helped many of us.

[To Employers p. 141]

CONSIDERATION

If we think about it, there is little difference in how we approach another alcoholic, whether he is our employee or not, should we choose to share all or part of our recovery story. Of course we may have the power to hire and fire, but in terms of explaining how we, or others, have found the A.A. solution does not change in a business relationship. If we do not wish to share our personal experience with alcoholism, we can respect anonymity and generically share the experience of other alcoholics we know who have tried A.A. This can be done with an attitude of support rather than condemnation. Naturally, we make clear to the alcoholic employee that the company will help as best as it is able if the employee will seek and engage in treatment. The number of times this approach is permitted will be up to senior company management, over which we may or may not have much influence or control.

Am I able to take an objective business approach when dealing with an alcoholic employee?

NOVEMBER 15

TO EMPLOYERS

Next he can be assured that you do not intend to lecture, moralize, or condemn...Say that you believe he is a gravely-ill person, with this qualification—being perhaps fatally ill, does he want to get well?....Will he take every necessary step, submit to anything to get well, to stop drinking forever? If he says yes, does he really mean it, or down inside does he think he is fooling you, and that after rest and treatment he will be able to get away with a few drinks now and then? We believe a man should be thoroughly probed on these points. Be satisfied he is not deceiving himself or you.

[To Employers p. 142]

CONSIDERATION

Experience has shown that it is prudent to qualify anyone we are planning to work with as a real alcoholic, whether inside or outside of the workplace, since that is where our experience lies. If we are the person's employer, it is unwise to become our employee's sponsor, but we can still be supportive. If we are an equal level co-worker and wish to sponsor our friend, we speak with our prospect not only about their drinking habits and consequences, but more importantly, their willingness to stop drinking forever, and seek ongoing treatment in A.A. or elsewhere. We, as fellow alcoholics and potential sponsors, must be convinced that the person we are offering to spend a lot of time and effort on is in fact willing to do the work to change. Since we almost always receive a positive response in this regard, we learn to trust our gut on whether or not we believe them. Some of us advocate using a trial period with the newcomer, to see if he or she will comply with suggested Big Book readings and other brief assignments prior to formally starting the 12 Step recovery coursework.

Before making decisions involving a newcomer, employee or not, do I first qualify them as a real alcoholic who is ready to stop drinking for good, and do all the work necessary to change their way of life?

NOVEMBER 16

TO EMPLOYERS

Whether you mention this book is a matter for your discretion. If he temporizes and still thinks he can ever drink again, even beer, he might as well be discharged after the next bender which, if an alcoholic, he is almost certain to have. He should understand that emphatically. Either you are dealing with a man who can and will get well or you are not. If not, why waste time with him? This may seem severe, but it is usually the best course.

[To Employers p. 142]

CONSIDERATION

Giving an employee, or any other alcoholic, an evenhanded chance to recover is fair and reasonable. However, wasting time with a person who is unready, unable or unwilling to take the actions needed to do their part in recovery is not the best use of our time. With so many suffering alcoholics in and outside the rooms of A.A., it is our duty to allocate our limited time and resources among those willing to do the work. Once we determine that a newcomer is not capable, for whatever reason, of engaging in the program, most of us move on quickly to the next candidate. We may not always be correct in our assessment of the newcomer, but after having a few frank and honest discussions with them, we should have a fairly good idea of where they stand.

Am I willing to spend enough time with a newcomer to come to my best judgement about their willingness to go to any length to treat their disease?

NOVEMBER 17

TO EMPLOYERS

After satisfying yourself that your man wants to recover and that he will go to any extreme to do so, you may suggest a definite course of action. For most alcoholics who are drinking, or who are just getting over a spree, a certain amount of physical treatment is desirable, even imperative. The matter of physical treatment should, of course, be referred to your own doctor. Whatever the method, its object is to thoroughly clear mind and body of the effects of alcohol. In competent hands, this seldom takes long nor is it very expensive. Your man will fare better if placed in such physical condition that he can think straight and no longer craves liquor. If you propose such a procedure to him, it may be necessary to advance the cost of the treatment, but we believe it should be made plain that any expense will later be deducted from his pay. It is better for him to feel fully responsible.

[To Employers p. 142]

CONSIDERATION

Most of the larger workplaces today have structured Employee Assistance Programs to initiate and facilitate the treatment process for alcoholics. Treatment may or may not involve formal medically supervised detoxification or in-patient rehabilitation. However, having an evaluation by a qualified medical professional is often recommended to avoid any potential life-threatening effects of withdrawal, followed by a tailored proposal for further addiction treatment. Smaller workplaces without formal assistance programs can still recommend or even require that their addicted employee seek medical and addiction recovery advice and treatment from competent professional sources of their own choosing or from others recommended in the community.

Do I have enough knowledge and resources, as an employer, to help my alcoholic employee get started on the road of recovery, if they are sincere, willing and able?

NOVEMBER 18

TO EMPLOYERS

If your man accepts your offer, it should be pointed out that physical treatment is but a small part of the picture. Though you are providing him with the best possible medical attention, he should understand that he must undergo a change of heart. To get over drinking will require a transformation of thought and attitude. We all had to place recovery above everything, for without recovery we would have lost both home and business.

[To Employers p. 143]

CONSIDERATION

The extent to which we, as a recovered alcoholic employer, share our personal story with an alcoholic employee is solely up to us. Some of us choose not to share any of our story, and simply lay out the company's formal position and available resources for the employee who is willing to undergo treatment. Others of us may wish to share some or all of our personal story, in the hopes that it will further motivate and encourage our alcoholic employee to obtain treatment, and provide some additional hope that full recovery is possible.

Have I impressed upon my employee that not drinking is the most important initial action they can take, and that it must be maintained above all else as they progress down the road of recovery?

NOVEMBER 19

TO EMPLOYERS

Can you have every confidence in his ability to recover? While on the subject of confidence, can you adopt the attitude that so far as you are concerned this will be a strictly personal matter, that his alcoholic derelictions, the treatment about to be undertaken, will never be discussed without his consent? It might be well to have a long chat with him on his return.

[To Employers p. 143]

CONSIDERATION

Part of the obligation of anonymity in A.A. is that we do not disclose, without permission, the full names or personal situations of fellow members publicly. Confidentiality is especially important in the workplace, despite the fact that most employees somehow discover an astonishing amount of private information about their co-workers. We may not be able to control the gossip of others, but we can set the example and not do it ourselves. We may openly discourage inappropriate chit-chat, but we can rarely prevent it. When in doubt about sharing someone's name or story, it is often better to error on the side of restraint.

Do I keep other people's identity and employment situation confidential?

NOVEMBER 20

TO EMPLOYERS

To return to the subject matter of this book: It contains full suggestions by which the employee may solve his problem. To you, some of the ideas which it contains are novel. Perhaps you are not quite in sympathy with the approach we suggest. By no means do we offer it as the last word on this subject, but so far as we are concerned, it has worked with us. After all, are you not looking for results rather than methods? Whether your employee likes it or not, he will learn the grim truth about alcoholism. That won't hurt him a bit, even though he does not go for this remedy.

[To Employers p. 143]

CONSIDERATION

Our approach with the alcoholic employee is little different than our approach with any other fellow alcoholic when it comes to how we share and encourage the A.A. solution that we have found for our own illness. We might remind ourselves and our fellow that A.A. may not be the only solution for every alcoholic, and that A.A. has no corner on the market. What matters is that our employee be able to admit they are sick and be willing to seek help from any reputable source. As a representative of a business or company, we can support our employee during the time they are under treatment, but make it clear that our support may not last forever if their treatment fails, since we have a business to run and obligations to others.

Am I willing to give a sincere alcoholic employee a reasonable chance at recovery without jeopardizing their job position?

NOVEMBER 21

TO EMPLOYERS

We hope the doctor will tell the patient the truth about his condition, whatever that happens to be. When the man is presented with this volume it is best that no one tell him he must abide by its suggestions. The man must decide for himself.

[To Employers p. 144]

CONSIDERATION

Few of us ever volunteer to do something we don't want to do, or don't believe in. Employees do not always feel they have a free choice when it is suggested they enter a recovery program. Often times, threats of dismissal from the company, divorce from a spouse or exile from the family are used as additional clubs to bully a sick alcoholic into recovery. This is not to say that all who enter rehabilitation are resistant, but the odds of successful recovery increase the more willing the alcoholic becomes to seek and accept help. Ironically, a few alcoholics who are court ordered into treatment can and do recover, yet some who willingly enter treatment never recover. Why one alcoholic recovers, and another does not, remains a mystery. Since no one can predict with certainty who will or will not progress during treatment, it seems reasonable to offer treatment to everyone at least once, and see how they respond.

Do I encourage all alcoholics to seek recovery, even when they are somewhat resistant?

NOVEMBER 22

TO EMPLOYERS

You are betting, or course, that your changed attitude plus the contents of this book will turn the trick. In some cases it will, and in others it may not. But we think that if you persevere, the percentage of successes will gratify you. As our work spreads and our numbers increase, we hope your employees may be put in personal contact with some of us. Meanwhile, we are sure a great deal can be accomplished by the use of the book alone.

[To Employers p. 144]

CONSIDERATION

We in A.A. always enjoy a good debate, especially when it comes to recovery issues. Someone asks, "Is it possible to find sobriety and a new way of living simply by reading our Big Book?" In other words, can that Eskimo in Greenland recover on their own just by reading a copy of our book? Of course, no one can answer this question with certainty, but it usually stimulates a lively conversation among us alcoholics. One thing we know for certain is that in this day and age of worldwide communication options, no one needs to be completely alone with only a Big Book in hand to support their recovery, unless it is their choice. Alcoholics can easily communicate with each other through cell phones, letters, email, texts, Skype, Facetime and on-line Internet forums and meetings. Regardless of our method of communication, the A.A. recovery message we carry remains unchanged. That message is that we need to undergo a spiritual awakening through the 12 Steps, which results in a drastic change in our attitudes and actions. Then we discover the power we need to maintain our sobriety. First is the people power of the Fellowship through meetings and sponsorship, which teach us a design for living using the 12 Step principles and Big Book instructions. Second is some type of spiritual Power, Force, Purpose or Principles of our own choosing that we can use for motivation, strength, guidance and direction as we progress in our new life.

Am I willing to use all the resources available to me to carry the A.A. message to others in need?

NOVEMBER 23

TO EMPLOYERS

The greatest enemies of us alcoholics are resentment, jealousy, envy, frustration, and fear. Wherever men are gathered together in business there will be rivalries and, arising out of these, a certain amount of office politics. Sometimes we alcoholics have an idea that people are trying to pull us down. Often this is not so at all. But sometimes our drinking will be used politically.

[To Employers p. 145]

CONSIDERATION

There are no excuses for not using all the principles of the A.A. program in every aspect of our life. Whether we are in the boardroom or on the shop floor, if we put aside our selfishness and self-centeredness, we often find we are much more content with life. No longer must we run the show and get our own way all the time. No longer are we ruled by our emotions. If we can let go of our pride, vanity and ego long enough to think of someone else and how our actions might affect them, we have come a long way in sobriety. Regardless of what others think of us, how they treat us or gossip about us, can we stick to practicing the 12 Step principles that have served us so well in the past? Can we think more of how we can help someone else and what we can bring to the party, whether in the workplace, the community or in the home, and think less of what we want to get out of the situation?

Wherever I am, if I start to drift into selfishness, dishonesty, resentment or fear, can I use the tools of the Fellowship and my spiritual power to get me back on the beam?

NOVEMBER 24

TO EMPLOYERS

One instance comes to mind in which a malicious individual was always making friendly little jokes about an alcoholic's drinking exploits. In this way he was slyly carrying tales. In another case, an alcoholic was sent to a hospital for treatment. Only a few knew of it at first but, within a short time, it was bill boarded throughout the entire company. Naturally this sort of thing decreased the man's chance of recovery. The employer can many times protect the victim from this kind of talk. The employer cannot play favorites, but he can always defend a man from needless provocation and unfair criticism.

[To Employers p. 145]

CONSIDERATION

No one, not even employers, can control the actions of anyone, including their employees. Those who choose to gossip maliciously about an alcoholic or anyone else often find a way to transmit their venom despite protests from others. All of us can be supportive, in a sensitive way, of folks who are subjected to the spite of another person. If we are the target of gossip ourself, we might first pause and determine if what they are saying is true. If what is repeated about us is accurate, such as "He talks down to his staff at meetings," it may present an opportunity for us to acknowledge and correct that arrogant character defect. If what is said about us is not true, we learn that although ignoring and rejecting the criticism of jealous or hateful people is difficult, it is essential if we are to remain sober. We can remind ourselves that they are sick individuals, just as we are, and wish better things for them, just as we would wish for ourselves.

Difficult as it is, can I not strike back in a hostile, resentful manner when I am the subject of gossip?

TO EMPLOYERS

After your man has gone along without drinking for a few months, you may be able to make use of his services with other employees who are giving you the alcoholic run-around—provided, of course, they are willing to have a third party in the picture. An alcoholic who has recovered, but holds a relatively unimportant job, can talk to a man with a better position. Being on a radically different basis of life, he will never take advantage of the situation.

[To Employers p. 146]

CONSIDERATION

One alcoholic carrying the message to another alcoholic is the foundation of the A.A. program. Doing so within the workplace may be less desirable than doing so outside the workplace, where everyone's time is their own. In this modern age most companies have an in-house employee assistance process to aid the addicted employee who seeks help. Whatever support that employee pursues outside of workplace hours is up to them. As alcoholics, mindful of our Twelve Traditions and anonymity suggestions, we may or may not feel it is appropriate to develop a recovery relationship with an employee. Careful thought and consultation with our sponsor and others experienced in such matters may help guide our final decision.

As an employer, will I first discuss with my sponsor my situation, and carefully review my options before becoming personally involved with an alcoholic employee in my company?

NOVEMBER 26

TO EMPLOYERS

Your man may be trusted. Long experience with alcoholic excuses naturally arouses suspicion. When his wife next calls saying he is sick, you may jump to the conclusion he is drunk. If he is, and is still trying to recover, he will tell you about it even if it means the loss of his job. For he knows he must be honest if he would live at all. He will appreciate knowing you are not bothering your head about him, that you are not suspicious nor are you trying to run his life so he will be shielded from temptation to drink. If he is conscientiously following the program of recovery he can go anywhere your business may call him.

[To Employers p. 146]

CONSIDERATION

Most alcoholics who are fully engaged in recovery quickly realize that honesty, the principle of our first Step, is critical in all aspects of their life, no matter where they work, or travel, or who they may encounter. Lying, or worse, not disclosing the entire truth of a situation may be tempting, but often leads to broader deceptions which are more damaging and difficult to undo. If we are honest with all persons, we no longer need to remember each lie we tell, and to which people we've told which lies. This makes our life much easier. Of course, we should always be humble and sensitive to the feelings of others and examine our motives before we speak. If we are asked our opinion on someone else's habits or actions, we can be gentle and diplomatic in our response, or we can choose to remain silent. Being brutally honesty in all circumstances is rarely considerate, nor does it reflect our spiritual principles. Kindness in speaking our mind takes practice, but is attainable. Say what we mean, mean what we say, but don't say it mean.

Can I be honest with my employer as I recover from my illness?

NOVEMBER 27

TO EMPLOYERS

In case he does stumble, even once, you will have to decide whether to let him go. If you are sure he doesn't mean business, there is no doubt you should discharge him. If, on the contrary, you are sure he is doing his utmost, you may wish to give him another chance. But you should feel under no obligation to keep him on, for your obligation has been well discharged already.

[To Employers p. 147]

CONSIDERATION

Most, but by no means all, alcoholics have a slip or two on their journey through recovery. A slip describes the alcoholic who is active in recovery, suddenly takes a few unplanned drinks but quickly returns to the program. It is like slipping on the stairs or an icy patch on a sidewalk. The unintentional fall is brief, and the person quickly gets back up with no permanent injury. These types of events, disappointing as they may be, are reviewed with a sponsor and hopefully will not recur. If an alcoholic has a relapse it is much more serious. A relapse means the alcoholic makes a conscious decision to abandon recovery, resume drinking and return to their old way of life. Recovery is still possible in either case, but is usually much more prolonged and torturous for the relapser. How far a company will tolerate a relapsing employee is up to them, but for the protection of the company and their customers, most habitual relapsers end up rightfully losing their job.

Do I understand the difference between a slip and a relapse?

NOVEMBER 28

TO EMPLOYERS

It boils right down to this: No man should be fired just because he is alcoholic. If he wants to stop, he should be afforded a real chance. If he cannot or does not want to stop, he should be discharged. The exceptions are few.

[To Employers p. 148]

CONSIDERATION

When we drink we don't care about the people we work for or the customers we serve. So we end up getting fired, as almost all of us have been at one time or another. The jobs we quit just before we know we will be fired count as firings too. Even jobs we leave by making that unsuccessful geographical move that we pretend will curtail our drinking can be counted. When we are fired we usually blame our boss, a co-worker or the company, playing the victim and denying that our drinking had anything to do with our dismissal. Even though we know our firing is justified, we pretend it isn't, and use this perceived injustice to drink even more now that we're unemployed. The periods between our steady employments grow longer as we spend more time drinking. All we care about is having enough money to get the next drink. After a while, we don't care about finding a job since we know we will lose it anyway. We just want to drink. It is not until we reach that jumping off place, enter recovery and begin to accept responsibility for our actions that we become an accountable person and a reliable employee.

Have I lost any resentments I have toward past employers for firing me?

NOVEMBER 29

TO EMPLOYERS

We think this method of approach will accomplish several things. It will permit the rehabilitation of good men. At the same time you will feel no reluctance to rid yourself of those who cannot or will not stop. Alcoholism may be causing your organization considerable damage in its waste of time, men and reputation. We hope our suggestions will help you plug up this sometimes serious leak. We think we are sensible when we urge that you stop this waste and give your worthwhile man a chance.

[To Employers p. 148]

CONSIDERATION

As an alcoholic, we often take pity on another alcoholic. We know what he or she is going through, and how difficult it is to admit defeat and enter recovery. We understand how important it is for an employee to have a steady job and source of income so they may support themselves and their family. But we must balance our desire to always give an alcoholic employee another chance with the odds that they will or will not damage the company, other employees, or customers in the interim. These are not easy decisions for any one person to make. Disrupting the alcoholic's employment is no small matter, and should only be taken after thoughtful deliberation. If we need to consult with our sponsor and others, we should do so.

Will I give due time and consideration to the alcoholic's situation before taking any formal company action against them?

NOVEMBER 30

TO EMPLOYERS

It is not to be expected that an alcoholic employee will receive a disproportionate amount of time and attention. He should not be made a favorite. The right kind of man, the kind who recovers, will not want this sort of thing. He will not impose. Far from it. He will work like the devil and thank you to his dying day.

[To Employers p. 149]

CONSIDERATION

We may wish to play favorites in business as we do in life. This is not always a good idea, especially concerning an alcoholic employee. If we extend special privileges to an alcoholic that we don't extend to a non-alcoholic, our favoritism will be quickly discovered and not appreciated by our employees. Their tolerance of our partiality will be short-lived. All will suffer. If we are the employee in recovery, we can make it clear we expect no special treatment from our employer, and will do our best to perform our work duties capably and competently just like any other employee.

Can I be objective in my treatment of the alcoholic in the workplace?

DECEMBER 1

A VISION FOR YOU

For most normal folks, drinking means conviviality, companionship and colorful imagination. It means release from care, boredom and worry. It is joyous intimacy with friends and a feeling that life is good. But not so with us in those last days of heavy drinking. The old pleasures were gone. They were but memories. Never could we recapture the great moments of the past. There was an insistent yearning to enjoy life as we once did and a heartbreaking obsession that some new miracle of control would enable us to do it. There was always one more attempt—and one more failure.

[A Vision For You p. 151]

CONSIDERATION

The saying, "Chasing the dragon," refers to the addict's constant pursuit of the feelings of their first high. But since the mythical dragon does not exist, we chase in vain for past experiences that can never be relived. Preoccupation with recalling our bygone glory days of drinking when we had some control over alcohol cannot extinguish the reality of our present situation. Reminiscing about what life was like as a moderate or hard drinker never changes our here and now as a real alcoholic. We can never catch our dragon, the ease and comfort of our past, no matter how hard we try.

Have I given up chasing the dragon?

DECEMBER 2

A VISION FOR YOU

The less people tolerated us, the more we withdrew from society, from life itself. As we became subjects of King Alcohol, shivering denizens of his mad realm, the chilling vapor that is loneliness settled down. It thickened, ever becoming blacker. Some of us sought out sordid places, hoping to find understanding companionship and approval. Momentarily we did—then would come oblivion and the awful awakening to face the hideous Four Horsemen—Terror, Bewilderment, Frustration, Despair. Unhappy drinkers who read this page will understand!

[A Vision For You p. 151]

CONSIDERATION

As we descend further into our alcoholic affliction, we quickly tire of being around people who either criticize us or try to help us. All we want to do is to drink in peace. As our shame grows we withdraw from life. We visit dive bars filled with doomed and deserted alcoholics just like us, but even those dismal places provide no relief. We can barely work, if at all. We rarely speak with our spouse, and stop seeing our family and friends. Phone calls go unanswered. Bills remain unpaid and appointments ignored. We close our drapes and blinds. When it is barely light outside after coming to from yet another blackout, we never know if it is dawn or dusk. We keep our TV set on twenty-four hours a day as distractive background noise. One terrible day we look up and find a huge herd of Horsemen surrounding us: Fear, Shame, Hopelessness, Desperation and Desolation. We have reached the bottom.

Have I met all my Horsemen yet?

DECEMBER 3

A VISION FOR YOU

Now and then a serious drinker, being dry at the moment says, "I don't miss it at all. Feel better. Work better. Having a better time." As ex-problem drinkers, we smile at such a sally. We know our friend is like a boy whistling in the dark to keep up his spirits.

[A Vision For You p. 151]

CONSIDERATION

How easy it is to delude ourselves. Despite spending most of our time drinking uncontrollably, on that rare occasion that we are able to not drink for a short period of time, we feel we have licked our problem. We wonder what all the fuss is about in the first place. Physically, we feel better, since our body is not currently being pickled by alcohol. Mentally, we pray that this will be the day we've got everything under control. Our pace quickens as we prance down the street toward the liquor store, trying to drown out the rumbling of our alcoholic obsession stirring from its sleep.

Am I still deceiving myself that I can drink normally?

DECEMBER 4

A VISION FOR YOU

He fools himself. Inwardly he would give anything to take half a dozen drinks and get away with them. He will presently try the old game again, for he isn't happy about his sobriety. He cannot picture life without alcohol. Some day he will be unable to imagine life either with alcohol or without it. Then he will know loneliness such as few do. He will be at the jumping-off place. He will wish for the end.

[A Vision For You p. 151]

CONSIDERATION

Terror, Bewilderment, Frustration and Despair. We met those four horsemen before and assume we have them safely corralled in their pen. But they keep jumping the fence every time we go back to our bottle and they track us down. So we just drink and drink and drink, wondering why we can no longer manage our alcoholic life or gain any pleasure from it. The thrill is long gone. We don't know how to live sober and we don't know how to live drunk. We drink ourselves into a stupor, but the uproar in our head persists. There is no way out. Our thoughts turn to suicide as the final solution, trying to figure out a way to kill ourselves as quickly and painlessly as possible, and in a manner that will bring the least amount of disgrace to our family. We practice sticking the barrel of a shotgun in our mouth, surprised by its bitter taste, while praying for the courage to pull the trigger. We look for high places from which we can jump, wondering what we might think about during those last few seconds before we hit the ground. We try to calculate how fast we have to drive our car to make sure we will die as we plow into a concrete bridge abutment along the freeway. But with our minds awash with alcohol, plans for our own death soon drift away as the drinks take hold.

How many times have I almost committed suicide?

DECEMBER 5

A VISION FOR YOU

We have shown how we got out from under. You say, "Yes, I'm willing. But am I to be consigned to a life where I shall be stupid, boring and glum, like some righteous people I see? I know I must get along without liquor, but how can I? Have you a sufficient substitute?" Yes, there is a substitute and it is vastly more than that. It is a Fellowship in Alcoholics Anonymous. There you will find release from care, boredom and worry. Your imagination will be fired. Life will mean something at last. The most satisfactory years of your existence lie ahead. Thus we find the Fellowship, and so will you.

[A Vision For You p. 152]

CONSIDERATION

Being naturally self-centered, most alcoholics really don't want to kill themselves. We just want the noise, static, chatter, chaos, pain and committee in our head to stop. When the booze stops working, or when we suffer enough consequences of our drinking, we come to three forks in the road. We must choose whether we are going to try to live a sober life, commit suicide, or let our disease slowly kill us. A.A. shows us, through the experience of millions of alcoholics over the years, that we can successfully stop drinking and find a better way of living. How can we deny the recovery experience of so many alcoholics who reached the end of their line, just as we have, yet were able to recover? If we can ignite a flicker of hope in our battered bodies and souls we have a chance. Maybe, just maybe, we really can get better.

Do I have even a speck of hope that I can recover?

DECEMBER 6

A VISION FOR YOU

You will be bound to them with new and wonderful ties, for you will escape disaster together and you will commence shoulder to shoulder your common journey. Then you will know what it means to give of yourself that others may survive and rediscover life. You will learn the full meaning of "Love thy neighbor as thyself." It may seem incredible that these men are to become happy, respected, and useful once more.

[A Vision For You p. 152]

CONSIDERATION

If we can hang on to our hope of recovery long enough to enter the rooms of A.A., we will have taken our first step toward sobriety. Even if we are not able to stop drinking immediately, we begin to hear the A.A. message and are introduced to a Fellowship of recovered men and women. Little of what is said or done in the rooms of A.A. makes sense at first, but our fellows can teach us how to stop drinking just for this day by sharing their own experience. Once we stop drinking one day at a time, we start to absorb the message of recovery, and can begin taking small steps toward a wonderful new way of living.

Am I willing to give A.A. a chance to help me find a new way of life?

DECEMBER 7

A VISION FOR YOU

How can they rise out of such misery, bad repute and hopelessness? The practical answer is that since these things have happened among us, they can happen with you. Should you wish them above all else, and be willing to make use of our experience, we are sure they will come. The age of miracles is still with us. Our own recovery proves that!

[A Vision For You p. 153]

CONSIDERATION

When we enter the rooms of A.A. it is difficult to deny that they are full of recovered alcoholics. Not everyone in the rooms has recovered, but if we seek out those who have and listen to their advice and experience, we have made a promising start. We soon learn that we have a lot in common with our recovered friends. Despite our different backgrounds and life history, we have in common a fatal disease for which we learn there is a common solution. All we have to do is be honest, open and willing enough to do the work to try to get better.

Am I willing to go to any length to treat my alcoholism?

DECEMBER 8

A VISION FOR YOU

Our hope is that when this chip of a book is launched on the world tide of alcoholism, defeated drinkers will seize upon it, to follow its suggestions. Many, we are sure, will rise to their feet and march on. They will approach still other sick ones and Fellowships of Alcoholics Anonymous may spring up in each city and hamlet, havens for those who must find a way out.

[A Vision For You p. 153]

CONSIDERATION

Most of us enter A.A. to get relief after alcohol stops working. Others arrive to dry out for a while, hoping to pick up a few tips on how to drink successfully. Some of us are compelled by our family, employer or courts into A.A., and we'll attend a few meetings just to get them off our back, counting down the days until we can go back and drink like we used to. We have little interest in reading the Big Book or starting 12 Step work, and it is all we can do just to sit still and pretend we are paying attention during meetings. A few of us come into A.A. with an honest desire to stop drinking for good and find a new life. We are willing to go to any length to treat our disease, dying and desperate to find a way out of our alcoholic hell.

Regardless of my real reason for being here, am I willing to stick with A.A., and keep coming back to the rooms to hear the message of how I can recover so that I may eventually pass it on to others in need?

DECEMBER 9

A VISION FOR YOU

Years ago, in 1935, one of our number made a journey to a certain western city. From a business standpoint, his trip came off badly. Had he been successful in his enterprise, he would have been set on his feet financially which, at the time, seemed vitally important. But his venture wound up in a law suit and bogged down completely. The proceeding was shot through with much hard feeling and controversy.

[A Vision For You p. 153]

CONSIDERATION

This re-telling of Bill Wilson's recovery story marks the turning point in his life when he met Dr. Bob Smith in Akron, Ohio, where the two men started what was to later become Alcoholics Anonymous. Bill was barely six months sober, and had been totally unsuccessful in recruiting any New York City alcoholics into the new, as yet unnamed Fellowship. His business adventures in Akron kept him there longer than he anticipated, and nothing turned out the way he had hoped. Business and financial failure can quickly lead to a resentment in any of us, and is an excellent excuse we use to drink. Bill's depressing situation turned out to be the acid test of his shaky sobriety, and the events that followed after the two men met is gift to all of us in A.A. today.

How often have I used work related disappointments as an excuse to drink?

DECEMBER 10

A VISION FOR YOU

Bitterly discouraged, he found himself in a strange place, discredited and almost broke. Still physically weak, and sober but a few months, he saw that his predicament was dangerous. He wanted so much to talk with someone, but whom?

[A Vision For You p. 154]

CONSIDERATION

Alone, tired, agitated, anxious, annoyed and disillusioned, Bill W. does not immediately reach for the bottle as he has in the past. He is able to pause long enough in his angst to remember that once he takes that first drink, his craving will return, and many more drinks are sure to follow. All his business problems will remain after he sobers up, and he will be back on that incessant treadmill of drinking and stopping, and drinking and stopping. Bill remembers that talking with other alcoholics kept him sober for the past six months, so he takes the only action he knows might help in his time of crisis—he seeks out one of his kind.

When I become obsessed with taking a drink, can I pause long enough to talk with another alcoholic before, rather than after, taking that first drink?

DECEMBER 11

A VISION FOR YOU

One dismal afternoon he paced a hotel lobby wondering how his bill was to be paid. At the end of the room stood a glass covered directory of local churches. Down the lobby a door opened into an attractive bar. He could see the gay crowd inside. In there he would find companionship and release. Unless he took some drinks, he might not have the courage to scrape an acquaintance and would have a lonely weekend.

[A Vision For You p. 154]

CONSIDERATION

Other than his business associates, Bill W. knows no one in Akron, Ohio. At the end of a long day he yearns to relax and partake of some human companionship. Like so many of us, he needs alcohol to give him the courage to approach strangers in unfamiliar places. He wants to make an acquaintance to hopefully keep him company over the weekend, but doesn't want to take a drink to get that company. He is on the horns of the alcoholic dilemma so familiar to us all—do I drink or not?

How many times have I debated with myself whether or not I should take that first drink?

DECEMBER 12

A VISION FOR YOU

Of course he couldn't drink, but why not sit hopefully at a table, a bottle of ginger ale before him? After all, had he not been sober six months now? Perhaps he could handle, say, three drinks—no more! Fear gripped him. He was on thin ice. Again it was the old, insidious insanity—that first drink. With a shiver, he turned away and walked down the lobby to the church directory. Music and gay chatter still floated to him from the bar.

[A Vision For You p. 154]

CONSIDERATION

Just like Jim the used car salesman described earlier in the Big Book, Bill starts to rationalize how he might be able to get away with taking a few drinks. After all, he has been sober a while and maybe his body will react differently to alcohol, even though it had never done so before. Perhaps he really can limit himself to just a few drinks, now that his body has healed physically and he feels mentally more confident than ever. Self-knowledge and a bit of extra will power might just do the trick this time! The sirens of the Mayflower Hotel bar beckon.

Do I continue to rationalize taking that first drink, thinking that this time it will be different?

DECEMBER 13

A VISION FOR YOU

But what about his responsibilities—his family and the men who would die because they would not know how to get well, ah—yes, those other alcoholics? There must be many such in this town. He would phone a clergyman. His sanity returned and he thanked God. Selecting a church at random from the directory, he stepped into a booth and lifted the receiver.

[A Vision For You p. 154]

CONSIDERATION

While living in New York City, Bill W. sought out other alcoholics to share his experience of recovery from alcoholism. Although none of them achieved sobriety, Bill had maintained his. This lesson is not lost on him in Akron as he struggles to choose between drinking or not drinking and seeking out the company of another alcoholic. Fortunately for us and all of A.A., he decides to push aside his selfishness and self-centeredness long enough to think of his family and other alcoholics he might help. He holds on to the hope that speaking with another alcoholic and carrying the message of recovery will continue to keep him sober and overcome his obsession to drink.

Will I immediately reach out to another alcoholic whenever I have an overwhelming urge to drink?

DECEMBER 14

A VISION FOR YOU

His call to the clergyman led him presently to a certain resident of the town, who, though formerly able and respected, was then nearing the nadir of alcoholic despair. It was the usual situation; home in jeopardy, wife ill, children distracted, bills in arrears and standing damaged. He had a desperate desire to stop, but saw no way out, for he had earnestly tried many avenues of escape. Painfully aware of being somehow abnormal, the man did not fully realize what it meant to be alcoholic.

[A Vision For You p. 155]

CONSIDERATION

During Bill Wilson's first meeting with surgeon Dr. Bob Smith of Akron, he discusses his experience with alcoholism and emphasizes that it is a hopeless, incurable medical illness. Despite being a physician, Bill's story and the medical basis of alcoholism is a revelation to Dr. Bob, who for the first time feels another person really understands what it is like to be an alcoholic like himself. This first meeting between Bill W. and Dr. Bob was the beginning of Alcoholics Anonymous and their lifelong friendship. Had that initial connection not been made between these two alcoholics, there would have been no opportunity for either of them to stay sober. It is our ability to relate, one-on-one, to another alcoholic that forms the foundation for all that follows. This is really the initial step in our recovery, for it is the step that opens our mind to listening, gives us a bit of hope for recovery, and stirs a willingness to change.

Will I remember that my first task when speaking with another alcoholic is to make that one-on-one personal connection, stressing that we share the same hopeless, incurable medical illness?

DECEMBER 15

A VISION FOR YOU

When our friend related his experience, the man agreed that no amount of will power he might muster could stop his drinking for long. A spiritual experience, he conceded, was absolutely necessary, but the price seemed high upon the basis suggested. He told how he lived in constant worry about those who might find out about his alcoholism. He had, of course, the familiar alcoholic obsession that few knew of his drinking. Why, he argued, should he lose the remainder of his business, only to bring still more suffering to his family by foolishly admitting his plight to people from whom he made his livelihood? He would do anything, he said, but that.

[A Vision For You p. 155]

CONSIDERATION

Fear of admitting that we are real alcoholics, combined with our lethal misconception that we can overcome our illness based on self-will and self-knowledge, is a strong argument for isolating and rejecting outside help. We think no one knows about our excessive drinking and the trouble we get into over it, but we are only fooling ourselves. Everyone knows of our plight, though they may not confront us with that knowledge. Coming up out of our basement, so to speak, is our first step towards recovery. We accept the truth about ourselves. We admit we have a hopeless illness, can't control our drinking, and that our life is a mess. Next we admit it to others. Then we admit we can't get better on our own. Then we ask for help. And finally, we become willing to accept that help.

Can I admit I'm a hopeless alcoholic, unable to manage my drinking or my life, and that I need help?

DECEMBER 16

A VISION FOR YOU

Being intrigued, however, he invited our friend to his home. Sometime later, and just as he thought he was getting control of his liquor situation, he went on a roaring bender. For him, this was the spree that ended all sprees. He saw that he would have to face his problems squarely that God might give him mastery. One morning he took the bull by the horns and set out to tell those he feared what his trouble had been. He found himself surprisingly well received, and learned that many knew of his drinking. Stepping into his car, he made the rounds of people he had hurt. He trembled as he went about, for this might mean ruin, particularly to a person in his line of business. At midnight he came home exhausted, but very happy. He has not had a drink since. As we shall see, he now means a great deal to his community, and the major liabilities of thirty years of hard drinking have been repaired in four.

[A Vision For You p. 155]

CONSIDERATION

Dr. Bob has a rapid spiritual awakening after spending time with Bill W. in Akron. Like Bill, he essentially goes through his 12 Step work in short order, including making his amends all in one day. Although his obsession to drink is not immediately removed, he remains sober by continuing his daily efforts to help other alcoholics just as he had been helped by Bill. Together, the two men start A.A. in Akron, and remain sober for the rest of their lives. Once again, it is their continuous, daily work with other alcoholics that keeps their foundation of sobriety intact.

After finishing the 12 Steps and having had a spiritual awakening, am I sponsoring other alcoholics?

DECEMBER 17

A VISION FOR YOU

But life was not easy for the two friends. Plenty of difficulties presented themselves. Both saw that they must keep spiritually active. One day they called up the head nurse of a local hospital. They explained their need and inquired if she had a first class alcoholic prospect. She replied, "Yes, we've got a corker. He's just beaten up a couple of nurses. Goes off his head completely when he's drinking. But he's a grand chap when he's sober, though he's been in here eight times in the last six months. Understand he was once a well-known lawyer in town, but just now we've got him strapped down tight." Here was a prospect all right but, by the description, none too promising. The use of spiritual principles in such cases was not so well understood as it is now. But one of the friends said, "Put him in a private room. We'll be down."

[A Vision For You p. 156]

CONSIDERATION

Bill Dotson, a lawyer from Kentucky living in Akron, becomes the third member of A.A. after a few visits from Bill W. and Dr. Bob. This was remarkable, since there was no Big Book, structured 12 Step program or formal A.A. Fellowship in 1935 when Bill and Dr. Bob first met. All the two alcoholics knew was when they accepted they had a hopeless medical illness, sought spiritual guidance, completed a moral inventory, shared their shortcomings, and made restitution to those they had harmed, that speaking with another alcoholic had kept them sober. Neither knew if sharing their recovery message would help anyone, but they knew it had helped them stay sober, so they continued their efforts.

Do I try to help another alcoholic on a daily basis?

DECEMBER 18

A VISION FOR YOU

Two days later, a future fellow of Alcoholics Anonymous stared glassily at the strangers beside his bed. "Who are you fellows, and why this private room? I was always in a ward before." Said one of the visitors, "We're giving you a treatment for alcoholism." Hopelessness was written large on the man's face as he replied, "Oh, but that's no use. Nothing would fix me. I'm a goner. The last three times, I got drunk on the way home from here. I'm afraid to go out the door. I can't understand it." For an hour, the two friends told him about their drinking experiences. Over and over, he would say: "That's me. That's me. I drink like that."

[A Vision For You p. 157]

CONSIDERATION

Just as Bill W. knew he had to first make some type of alcoholic connection with Dr. Bob before sharing his experience of recovery, both men knew they had to do the same with Bill Dotson, the third member of A.A., and nicknamed "The Man in the Bed" in Akron City Hospital. If sharing our experience as an alcoholic connects us with a newcomer, they will usually be willing to listen to how we got better. If we don't connect, they quickly tune out. If we can at least pass on to our alcoholic newcomer that although they may feel hopeless now, there is hope for their future. No matter how bad things are they can get better, and no one is too sick or too hopeless to recover if they are willing to do the 12 Step work. We share our stories to make that alcoholic connection. We share that we have a chronic medical illness, but that it is treatable on a daily basis. Then we share our experience with the solution.

Do I make Twelfth Step calls?

DECEMBER 19

A VISION FOR YOU

The man in the bed was told of the acute poisoning from which he suffered, how it deteriorates the body of an alcoholic and warps his mind. There was much talk about the mental state preceding the first drink......The two friends spoke of their spiritual experience and told him about the course of action they carried out. He interrupted: "I used to be strong for the church, but that won't fix it. I've prayed to God on hangover mornings and sworn that I'd never touch another drop but by nine o'clock I'd be boiled as an owl."....On the third day the lawyer gave his life to the care and direction of his Creator, and said he was perfectly willing to do anything necessary....He had begun to have a spiritual experience.

[A Vision For You p. 157]

CONSIDERATION

Once the medical aspect of alcoholism is explained to Bill Dotson, A.A. member number three, along with the peculiar mental twist and obsession to drink that afflicts all alcoholics, Bill W. and Dr. Bob share how their life improved after they took certain actions. Like Dr. Bob, Bill D. felt that God, faith, regular church attendance and vigorous prayer was the only thing necessary to get sober. The experience of Bill W. and Dr. Bob confirmed that was not true. No one gets sober through God alone. Prayer, worship and faith, either religious or spiritually based, must be accompanied by additional unselfish actions to be successful. We start each day by not drinking. Next we set aside a quiet time to improve our conscious contact with our chosen spiritual Power, Purpose or Principles in our life. Throughout the day we address our shortcomings, spot-check our inventory, make amends if needed, try to practice all the 12 Step principles while doing the next right thing, and make an effort to carry the message to those that still suffer. By taking these additional actions, odds are excellent that we will stay sober this day.

Do I have a daily routine to try to maintain my spiritual condition?

DECEMBER 20

A VISION FOR YOU

On the third day the lawyer gave his life to the care and direction of his Creator, and said he was perfectly willing to do anything necessary. His wife came, scarcely daring to be hopeful, though she thought she saw something different about her husband already. He had begun to have a spiritual experience.

[A Vision For You p. 158]

CONSIDERATION

Very few of us have had sudden, abrupt shifts or psychic changes in our personality that instantly removes our obsession to drink and rockets us headlong into sobriety. These are usually called spiritual experiences. For most of us, our personality change comes slowly over time as it did for Dr. Bob. This type of change is described in "Appendix II—Spiritual Experience" of the Big Book, and is more commonly known as a spiritual awakening. Gradually, we develop a change in our attitudes and actions as we complete our 12 Step work. We lose our God-cape. We give up being the center of our world. We are no longer Director of the Universe. Selfishness and self-centeredness stop driving all our actions and consuming our life. Emotions no longer rule us. Resentments disappear. Our fears diminish. Relationships improve. Shame and guilt leave us. Dignity and self-esteem return. We are more comfortable in our own skin. We welcome the opportunity to help a fellow sufferer. This is our spiritual awakening.

Have I had a spiritual experience or spiritual awakening yet?

DECEMBER 21

A VISION FOR YOU

That afternoon he put on his clothes and walked from the hospital a free man. He entered a political campaign, making speeches, frequenting men's gathering places of all sorts, often staying up all night. He lost the race by only a narrow margin. But he had found God—and in finding God had found himself. That was in June, 1935. He never drank again. He too, has become a respected and useful member of his community. He has helped other men recover, and is a power in the church from which he was long absent.

[A Vision For You p. 158]

CONSIDERATION

Our book speaks of being free of the bondage of self, and of being given the keys to the kingdom once we have recovered. Indeed, the freedom to not-drink, to no longer have that unrelenting obsession for alcohol, to have the key of willingness that unlocks the doorway to sanity, sobriety and a new way of living; these are precious gifts. No one needs to seek or find God to get sober. No one needs to return to old-time religion to get sober. But we do need to seek our own spiritual bridge to sobriety, and a new way of living through our willingness to change. We become willing to draw on the dual powers of A.A.—the people power of our Fellowship and some type of non-human spiritual Power, Purpose, Force, or Principles of our own creation—to give us the motivation, strength, direction and courage to change.

Have I found, and do I use the power of the Fellowship and my spiritual power, to keep me sane and sober in my new life?

DECEMBER 22

A VISION FOR YOU

So, you see, there were three alcoholics in that town, who now felt they had to give to others what they had found, or be sunk. A fourth turned up...He proved to be a devil-may-care young fellow whose parents could not make out whether he wanted to stop drinking or not...He suffered horribly from his sprees, but....He consented, however, to go to the hospital, where...He had three visitors. After a bit, he said, "The way you fellows put this spiritual stuff makes sense. I'm ready to do business. I guess the old folks were right after all." So one more was added to the Fellowship.

[A Vision For You p. 158]

CONSIDERATION

In Akron, Bill and Bob realized that other alcoholics could stay sober if they did what they did. Absent a formal A.A. program or Big Book in 1935, most early members kept their focus on not drinking, praying to God, meeting with other alcoholics regularly, taking inventory, making amends, and passing on how they stayed sober to their fellow sufferers. The fourth Akron A.A. member was Ernie Galbraith, a devil-may care fellow who briefly got sober after being visited by Bill W., Bill D. and Dr. Bob. He also became the first husband of Dr. Bob's daughter Sue, but unfortunately his drinking continued and he never recovered. Those early A.A. pioneers learned their efforts may not work every time or with every alcoholic, but enough alcoholics do get sober that witnessing and sharing the A.A. solution continues throughout the world today. Giving personal testimony on how we recover from our hopeless state of mind and body is one of the most powerful tools we can use to help another alcoholic. Whether or not our newcomer succeeds with sobriety doesn't really matter, in the sense that we humans do not have enough power to get anyone sober or get them drunk. What matters is that we always continue our outreach efforts, stay away from that first drink ourselves and remain a full, active member of our Fellowship.

Am I an active member of A.A.?

DECEMBER 23

A VISION FOR YOU

These men had found something brand new in life. Though they knew they must help other alcoholics if they would remain sober, that motive became secondary. It was transcended by the happiness they found in giving themselves for others.

[A Vision For You p. 159]

CONSIDERATION

Most of us admit that the most rewarding activity we do is working with a fellow alcoholic. We hope the obsession to drink will leave them, and that after completing the 12 Steps they will find some health, happiness and peace. Should that happen, few experiences surpass our pleasure and joy in witnessing this spiritual transformation. It brings us more pleasure than drinking ever did, even if our fellow slips or relapses. At least we tried. Regardless of the outcome, we have no desire to relinquish our quest to serve the next alcoholic that comes our way. We remain bound to A.A. as closely as we ever were, and are forever grateful for what we were so freely given.

Do I continue to help the new alcoholic, regardless of the results of my past efforts?

DECEMBER 24

A VISION FOR YOU

A year and six months later these three had succeeded with seven more. Seeing much of each other, scarce an evening passed that someone's home did not shelter a little gathering of men and women, happy in their release, and constantly thinking how they might present their discovery to some newcomer. In addition to these casual get-togethers, it became customary to set apart one night a week for a meeting to be attended by anyone or everyone interested in a spiritual way of life. Aside from Fellowship and sociability, the prime object was to provide a time and place where new people might bring their problems.

[A Vision For You p. 159]

CONSIDERATION

As A.A. membership grew, in 1937 a few regular A.A. gatherings were supplemented by a separate weekly meeting where alcoholics and anyone else, including non-alcoholics or other addicts, could go to discuss their problems and pursue a spiritual way of life. Eighty years later, in different areas of the country, there are still various Step Study and Big Book groups who welcome alcoholics and any other folks who wish to enlarge their spiritual life using A.A.'s 12 Step approach. Early in A.A., most traditional meetings eventually became Home Groups, the first of which was Dr. Bob's Akron A.A. Group #1, initially held in his Ardmore Avenue residence. In 1940, the group moved that meeting to the King Elementary School, where it endures today as the oldest continuously held A.A. meeting in the world.

Do I regularly attend and support my A.A. Home Group?

DECEMBER 25

A VISION FOR YOU

But life among Alcoholics Anonymous is more than attending gatherings and visiting hospitals. Cleaning up old scrapes, helping to settle family differences, explaining the disinherited son to his irate parents, lending money and securing jobs for each other, when justified—these are everyday occurrences. No one is too discredited or has sunk too low to be welcomed cordially—if he means business. Social distinctions, petty rivalries and jealousies—these are laughed out of countenance. Being wrecked in the same vessel, being restored and united under one God, with hearts and minds attuned to the welfare of others, the things which matter so much to some people no longer signify much to them. How could they?

[A Vision For You p. 161]

CONSIDERATION

At some point all alcoholics want relief from the miserable life they are living. Newcomers may be confused about wanting to stop drinking, or question if they are really an alcoholic. Most of them figure it out after a few meetings and the passage of time. Even if newcomers are not sure if they have a desire to stop drinking for good, or if they do, whether that desire is honest or sincere, it does not matter. A.A. welcomes all who share our common problem and seek our common solution. Of course A.A. cannot carry the alcoholic by acting as therapist, doctor, lawyer, banker, employer, marriage counselor, or family restorer. But we are responsible for carrying our message of hope and recovery to our fellow sufferers. Whether or not the newcomer is successful in recovery is beyond our control, but we keep the door open to all.

Am I doing my best to carry the A.A. message of hope and recovery?

DECEMBER 26

A VISION FOR YOU

Under only slightly different conditions, the same thing is taking place in many eastern cities. In one of these there is a well known hospital for the treatment of alcoholic and drug addiction. Six years ago one of our number was a patient there. Many of us have felt, for the first time, the Presence and Power of God within its walls. We are greatly indebted to the doctor in attendance there, for he, although it might prejudice his own work, has told us of his belief in ours.

[A Vision For You p. 161]

CONSIDERATION

In "Bill's Story," he tells of his fourth and final visit to Towns Hospital in New York City in December, 1934, where he has an unexpected hot flash event he describes as "a clean wind of a mountain top blew through and through." This incident causes Bill to conclude he has found God, just as his grandfather had years before when Bill was a child. Surprisingly, his physician Dr. Silkworth does not attribute Bill's sudden religious conversion as being the result of the hallucinogen belladonna, which he prescribed to detoxify Bill, or from alcoholic hallucinosis due to alcohol withdrawal. Instead, Silkworth simply encourages Bill to hang on to his experience. Few of us alcoholics have undergone a sudden conversion event. Most of us just come to the slow realization over time that we need a physical, mental and spiritual solution for our illness. We must stop drinking, change our lifelong way of thinking, clean up our past, take actions we never considered before, help our fellow man in an unselfish manner, and learn how to engage with some type of spiritual power to help us live sane and sober in our new life.

Am I treating my alcoholism in all three areas of my life—physical, mental and spiritual?

DECEMBER 27

A VISION FOR YOU

Every few days this doctor suggests our approach to one of his patients. Understanding our work, he can do this with an eye to selecting those who are willing and able to recover on a spiritual basis. Many of us, former patients, go there to help. Then, in this eastern city, there are informal meetings such as we have described to you, where you may now see scores of members. There are the same fast friendships, there is the same helpfulness to one another as you find among our western friends. There is a good bit of travel between East and West and we foresee a great increase in this helpful interchange.

[A Vision For You p. 162]

CONSIDERATION

With Bill Wilson in New York City and Dr. Bob Smith in Akron, Ohio, the 450 miles between them seems to shrink as more and more cities form their own A.A. groups. Initially, A.A. expands from hospitals into the community as new members are referred by physicians, but over time most come by their own accord through word of mouth. In 1939, the first community Intergroup central office was created in Cleveland, Ohio to attract, educate and support a wider audience of alcoholics. During the 1940s, many more Intergroup offices were established around the country. As our service functions grow, so does our opportunity to reach more sufferers in the hopes they will join our Fellowship and find a new way of life.

Am I helping my A.A. community carry the message by volunteering for Intergroup and other service work?

DECEMBER 28

A VISION FOR YOU

Some day we hope that every alcoholic who journeys will find a Fellowship of Alcoholics Anonymous at his destination. To some extent this is already true. Some of us are salesmen and go about. Little clusters of twos and threes and fives of us have sprung up in other communities, through contact with our two larger centers. Those of us who travel drop in as often as we can. This practice enables us to lend a hand, at the same time avoiding certain alluring distractions of the road, about which any traveling man can inform you. Thus we grow. And so can you, though you be but one man with this book in your hand. We believe and hope it contains all you will need to begin.

[A Vision For You p. 162]

CONSIDERATION

Just because we travel away from our home town and our A.A. Home Group, it does not mean we forget about A.A. Few of us can afford to take a hiatus from A.A. for very long. There is little substitute for the face-to-face meetings we regularly attend, either at home or elsewhere. Visiting new meetings during our travels brings us the opportunity to share the A.A. message of hope and recovery with a new group of fellows. If we are spiritually fit, there is no place we should be hesitant or afraid to visit during our journey. By planning ahead and identifying which meetings we might be able to attend while on the road, we acquire a sense of safety and security that we never have to be alone as we go about our business in another city or country. We are grateful for the availability of A.A. meetings worldwide, and are always willing to share our story at those meetings so that we may possibly help a fellow alcoholic.

As I travel throughout the country and the world, do I continue to carry the A.A. message to alcoholics in the communities I visit?

DECEMBER 29

A VISION FOR YOU

We know what you are thinking. You are saying to yourself: "I'm jittery and alone. I couldn't do that." But you can. You forget that you have just now tapped a source of power much greater than yourself. To duplicate, with such backing, what we have accomplished is only a matter of willingness, patience and labor.

[A Vision For You p. 163]

CONSIDERATION

Pride, fear, or timidity should never prevent us from reaching out to another alcoholic who is still suffering. We are responsible, as a Fellowship and as an individual, to reach out our hand to those in need. Our shared experience in recovery can literally save another alcoholic's life. We possess a unique and powerful tool, and it is the daily reprieve we receive from our involvement in A.A. We were given the keys to the kingdom, and there should be no hesitation on our part not to pass on what we have learned and experienced. No one is beyond hope, no one is too undeserving of our attention, and no one should be denied our efforts as we share our experience, strength and hope. Carrying the message is the very least we can do to show our gratitude for what we have been so freely given.

Am I going to any length to carry the message of A.A. to others?

DECEMBER 30

A VISION FOR YOU

Our book is meant to be suggestive only. We realize we know only a little. God will constantly disclose more to you and to us. Ask Him in your morning meditation what you can do each day for the man who is still sick. The answers will come, if your own house is in order. But obviously you cannot transmit something you haven't got. See to it that your relationship with Him is right, and great events will come to pass for you and countless others. This is the Great Fact for us.

[A Vision For You p. 164]

CONSIDERATION

Our Big Book says it is suggestive only, but we must admit it has some fine suggestions. Those suggestions continue to save our life. They show us how we can be reborn into a new way of living by changing our attitudes and actions. They allow us to get honest with ourself and others, to clean up our past and make restitution for yesterday's wrongs. They allow us to identify and address our character defects so that we can better live in this day. They teach us how to find a spiritual power of our own design which we can consciously use, each and every day, to guide and direct our thinking and actions, giving us the serenity and strength to live life on life's terms. They show us how we can best carry the message of recovery to our fellow sufferers, which keeps us sane and sober, if nothing else. They teach us that anonymity and humility mean it's not always about me-me-me, and we no longer must prove to the world we are important. We learn that by having an attitude of gratitude and practicing all the principles of the 12 Steps, regardless of what is happening right this minute, our fears and resentments fade away. Above all, the Big Book suggestions release us from the bondage of self, and our need to be the Director of the Universe. Now freed, we can live and enjoy our new life to the fullest.

Do I ask myself each and every day what I can do for the man who is still sick?

DECEMBER 31

A VISION FOR YOU

Abandon yourself to God as you understand God. Admit your faults to Him and to your fellows. Clear away the wreckage of your past. Give freely of what you find and join us. We shall be with you in the Fellowship of the Spirit, and you will surely meet some of us as you trudge the Road of Happy Destiny. May God bless you and keep you—until then.

[A Vision For You p. 164]

CONSIDERATION

We finally fit it. We are human again and are all one and the same. We suffer together. We recover together. We cry and laugh together. We make mistakes together, and make amends together. We celebrate together. We remain imperfectly human together. We may walk our road alone, yet we are all on the same journey hand-in-hand, all heading in the same direction. No longer must we drag our past along with us, or fear what is around the next corner. We're not certain of what lies ahead, but we keep trudging anyway, head held high, full of gratitude, purpose, confidence, decency, dignity and integrity.

Am I finally able to fit in this magnificent stream of life, comfortable in my own skin, staying true to myself, and being forever grateful for the new life I've been given?

VARIOUS
MUSINGS

Various Musings

The Tenth Tradition of Alcoholics Anonymous states that A.A., the Fellowship, has no opinion on outside issues. However, I've discovered that individual A.A. members, including myself, have lots of opinions on just about every issue. What follows are a few good-natured ramblings of mine.

ALCOHOLISM & ADDICTION

ALCOHOLICS

A.A. MEETINGS

THE BIG BOOK OF ALCOHOLICS ANONYMOUS

BIG BOOK & STEP STUDIES

MONEY, POWER, PRIDE, PROPERTY & PRESTIGE

CHARACTER DEFECTS & SHORTCOMINGS

ANONYMITY & HUMILITY

DESIGN FOR LIVING

SERVICE WORK

FAITH

RELIGION

GOD

HIGHER POWER

PRAYER & MEDITATION

SPIRITUAL EXPERIENCE & AWAKENING

LIFE

DEATH

UNIVERSE

LOVE

ALCOHOLISM & ADDICTION

The subject presented in this book seems to me to be of paramount importance to those afflicted with alcoholic addiction. I say this after many years' experience as Medical Director of one of the oldest hospitals in the country treating alcoholic and drug addiction.

The Doctor's Opinion, p. xxv

The tremendous fact for every one of us is that we have discovered a common solution. We have a way out on which we can absolutely agree, and upon which we can join in brotherly and harmonious action. This is the great news this book carries to those who suffer from alcoholism.

There Is A Solution, p. 17

Alcoholism and addiction are chronic brain diseases. Period.

Almost 10% of the U.S. population suffers from some type of addiction. As a retired Internal Medicine physician with no formal credentials in addiction medicine, I try to keep up with the current medical literature anyway, and know that one major component of alcoholism involves massive changes in our brain chemistry.

When I think back to why I really started drinking, I never wanted to get drunk and pass out. I simply wanted to feel more a part of whatever group of people I was with at the time. I wanted to feel connected to my fellow human beings; I wanted their approval and acceptance. I wanted to feel comfortable in my own skin. Being perpetually restless, irritable and discontented, I just wanted to feel normal. I wanted to be on a level emotional playing field with my peers.

When I learned that drinking initially increases dopamine and serotonin, some feel good brain chemicals, it started to make sense to me. As one professional explained, I was born "a quart low" with some of those brain chemicals, and had spent a lifetime trying to find anything that would boost my chemicals up to the "normal" line so that I'd be playing on the same team as everyone else. Compared to others around me, I felt like I was living life slightly out of focus, and seemed to be perpetually drowsy, or never fully awake, so I could be present, be in the moment, and participate in the day.

My professional friend was right. As a teenager, I discovered that a variety of activities seemed to add a quart or two to my emotional reservoir. Certain drugs, gambling, food, sex, caffeine, nicotine, exercise, sports, shopping, stealing, overworking, reckless driving, risky behavior and family conflict worked to some extent, but alcohol rocketed me up to that normal level quicker and better than anything else, so I stuck with it.

My problem is, of course, that I'll always be a quart low. My natural state will forever be restless, irritable and discontented. I have the perpetual "divine dissatisfaction" that Father Ed Dowling recognized in Bill Wilson, so I need to find something other than alcohol to keep nudging my brain chemicals into the "I feel pretty normal" range.

Once I entered A.A., stopped drinking, completed the 12 Step work, had a spiritual awakening resulting in a change in my attitudes and actions, and began sponsoring other alcoholics, I started to feel more at ease with people both inside and outside the Fellowship. I wasn't cured of my illness, but it became much more manageable, and I found I could begin to enjoy my new life and actually have some fun without liquor.

I'm not sure if my brain chemicals ever rise to a normal level today, but I know that I feel a lot better after every A.A. meeting I attend, and after spending time with my friends in the Fellowship.

ALCOHOLICS

I adore alcoholics, but who are we really? Even in solid sobriety, my experience has shown that we remain some of the most lovable, but skittish and befuddled people out there.

For fun, I carry a mental "Alcoholic Chat Meter" in my head that automatically engages whenever I am speaking with any alcoholic, whether they are drunk or sober. There is a little arrow on it, and when it deflects all the way to the left, it reads "Bullshit." When it deflects all the way to the right, it reads "Victim." When the arrow points straight up, it reads "Maybe telling the truth." The beauty of my mental meter is that it works regardless of who's speaking. My words are measured as well, and the arrow usually swings wildly back and forth, all over the dial, during any conversation.

A number of books and articles have been written on the alcoholic personality, but I particularly enjoy the comments of Drs. Silkworth and Tiebout, and Bill's own words from Step 12 in the *Twelve Steps and Twelve Traditions.*

Dr. Silkworth spoke of five types of alcoholics in "The Doctors Opinion" (xxviii): "The classification of alcoholics seems most difficult, and in much detail is outside the scope of this book. There are, of course, the [1] psychopaths who are emotionally unstable. We are all familiar with this type. They are always going on the wagon for keeps. They are over-remorseful and make many resolutions, but never a decision. [2] There is the type of man who is unwilling to admit that he cannot take a drink. He plans various ways of drinking. He changes his brand or his environment. [3] There is the type who always believes that after being entirely free from alcohol for a period of time he can take a drink without danger. [4] There is the manic-depressive type, who is, perhaps, the least understood by his friends, and about whom a whole chapter could be written. [5] Then there are types entirely normal in every respect except in the effect alcohol has upon them. They are often able, intelligent, friendly people."

Bill W., writing on Step 12 in the *Twelve Steps and Twelve Traditions,* reported that psychologists and doctors described alcoholics as "childish, emotionally sensitive, and grandiose."

Modern clinicians have endless descriptions of the active alcoholic's personality traits: sensitive, impulsive, anxious, fearful, perfectionist, blaming, co-dependent, easily frustrated, low tolerance, low self-esteem, feelings of guilt and shame, full of self-pity, plays the victim, has a sense of injustice and under-achievement, and unable to receive love. And that's just a few.

My favorite description of the alcoholic, which fits me perfectly, was used by Bill's psychiatrist, Dr. Harry Tiebout. In 1943, he said that Bill W. had spent his life trying to live out his infantile, grandiose demands in the manner of Freud's "His Majesty the Baby." We fancy ourselves as kings, but behave like narcissistic infants. I've found this universal character defect in all of us never completely disappears.

On a final note, there are very few pure alcoholics out there today. Many rehabilitation facility statistics report that about 5% of their patients are addicted only to alcohol, 5% only to drugs, and 90% to both. This makes sense, since both alcohol and drugs can boost our feel good brain chemicals, and we alcoholics and addicts will find and use anything that will help us feel more normal.

A.A. Meetings

My experience with A.A. meetings ranges from the worst, to the best, to the ordinary.

By far the worst experience I've ever had in A.A. came at the end of the final meeting of the 2015 A.A. International Convention in Atlanta, Georgia, when the New York City General Service Office moderator, representing A.A. worldwide, stood up, thanked the audience, and proceeded to instruct the 61,000 attendees in the Georgia Dome Stadium to stand and close out the Convention by saying the Lord's Prayer instead of our A.A. Responsibility Statement.

I felt truly sick at the time, and was so angry it was all I could do to keep my mouth shut and not start booing. It was beyond disgraceful that A.A. exhibited such profound insensitivity to the thousands of non-Christian alcoholics who travelled from over eighty countries to participate in the otherwise outstanding international event.

After I returned home, I called and wrote the New York General Service Office several times to share my concerns, but they repeatedly refused to even acknowledge or respond in any way to my complaint. Shame on them and the A.A.W.S.

One of the best meetings I attended was one organized by my local Intergroup Accessibility Committee, which has a service program to take a one hour, standard A.A. meeting to alcoholics that are temporarily unable to attend their regular meetings for various reasons, usually related to health or legal issues. Meetings are held in homes, hospitals, nursing facilities, or other locations, and the program allows A.A. volunteers to make "house calls" on those in need.

One day we were called to see an impoverished single mom who was under court ordered Home Incarceration and living in a run-down, dilapidated motel room located in a depressed area of town. She was distraught being essentially locked up and having had her children removed from her custody.

Though new to A.A., incredibly she was able to think of someone other than herself. She never said a word, but it was obvious that she had made a very special effort to welcome us by cleaning up her tiny motel room as best she could, clearing off the clutter so folks could sit on her bed and floor, having a tiny pot of coffee she couldn't afford warming on a hotplate, and offering us her only muffin that was all she had to eat for breakfast. She owned no Big Book, but brought out a notepad full of recovery advice she had written down during meetings she had previously attended. After our meeting we gave her a Big Book and one of our female volunteers offered to be her support person. The meeting was extremely moving for all of us, and we were so grateful we had been given the opportunity to meet her.

The ordinary A.A. meetings are the ones I attend most frequently. They are the result of everyday alcoholics like you and me being responsible enough to show up every week to make sure that someone is available to share A.A.'s message of hope and recovery with any stray alcoholic that wanders in.

A while ago I attended one of my ordinary meetings, which turned out to be anything but ordinary. I've been to thousands of A.A. meetings and I am well acquainted with the diversity of emotions that members express while sharing their stories.

On average, I attend six or seven A.A. meetings every week, and somehow end up chairing about one of them each week. So I thought nothing could surprise me anymore, until I lead a meeting during which one long time A.A. member shared about the resentment she once held against her father for violently and vindictively killing her pet dog in front of her when she was a little girl.

As this lady, who was now in her mid-50s, began telling her story, her eyes slowly glazed over and she seemed to actually travel back in time and relive the events surrounding the killing of her dog when she was a child. Her voice physically changed into the high pitched cry of a terrified young girl. Her fear and panic were palpable; she began trembling and crying. She was transformed into the child of her story before our eyes. She *became* that child. This went on for some time, as every painful detail of her suffering spilled out.

This was not some mentally ill person having a breakdown, but a grown woman with over thirty years of solid, uninterrupted sobriety. I had never experienced anything like it before. She openly bled from her emotional wounds in a way I've never witnessed, and there was not a dry eye in the room. No one was able to speak. All of us were emotionally consumed.

When she finished, she wiped her eyes and talked about how A.A. had helped her let go of her deep hate and resentment against her father, which in turn helped her get sober decades ago. Her story was a stunning testimony of the transforming spiritual healing power of our program.

My A.A. Intergroup area straddles two states, encompasses eleven counties, extends over 3,200 square miles, and hosts just under 500 different A.A. meetings each week. Early in sobriety, for reasons yet obscure other than I really wanted to stay sober, I decided to visit one new A.A. meeting each week that I had never previously attended, in addition to attending my regular meetings. Over the next eight years I visited every single one of those Intergroup meetings, expect for the women's meetings. And yes, I'm doing a bit of prideful bragging, so be impressed! I continue to visit each new A.A. meeting as soon as they are listed, simply because I absolutely love visiting new meetings, chatting with new folks, and most importantly, it's just plain fun.

Having attended well over 450 different meetings in my area so far, I was amazed with the consistency of the meetings. All were very welcoming, and except for about a dozen, each one followed the standard A.A. meeting format. As a new visitor, I was rarely ignored and always made to feel at ease. It made me so proud of A.A., and the gentle humanity of our broad and open Fellowship.

Meetings were held in the usual assortment of church basements, schools, clubs, gymnasiums, public buildings, restaurant back rooms, hospital classrooms, rehabilitation centers, recovery houses and jails.

One group met outdoors in broken down lawn chairs underneath a huge oak tree, high on a hill, overlooking a stunning countryside where members shared as the sun set over farm fields of corn and rye.

Another small town meeting was held on the tiny back porch of the local post office, with extension cords running through the window to pots brewing coffee on the outdoor stoop.

Depending on which geographic area I visited, the culture of the meetings varied. At some rural meetings members arrived on tractors and shared the daily weather and farm report along with other A.A. announcements, which was informative and always brought on a chuckle from this city guy. Meetings in one part of town were all "Halleluiah and praise the Lord," in a rollicking, enthusiastic, revivalist fashion. Meetings in another area took the more direct "You need to do the Steps, and we'll kick your butt if you whine about it" approach. A third area used a more didactic approach to the Big Book suggestions, with debate over words, sentences and meanings filling the rooms. One distant county laughingly, and quite accurately, described themselves as the land of "soybeans, meth labs and double-wides."

Alcoholics of all ages come into our rooms in various shapes and sizes, and with diverse backgrounds. Many have more than one addiction. Some are newcomers, some not so new. With few exceptions, there are always more males than females at any given meeting. In some meetings there are just the two of us present, in others there are hundreds. A number of meetings have no coffee, food or even electricity, while others provide delicious five course, home-cooked meals. Several locations had no heat, air-conditioning or indoor plumbing, which for some reason seemed to keep members more grateful and attentive.

None of this matters. Whatever the setting, people, material comforts, or lack of them, all that matters is the sharing of the A.A. message of hope and recovery, one alcoholic directly with another.

THE BIG BOOK OF ALCOHOLICS ANONYMOUS

In 2012, the National Library of Congress selected 88 "Books That Shaped America," and our book *Alcoholics Anonymous* was rightly listed among them.

To show other alcoholics precisely how we have recovered is the main purpose of this book.

Foreword to First Edition, p. xiii

He accepted the plan outlined in this book.

The Doctor's Opinion, p. xxxi

Once I read how millions of alcoholics had recovered before me, all I had to do was give it a try. If I did what they did, maybe it would work for me. My first thought was, "What do I have to lose by trying?" but later on it was "What can I gain if I'm successful?"

In "The Doctor's Opinion," I noticed Dr. Silkworth suggested accepting the A.A. program rather than submitting to it. Habit and pride usually prevents me from submitting to anything I don't want to unless there is a gun at my head, but if I can become open-minded enough to accept that something might work for me, I find that I'm much more willing to give it a try. Tell me what I must do to get sober and I'll rebel. Tell me how you got sober, and I'll listen.

I'm not so much a Big Book thumper as I am a Big Book believer. I discovered when I followed the suggestions in the Big Book and they began to work for me, I started to pay attention. I listened as others shared their experience in meetings. I turned off my cell phone before each meeting, and still do today. There is no reason I cannot be fully attentive and present at a one hour A.A. meeting each day that continues to enlarge my life.

When I don't like the way I feel, I know where to look in the Big Book for the solution. I know who to call when I become seriously agitated. I know where to go if I start thinking maybe I can drink normally today, and turn myself from a pickle back into a cucumber.

I absolutely love the four Big Book stories in "More About Alcoholism." There is the foolish jaywalker, Jim the resentful used car salesman, Fred the happy accountant, and the clueless man of thirty. I see parts of myself in each of those men, and frequently re-read those stories.

I no longer get hysterical about the archaic Big Book language used from the 1930s, or the sexist approach of Bill's writings. It doesn't matter to me that Bill would not let his wife Lois or another woman author the "To Wives" chapter, or that Hank Parkhurst wrote the "To Employers" chapter.

I finally stopped complaining about all the "God stuff" cropping up on every page of the Big Book, and the religious Christian arrogance of the "We Agnostics" chapter. I focus instead on how my spiritual purpose and principles can help me maintain a sane, sober and serene life in this day. When I cease fighting everything and everyone, including what I don't agree with in A.A., my life gets a whole lot better.

BIG BOOK & STEP STUDIES

Various members in many A.A. communities host Step Study groups, which technically are not A.A. meetings in the A.A. Group sense so they need not follow the Twelve Traditions. Meetings are simply a few A.A. members gathering together to help each other go through the 12 Steps or read and discuss the Big Book.

Over eight years I participated in two eighteen-week long Step Study sessions and 35 eight-week long sessions. The hosts of the eight week sessions noticed that it took so long for newcomers to get relief doing the 18 week courses that many dropped out and drank before finishing. Remembering that Bill W. essentially did his Step work over one week in Towns Hospital, and Dr. Bob did much of his in one day, they felt shortening the length of the Step Study from 18 to 8 weeks might prevent more newcomers from dropping out, and they were right.

Statistics from the 35 eight-week Step Study sessions indicated that during those years, 479 members attended, and on average 44% completed the entire session. The completion rate for newcomers with less than one year was 42%, for those with 2 to 5 years it was 65%, those with 5 to 10 years 50%, those with 10 to 20 years 71%, and of those with over 20 years, only 28% completed the course. On average, 13 members started each Step Study group, and 6 completed the entire session. There were usually twice as many males as females at the sessions.

Big Book Study meetings I've enjoyed vary from those with a more detailed and educational focus to those with a lighter open discussion format after reading a few pages from the Big Book. Some groups read only the first 164 pages of the book, while others read the entire book, including all the stories in the back.

A few Big Book meetings do not restrict themselves to the Big Book. One meeting I attended was reading the entire *Twelve Steps and Twelve Traditions* book. Another group I found read the long 1941 Jack Alexander article from the Saturday Evening Post, and was getting ready to read the book *Drop the Rock* by Bill Pittman.

Some Big Book study meetings are focused specifically on the newcomer, with more experienced members occasionally using chalk boards to outline Big Book suggestions and directions, followed by a question and answer period.

Many Big Book discussions seem to center on the more challenging parts of the book for the newcomer, such as the "God stuff" in Steps 2, 3, and 11, inventory and admission in Steps 4 and 5, and the amends process in Steps 8 and 9.

Personally, the most challenging Steps for me are 6 and 7, because I simply don't want to change. I really enjoy the first 164 page educational Big Book meetings the most, but I've never been disappointed in any meeting I've attended.

Regardless of meeting format or style, the emphasis is always on the specific suggestions outlined in the Big Book, which is as it should be.

Money, Power, Pride, Property & Prestige

Tradition Six warns me that problems of money, property and prestige will divert me from my primary purpose of carrying the A.A. message of hope and recovery to other alcoholics. I would add the problems of power and pride to that list.

My natural instincts drive my ego, vanity, greed, and emotional gluttony to trample everything and everyone in my path. I want to be the Director of the Universe, with no whining from anyone. I want what I want when I want it, and when I step on your toes to get it, you better not retaliate. Of course, my selfish and self-centered desires are a fantasy, and I can laugh about them today. It's back to Step One. I have no control over anyone or anything other than my own actions.

If I model my behavior on the spiritual principles of the 12 Steps, which some in A.A. say all boil down to the Golden Rule, treating others the way I want to be treated, I discover that my life is much more peaceful and productive.

I find that when the committee in my head suddenly calls a meeting to discuss why I'm not getting my fair share of money, power, property, recognition and approval, I can go back to Step Ten, but it helps me to have a quick, reflexive response available as well. So I repeat the Serenity Prayer (omitting God) along with some of A.A.'s mottos, such as One Day at a Time, First Things First, Live and Let Live, Easy Does It and Attitude of Gratitude.

I also use an acronym I made up of G-P-S (Gratitude-Prayer-Service) to help me get back on track. I know my GPS unit keeps me going in the right direction when driving my car, so it's easy to remember.

Gratitude reminds me of the gifts I've freely received in sobriety, and I can list those material and emotional gifts in my head or on paper. For fun I sometimes list them alphabetically: A is for A.A., B is for Big Book, C is for Cats (my pets), D is for Daily (living one day at a time), E is for Empathy (I feel your pain), and so on.

Prayer reminds me that I need to ask for help from the two powers that will keep me sane and sober today: the people power of the Fellowship, and the spiritual power of my own choosing that I can connect with to motivate, aid and guide me through life. My spiritual power is embodied in the principles of the 12 Steps.

Service reminds me that it's not all about me all the time. When I think about what I can do for someone else, I'm not thinking about what I need to do for me-me-me, and don't develop toilet-seat rings on my rear end from sitting too long on my pity-pot.

When I navigate each day using the 12 Step principles and my G-P-S system, living life on life's terms becomes much easier.

Character Defects & Shortcomings

If we can answer to our satisfaction, we then look at Step Six. We have emphasized willingness as being indispensable. Are we now ready to let God remove from us all the things which we have admitted are objectionable? Can He now take them all—every one? If we still cling to something we will not let go, we ask God to help us be willing.

Into Action, p. 76

When ready, we say something like this: "My Creator, I am now willing that you should have all of me, good and bad. I pray that you now remove from me every single defect of character which stands in the way of my usefulness to you and my fellows. Grant me strength, as I go out from here, to do your bidding. Amen." We have then completed Step Seven.

Into Action, p. 76

If I want God to remove my character defects, I'll have to stop doing them.

A.A. Thoughts For The Day - July 21

At an early age, I discovered there was no Santa Claus or Tooth Fairy. Imaginary beings never put presents under my Christmas tree, or left a quarter under my pillow. As an adult in A.A., I discovered that neither God nor any other Higher Power ever removed any of my character defects. Believing that some magical friend or spiritual power will actively intervene to remove my character defects if I am willing to "turn them over" is beyond my imagination.

So how do I deal with my character defects, which will destroy my new life and lead me back to drinking if left unchecked? Do I arrogantly dismiss Steps Six and Seven simply because I don't believe in God? Of course not.

Nothing will diminish my defects of selfishness, dishonesty, resentment and fear more effectively than a conscious daily effort to change my behavior in these areas using the tools of the program. The help I need to change my behavior is rooted in the Big Book guidelines outlined in Steps Ten and Eleven that suggest specific actions I can take to try to maintain a fit spiritual condition from the time I wake up in the morning, throughout the day, and upon retiring. Those inventory activities easily blend into my own concept of the spiritual power and principles that guide my life. They are part of my kit of spiritual tools.

Surprisingly, I found that the Oxford Group's Four Absolutes—Honesty, Unselfishness, Love and Purity—can also help direct my conduct throughout the day. Is my behavior honest and unselfish? Are my motives for my actions loving and pure, free of self-centered motivation and a desire to manipulate others to my own wants? Do I spend my day thinking only of myself to the exclusion of others?

I also use a humorous cartoon image to help me stay centered in my day. Imagine a person sitting at a desk with two separate, but very large, red push buttons on the desk top in front of them. The button on the left says "Be a Dick." The button on the right says "Don't be a Dick." The cartoon caption reads: "The Everyday Struggle." It's always my choice. You get the picture.

My experience in addressing my own shortcomings has shown me that using my own will to take corrective action works for me. If I want my defects removed, I need to change my behavior and stop doing them.

Today, I still have my character defects, but they no longer rule my day or anyone else's, nor are they as deep and broad as they once were.

Just ask my family if you don't believe me.

ANONYMITY & HUMILITY

As we know, all A.A. progress can be reckoned in terms of just two words: humility and responsibility. Our whole spiritual development can be accurately measured by our degree of adherence to these magnificent standards. Ever deepening humility, accompanied by an ever greater willingness to accept and to act upon clear cut obligations—these are truly are touchstones for all growth in the life of the spirit. They hold up to us the very essence of right being and right doing. It is by them that we are enabled to find and to do God's will.

Our Great Responsibility, The Guidance of A.A.'s World Affairs, by Bill W., General Service Conference, 1965; (Grapevine, January 1966)

Tradition Twelve says that the principle of anonymity has an immense spiritual significance, is the spiritual foundation of all our traditions, and reminds us to place principles before personalities.

Anonymity, of course, means being anonymous, unknown, and without any name. When I read Tradition Twelve for the first time, I didn't understand it, and thought it only meant not to divulge anyone's name outside the rooms of A.A. The principle was secrecy over disclosure. I was partially correct.

After reading all of Bill Wilson's Grapevine articles on the Traditions, I learned that anonymity is really about humility, which was another term I didn't understand, and always confused with humiliation. But at the end of the day all roads lead to Rome.

In A.A., anonymity and humility are very similar, as I discovered during my fourth and fifth Step work. Humility means I'm not God, I'm not the Director of the Universe, the world does not revolve around me, and no one exists to do my bidding. If I remain selfish and self-centered, I'll never understand or acquire any anonymity or humility. Those two words simply mean it's not all about promoting me-me-me all the time.

In the *Twelve Steps and Twelve Traditions*, Bill W. said that the spiritual substance of anonymity is sacrifice. He said that anonymity is real humility at work, and that we should try to give up our natural desire for distinction both within A.A. and before the general public.

So when I see myself as no one special, just another sick alcoholic trying to recover like everyone else, no better or worse than the next fellow, life goes much better since I no longer have to prove to the world I'm important.

DESIGN FOR LIVING

We, in our turn, sought the same escape with all the desperation of drowning men. What seemed at first a flimsy reed, has proved to be the loving and powerful hand of God. A new life has been given us or, if you prefer, "a design for living" that really works.

There Is A Solution, p. 28

My wife and I abandoned ourselves with enthusiasm to the idea of helping other alcoholics to a solution of their problems...I was not too well at the time, and was plagued by waves of self-pity and resentment. This sometimes nearly drove me back to drink, but I soon found that when all other measure failed, work with another alcoholic would save the day. Many times I have gone to my old hospital in despair. On talking to a man there, I would be amazingly lifted up and set on my feet. It is a design for living that works in rough going.

Bill's Story, p. 15

I grew up as an only child in the 1950s. My alcoholic father was a chemical engineer who provided all my material comforts, but no emotional sustenance. My mother controlled my life using a punishing conditional love, so I learned to endure my surroundings by adopting the "don't talk, don't trust, don't feel" defense. Children of alcoholics and sick families understand.

My design for living was emotional survival, with the goal of getting out of the house as soon as possible. Around age ten I invited alcohol into my life, which prevented me from killing myself during my teenage years which were consumed by fear, anger, anxiety and depression. I used my alcohol design for living for forty more years, until that strategy failed me. Alcohol stopped working, so I had to find something else to help me survive in the real world.

Adopting the A.A. design for living allows me to live a full, honest, sober, and mostly serene life today. Guided by the spiritual 12 Step principles, I can look myself in the mirror again. Self-esteem, sprinkled with a touch of dignity and decency, has returned. I am comfortable in my own skin, and try to wear it loosely so I don't get too tightly wrapped up in me-me-me.

I no longer pray that I won't wake up in the morning, and I haven't had the bitter taste of the end of a shotgun in my mouth for well over a decade. My G-P-S of Gratitude-Prayer-Service keeps me on the beam most days, along with my daily quiet time rituals and touching at least one alcoholic every day by phone, email, text or in person. An alcoholic a day keeps my insanity and obsession away, I say.

I've discovered that any and all of us can adopt a new way of life, and recharge our design for living any time we choose.

Service Work

Practical experience shows that nothing will so much insure immunity from drinking as intensive work with other alcoholics. It works when other activities fail. This is our twelfth suggestion: Carry this message to other alcoholics! You can help when no one else can. You can secure their confidence when others fail. Remember they are very ill.

Working With Others, p. 89

The Third Legacy in A.A. is called Service. Defining service work, Bill Wilson said that Step Twelve, carrying the message, was the basic task of A.A., its principal aim, and the main reason for A.A.'s existence. He said A.A. was not only a set of principles, but a society of alcoholics in action, whose job was to carry the message so that we personally don't wither, and those who haven't been given the truth won't die. He said that A.A. service is anything that helps the Fellowship to reach a fellow sufferer, including individual Twelfth Step work, all the way up to the services provided by the New York General Service Office.

Service work keeps me sober today. So do many other A.A. Big Book suggestions and rituals, but at the end of the day, if I'm connecting with at least one alcoholic each day, I'm probably not going to be drinking that day.

In the Big Book story "Dr. Bob's Nightmare," the good doctor said "I spend a great deal of time passing on what I learned to others who want and need it badly. I do it for four reasons: 1. Sense of duty. 2. It is a pleasure. 3. Because in so doing I am paying my debt to the man who took time to pass it on to me. 4. Because every time I do it I take out a little more insurance for myself against a possible slip."

I know I must keep growing in A.A. in order to survive and continue the good life. Simply not drinking, attending an occasional meeting, adopting a sponsor, playing at Step work, skimming through the Big Book and setting out a few chairs at meetings is not enough.

Like Dr. Bob, I had to get involved in sponsorship and A.A. service work. So after my first year in A.A., I committed to myself that every year I would take on a new A.A. service project in addition to my regular A.A. activities. I called our Intergroup Office and asked "what can I do for A.A.?" Through our Intergroup I learned of a dozen local A.A. community service committees that needed volunteers, and how I could become involved. I learned how I could become an Intergroup or General Service Representative for my Home Group, and what that meant. I learned how to volunteer for Twelfth Step calls, how to become a temporary or not so temporary sponsor, how to agree to speak at meetings, and how to help host local A.A. conventions and other functions. Being a writer, I learned how to submit articles to the A.A. Grapevine magazine and our Area Newsletter.

Loving A.A. meetings and the people who inhabit them, over a period of eight years, I attended every directory listed A.A. meeting in our Intergroup service area except the women's only meetings—well over 450 of them in total. I continue to visit each new A.A. meeting in our area shortly after they start up to offer support and encouragement, but primarily just to have a good time.

Participating in Intergroup service activities, sponsoring numerous men, helping to host Step Study and Big Book groups, attending A.A. meetings almost every day, trying to practice the A.A. principles, and making sure I touch another alcoholic each and every day, has kept me sane and sober for a number of years. It has brought me the good life.

Despite all my A.A. activities, I have also tried to responsibly balance service work with my personal home and work life. It is easier to do so now that I am retired, but I was far from retired when I came into A.A., and had to make sure I did not neglect my non-A.A. obligations. That was a learning experience, but I received wise counsel from my sponsor and support group.

Today, my A.A. life and personal life are integrated into one wonderful experience. No longer are they separate, and I find I can be generous with my time and effort with both my A.A. family and my personal family of choice. At last I fit in.

FAITH

Even though your protégé may not have entirely admitted his condition, he has become very curious to know how you got well...Tell him exactly what happened to you. Stress the spiritual feature freely. If the man be agnostic or atheist, make it emphatic that he does not have to agree with your conception of God. He can choose any conception he likes, provided it makes sense to him. The main thing is that he be willing to believe in a power greater than himself and that he live by spiritual principles. When dealing with such a person....he will be curious to learn why his own convictions have not worked and why yours seem to work so well. He may be an example of the truth that faith alone is insufficient. To be vital, faith must be accompanied by self-sacrifice and unselfish, constructive action.

Working With Others, p. 93

In religion, faith means to have a strong belief in certain religious doctrines based on conviction rather than proof. More generally, it means to have complete trust or confidence in someone or something.

My faith requires no God. My faith is simply placed elsewhere, and is based on my experience, even if I have no proof. I have faith that if I follow the guidelines of the A.A. program I will remain sane, sober and emotionally balanced while I celebrate a wonderful new life. I have faith the sun will come up tomorrow morning. I have faith that the world is basically a good place, and that life is worth living, despite some setbacks and difficult situations. I have faith that if I live my life by the spiritual 12 Step principles and the Golden Rule, I will end up helping myself and perhaps someone else live their life more fully.

In relation to A.A., I know that having faith alone will never get or keep anyone sober. I know it because I've seen it over and over again, just as Bill W. and Dr. Bob said it and saw it. Faith is a word of action, not a state of mind. If I have God, or some other supreme deity, or a Higher Power, or Higher Principles, or a Higher Purpose in my life, simply declaring my faith without taking action to demonstrate my faith is pointless. Faith without works is indeed dead. Faith without action is worthless. If I do not strive to practice my guiding life principles, why am I here?

RELIGION

Alcoholics Anonymous is not a religious organization. Neither does A.A. take any particular medical point of view, though we cooperate widely with the men of medicine as well as with the men of religion.

Foreword to the Second Edition, p. xx.

The door opened and he [Ebby] stood there, fresh-skinned and glowing. There was something about his eyes. He was inexplicably different. What had happened? I pushed a drink across the table. He refused it. Disappointed but curious, I wondered what had got into the fellow. He wasn't himself. "Come, what's all this about?" I queried. He looked straight at me. Simply, but smilingly, he said, "I've got religion."

Bill's Story, p. 9

Instead of regarding ourselves as intelligent agents, spearheads of God's ever advancing Creation, we agnostics and atheists chose to believe that our human intelligence was the last word, the alpha and the omega, the beginning and end of all. Rather vain of us, wasn't it? We, who have traveled this dubious path, beg you to lay aside prejudice, even against organized religion. We have learned that whatever the human frailties of various faiths may be, those faiths have given purpose and direction to millions.

We Agnostics, p. 49

Religion is defined as the belief in, and worship of, a superhuman controlling power—a personal God or gods.

Bill W. reports he began life as an agnostic. Luckily for us, his hot flash experience in Towns Hospital in 1934, along with Dr. Silkworth's non-judgmental comments, resulted in the creation of a remarkable Fellowship that continues to save the lives of countless alcoholics.

As a physician, I am completely convinced that Bill's white flash experience was caused by his belladonna treatment and alcoholic hallucinosis from withdrawal rather than some transcendent deity, but I'll yield to Dr. Silkworth's astute response when he said something like "Whatever you've got now Bill, you'd better hold on to it. It's so much better than what you had only a couple of hours ago."

So Bill got religion, in a way, just like his friend Ebby Thacher had in his early days. Bill found sobriety and a new life for the rest of his own life, unlike poor Ebby, who became resentful, bitter, unwilling to help others and repeatedly got drunk. Bill was God-struck, but did not attend church regularly or join any traditional religious community. His Oxford Group experience taught him how to organize and structure A.A., and a number of the Oxford Group's principles and practices contributed to A.A.'s 12 Steps and design for daily living.

I used to dismiss religion as the most magnificent human hoax. We live a life of sin, suffering, injustice and misfortune, but don't worry, it will all get better after we're dead and are released from Purgatory, provided we don't make too much of a fuss in this life, read the Bible, obey the Ten Commandments, repent our sins, and give generously to the church. As you suffer and your fellows trample you down, don't despair, God loves you even if no one else does, so long as you don't complain, confess on a regular basis and continue giving money to the church. If you do what you're told, after you're dead you'll eventually end up in Heaven with all your friends and relatives, and maybe even that loyal old dog you grew up with.

What a deal! Everything good happens to you after you're dead, unless you've been really, really bad and unrepentant; then you get to spend an eternity roasting in Hell.

I'd think to myself, "Who could possibly believe all this gibberish? Those religious folks must be idiots, so easily falling prey to grifters and charlatans who just want their money and obedience."

What I failed to appreciate is that somehow religion saves lives too, just like A.A. When people have something to believe in and hold on to, whether it's during times of desperation or joy, how can that be a bad thing? Hope matters, regardless of its source. Having something other than our own human power to believe in is necessary for all of us, religious or not. So I am grateful for any religious or spiritual solution out there, and try to keep most of my dismissive opinions on religion to myself.

GOD

In talking to a prospect, stress the spiritual feature freely. If the man be agnostic or atheist, make it emphatic that he does not have to agree with your conception of God. He can choose any conception he likes, provided it makes sense to him. The main thing is that he is willing to believe in a Power greater than himself and that he live by spiritual principles.

Working With Others, p. 93

The God of my understanding is not God. I never believed in God. Ever. I couldn't help it, and never saw anything wrong with it, until I experienced some of the religious bias in A.A. and elsewhere. I didn't make a conscious choice not to believe in God—I was just born that way. I don't hate God or those that do; God is just not part of my life, and never has been.

I grew up in the Episcopal Church. My parents called it "Catholic lite." I resented having to wear a coat and tie to church, but loved the organ music and service rituals, which I knew by heart. I felt like a big deal when I was selected as the head acolyte, getting to light all the altar candles and lead the choir in and out of the church.

If there was extra wine left over after Communion, I helped the rector drink whatever remained, although he never knew it. I basically loved everything about the church itself, but for some reason never felt the slightest connection with the God they worshipped. I tried so hard to relate to the few biblical stories I was taught in Sunday school, especially from the New Testament, but never really could, other than the Golden Rule, a bit of the Sermon on the Mount, and four of the Ten Commandments.

Whenever the topic of God would come up with the adults, I'd ask "If God created everything, knows everything and runs everything, then who made God?" The stammering responses I received were never enough to convince me to believe in this imaginary friend of so many.

A.A. may not be religious, but the word God appears on 142 of the first 164 pages of the Big Book, and 156 times on the 104 Twelve Step pages of the *Twelve Steps and Twelve Traditions* publication.

This means Bill Wilson referenced God 298 times on 268 pages, or more than once per page, in his two most influential books. Food for thought.

The elephant that remains in the rooms of A.A. is God. God as the required Higher Power is never, ever questioned or discussed where I come from in A.A., because it seems everyone knows and believes that God is the only Higher Power necessary for alcoholics. If someone says they don't believe in God, the silence is deafening, and a few of the old-timers will mumble something like "I never did either, but once I completely accepted the program, I came to believe." This is followed by numerous stories of how once doubting members found God and sobriety. On their way out the door, skeptics are stamped with the scarlet letter "A" for Atheist or Agnostic.

When A.A. members ask me today if I believe in God, I chuckle and say "I'm a happy Christian atheist," which really gets them confused. This is instantly followed by a variety of quizzical and sometimes disgusting looks implying "What's wrong with you," or "You need to keep coming back," or "I can't believe you're still sober."

Early in A.A. I actually felt ashamed that my spiritual Higher Power was not the God of so many in the Fellowship. The fact that I lived in the Bible Belt didn't help either. I quickly became resentful at the smug, self-righteous dismissal by many in the Fellowship of anyone who did not believe in their God. Learning to accept that those fearful, insecure and judgmental alcoholics are sick people just like me helped me let go of my resentments.

Today, I don't care what others think about my personal concept of my guiding spiritual life principles. I'm sane, sober and relatively serene. I'm far less selfish than I ever was, and enjoy working with other alcoholics. My life is worth living, and I've stopped praying to not wake up in the morning. Grudges have been forgotten, and most fears removed. I'm happy to be alive and free of the obsession to drink. I've recovered from a hopeless state of mind and body. I'm grateful for every morsel of the spiritual gifts I've received. Whenever I'm able to live in this moment, I'm joyous. What more could I ask for?

HIGHER POWER

We could wish to be moral, we could wish to be philosophically comforted, in fact, we could will these things with all our might, but the needed power wasn't there. Our human resources, as marshalled by the will, were not sufficient; they failed utterly. Lack of power, that was our dilemma. We had to find a power by which we could live, and it had to be a Power greater than ourselves. Obviously. But where and how were we to find this Power? Well, that's exactly what this book is about. Its main object is to enable you to find a Power greater than yourself which will solve your problem. That means we have written a book which we believe to be spiritual as well as moral.

We Agnostics, p. 45

Follow the dictates of a Higher Power and you will presently live in a new and wonderful world, no matter what your present circumstances!

Working With Others, p. 100

Much to our relief, we discovered we did not need to consider another's conception of God. Our own conception, however inadequate, was sufficient to make the approach and to effect a contact with Him. As soon as we admitted the possible existence of a Creative Intelligence, a Spirit of the Universe underlying the totality of things, we began to be possessed of a new sense of power and direction, provided we took other simple steps. We found that God does not make too hard terms with those who seek Him. To us, the Realm of Spirit is broad, roomy, all inclusive; never exclusive or forbidding to those who earnestly seek. It is open, we believe, to all men.

We Agnostics, p. 46

I had never heard the term Higher Power until A.A. It sounded like a fudge factor for God. In reading the first 164 pages of the Big Book, Higher Power is mentioned only two times, whereas the word God appears 142 times, or 71 times more frequently. Especially in the chapter "We Agnostics," Bill intermingles and entangles the words God and Higher Power, implying they are one in the same, which in my experience, they are not.

In the *Twelve Steps and Twelve Traditions*, Bill W. suggested that members could temporarily make their A.A. Group their Higher Power until they came around to believing in God. Others in A.A. talk about God as "Good Orderly Direction," or a "Group Of Drunks."

The Higher Power of my understanding has never been God. In my experience I interpret the term Higher Power as completely non-religious and spiritual in nature. It represents my ideal way of living and behaving, not as some intervening god-like being or entity.

Some people's Higher Power may manifest as a Higher Force, such as the power of Love, Good, Justice, Harmony and Humanity in the world.

Others may view their Higher Power as a Higher Purpose in life, such as helping the less fortunate and those in need, being true to one's self, being comfortable in one's own skin, doing the next right thing, treating others as you wish to be treated, or being able to live honorably in this day.

My own spiritual Higher Power represents the Higher Principles of living to which I aspire, many of which are outlined in the 12 Steps: Honesty, Hope, Faith, Courage, Integrity, Willingness, Humility, Forgiveness, Justice, Perseverance and Service.

The bottom line is that I cannot be my own Higher Power. I'm not God or any god. I'm not the perfect Force, Purpose or Principle in this world. I'm not the Director of the Universe.

Today, I accept I'm no longer totally self-sufficient and self-reliant. I live by a set of spiritual principles, or values, that I can actively connect with and aspire to enlarge. The spiritual power I draw on comes from deep within me, and is unexplainable, untouchable and not material. I have no idea where it comes from, and I don't care. If it leads me to a better life for myself and those around me, and if it motivates me to be less selfish and self-centered in my actions, I'll stick with it.

Prayer & Meditation

Step Eleven suggests prayer and meditation. We shouldn't be shy on this matter of prayer. Better men than we are using it constantly. It works, if we have the proper attitude and work at it. It would be easy to be vague about this matter. Yet, we believe we can make some definite and valuable suggestions.

Into Action, p. 85

When reading Step 11 aloud at meetings, and I accidentally say prayer and medication, rather than prayer and meditation, I always chuckle to myself. Even unintentional mistakes contain a bit of wishful truth.

Step 11 suggests I take some time each day to put aside material matters and reflect on spiritual matters. I take Step 11 very seriously, but somehow it always reminds me of a member who once asked me my sobriety date. After I told him, he said "No, I mean your emotional sobriety date." I laughed and said "maybe tomorrow."

Members of the Christian based Evangelical Oxford Group movement, out of which A.A. grew, had a daily practice called Quiet Time. Dr. Bob's marvelous wife, Anne Smith, maintained a journal between 1933 and 1939, and described Quiet Time practices in detail. Oxford Group members read Biblical and other inspirational religious passages, and practiced "Two-way prayer." Prayer was speaking to God, and meditation during Quiet Time was listening to God.

Quiet Time was "A period in which man can receive Divine Guidance and be sensitive to the sway of the Spirit." Quiet Time was how the Oxford Group members meditated. Even though they became silent for a short period of time to listen to God, their meditation was an active process of thought and reflection, rather than trying to make their minds go blank of all conscious thought.

Many newcomers in A.A. read Step 11, and incorrectly assume they are expected to sit cross-legged on the floor, hands cupped and eyes closed, humming some Buddhist mantra. Some call this behavior contemplation. It may be helpful, but it is not meditation.

Many in the Fellowship will passionately debate the difference between contemplation and meditation, convinced that their view is the only correct one, but my experience suggests that what matters is not the definition but the action.

So I take some quiet time each day to consciously connect with my spiritual values and beliefs. I go somewhere private where I won't be interrupted or distracted, turn off the TV and put away my cell phone, read something with a spiritual focus and consciously reflect on it for a few minutes.

Each morning when I get up I recite my personal version of "On awakening" from page 86 of the Big Book, and ask to "Be relieved of the bondage of self." I read the day's *Daily Reflections, Twenty-Four Hours A Day* page, the *A.A. Thought For The Day*, a page from *As Bill Sees It*, one from Mel B.'s *Walk In Dry Places* and one from Joe C.'s *Beyond Belief Agnostic Musings for 12 Step Life*.

Of the six readings, something will always inspire me to ask myself "How am I doing with this?" I then sit quietly for a few minutes and consciously reflect on it. It's almost like doing a spot-check inventory.

At the end of each day I have a short personal prayer I say to no one, and review my day more or less as suggested in "When we retire at night" on page 86 of the Big Book.

These repetitive daily rituals keep me trudging the never ending Broad Highway. I still don't know where it will take me, but so far I'm enjoying the journey.

Spiritual Experience & Spiritual Awakening

The terms "spiritual experience" and "spiritual awakening" are used many times in this book which, upon careful reading, shows that the personality change sufficient to bring about recovery from alcoholism has manifested itself among us in many different forms.

Appendix II—Spiritual Experience, p. 569

I've had four momentary, fleeting spiritual occurrences in my life, during which I was totally connected and at peace with the world.

❖ Watching the sun set over the vast Serengeti Plain in northern Tanzania.

❖ Solo flying a small Cessna plane high above west Boston at sunset.

❖ Travelling through Texas, watching my sister nap in the back seat of my mother's car, with her two small children asleep in her lap.

❖ Sitting silently on a Florida beach with my sister, looking up at the magnificent Milky Way on a calm, clear night.

None of those episodes had anything to do with God or a Higher Power. None helped get me sober, but they do help keep me sober. They remind me that life is still worth living, despite the slings and arrows we all suffer along the way.

I am much less selfish and self-centered than I used to be. I stopped playing the victim. I stopped pretending to be the person I think you want me to be. I am more honest than ever, and usually when I lie it's a conscious decision based on unselfish motives—but not always!

I'm more tolerant and accepting of others, and try not to control and criticize their actions, although I may silently judge their behavior. My expectations center on my actions, not yours. I actually care about people, and will help out wherever I am able, even when I don't want to. I try to do the next right thing with whatever tools are in my tool kit this day.

One of my most significant spiritual awakenings in A.A. came after I completed Step Nine, when I had finished making my amends to all those I had harmed. I woke up one morning and realized that for the first time in over forty years, I had not thought about taking a drink at any time the day before. My alcoholic obsession was gone, and has never returned. This was a striking personality change I had never experienced, but was the result of becoming deeply involved with all aspects of A.A., following A.A.'s suggestions, putting in the work required to do the 12 Steps and being willing to help someone else.

Many other small awakenings, or realizations, followed as I finished up my Step work. Today, I still experience changes for the better as my attitudes and actions continue to improve during my stroll down the road of Happy Destiny.

LIFE

He cannot picture life without alcohol. Some day he will be unable to imagine life either with alcohol or without it. Then he will know loneliness such as few do. He will be at the jumping-off place. He will wish for the end. We have shown how we got out from under. You say, "Yes, I'm willing. But am I to be consigned to a life where I shall be stupid, boring and glum, like some righteous people I see? I know I must get along without liquor, but how can I? Have you a sufficient substitute?" Yes, there is a substitute and it is vastly more than that. It is a fellowship in Alcoholics Anonymous. There you will find release from care, boredom and worry. Your imagination will be fired. Life will mean something at last. The most satisfactory years of your existence lie ahead. Thus we find the fellowship, and so will you.

A Vision For You, p. 152

The first requirement is that we be convinced that any life run on self-will can hardly be a success. On that basis we are almost always in collision with something or somebody, even though our motives are good. Most people try to live by self-propulsion. Each person is like an actor who wants to run the whole show; is forever trying to arrange the lights, the ballet, the scenery and the rest of the players in his own way. If his arrangements would only stay put, if only people would do as he wished, the show would be great. Everybody, including himself, would be pleased. Life would be wonderful.

How It Works, p. 60

As an optimistic cynic, I believe that my life is whatever I choose to make it this day, and that I can start my day over at any time.

Being in the present, the present of the present, is one of my greatest challenges. Anguish over yesterday's failings and fear of tomorrow's unknowns are always on the agenda of the committee in my head. Too much worrying about my past or future prevents me from living in this day. A.A. gives me a way to correct yesterday's mistakes and plan for tomorrow, without having to plan tomorrow's outcomes.

No longer must I try to be the person I think you want me to be, so that you will like me and I will be able to manipulate you to my will. I don't have to lie to you anymore, or remember which lies I've told you and others. I don't have to wear a mask so that you won't see who I really am, then use that knowledge against me when you want something from me. I no longer live in shame and self-pity, unable to look myself in the mirror every morning. I don't hate myself anymore. Slowly, I can begin to trust those around me, and start to accept my feelings without having to bury, deny or change them.

No longer must I be the Director of the Universe, becoming angry when you retaliate after I step on your toes. Your business is no longer my business. I can play inside my hula-hoop, and you can too if I trust you enough.

I can live without most of the things that help me change the way I feel: alcohol, drugs, random sex, gambling, binge eating, binge shopping, reckless behavior or obsessive exercising. However, I still readily abuse tobacco and chocolate to make myself feel better. Reading and writing soothes my soul and is always a part of my daily activity, so I guess that's healthy.

I have no children, no spouse, few family members and a very small handful of close friends who complete my extended family. My work in A.A. and with other alcoholics brings me enormous pleasure and relief from a totally self-centered existence.

I've discovered that my non-A.A. life and my A.A. life have slowly merged during my sobriety. Today they are essentially the same, so I don't need to figure out how to live in two separate worlds.

Living life through my G-P-S: Gratitude, Prayer and Service, keeps me well centered most days. Or another way of putting it: Ask for help (prayer), accept help (gratitude), and be helpful (service). It works, it really does.

DEATH

Most of us have been unwilling to admit we were real alcoholics. No person likes to think he is bodily and mentally different from his fellows. Therefore, it is not surprising that our drinking careers have been characterized by countless vain attempts to prove we could drink like other people. The idea that somehow, someday he will control and enjoy his drinking is the great obsession of every abnormal drinker. The persistence of this illusion is astonishing. Many pursue it into the gates of insanity or death. We learned that we had to fully concede to our innermost selves that we were alcoholics. This is the first step in recovery. The delusion that we are like other people, or presently may be, has to be smashed.

More About Alcoholism, p. 30

I love this description of the first Step. It perfectly describes my obsession and delusion of one day becoming a normal drinker. It suggests I will eventually die from my alcoholism unless I face reality. Unfortunately, those ominous warnings never scared me sober. I was immortal, and threats of dying from my disease, if I actually had one, were meaningless.

I'm a physician, scientist and atheist, so I think I know all about death. I don't. The life cycle of all living things remains a mystery and miracle to me. But I do know that when we are dead, we are dead. Dust to dust, ashes to ashes. No afterlife. No pearly gates guarded by St. Peter. No dead relatives in Heaven waving to me from behind the white picket fence of my childhood home. No reincarnation. No Buddhist samsara or nirvana.

In death, we rot and dissolve into the atoms that came together to form us in the first place, and some of my atoms may eventually combine to create another new human being or other living organism.

We are connected in life and death not to God in Heaven, but to each other on Earth through a collective unconscious as Jung describes, and shared physical particles that create and sustain all life, human or otherwise. So, in some cosmic, ironic way, we are all part of each other and the universe as a whole, in both life and in death.

UNIVERSE

The atoms of our bodies are traceable to stars that manufactured them in their cores and exploded these enriched ingredients across our galaxy, billions of years ago. For this reason, we are biologically connected to every other living thing in the world. We are chemically connected to all molecules on Earth. And we are atomically connected to all atoms in the universe. We are not figuratively, but literally stardust.

Neil deGrasse Tyson

Could we still say the whole thing [life] was nothing but a mass of electrons, created out of nothing, meaning nothing, whirling on to a destiny of nothingness?

We Agnostics p. 54

Yes, my dear Bill Wilson, I sure can say that. Not that life is nothing to me, but that it is to the universe. In the grand scheme of things, my life doesn't matter at all.

As a single individual, I cannot transform our planet as it circles our sun, nor can I alone change the progression of evolution, or the fate of our world. I cannot predict the future or travel through time.

But as a single individual I can affect the life of another human being through love, tolerance, empathy, kindness and service. As an active A.A. member perhaps something I do or say may make a difference to a fellow sufferer. Who knows? But it's worth a try.

I know all I have right now in my universe is this tiny moment called a second, or maybe a millisecond. I wish for many more, but cannot control my destiny. What I can do is appreciate and in some small way try to contribute to the universe I live in each and every day.

When Bill W. was filled with awe and wonder, enchanted by a starlit night, and thought about who made all of this, he was looking at the universe. I experience the same awe and wonder that he did when I look out at the Milky Way on a clear night, but I don't think about who made it. I know I didn't make it, and no God made it. It exists for me to savor in this moment, and I remain grateful for all the beauty I'm blessed to experience in my small, tiny, transient little world.

LOVE

So we clean house with the family, asking each morning in meditation that our Creator show us the way of patience, tolerance, kindliness and love.

Into Action, p. 83

Since the home has suffered more than anything else, it is well that a man exert himself there. He is not likely to get far in any direction if he fails to show unselfishness and love under his own roof.

The Family Afterward, p. 127

This thought brings us to Step Ten, which suggests we continue to take personal inventory and continue to set right any new mistakes as we go along. We vigorously commenced this way of living as we cleaned up the past. We have entered the world of the Spirit. Our next function is to grow in understanding and effectiveness. This is not an overnight matter. It should continue for our lifetime. Continue to watch for selfishness, dishonesty, resentment, and fear. When these crop up, we ask God at once to remove them. We discuss them with someone immediately and make amends quickly if we have harmed anyone. Then we resolutely turn our thoughts to someone we can help. Love and tolerance of others is our code.

Into Action, p. 84

Our Twelve Steps, when simmered down to the last resolve themselves into the words love and service. We understand what love is, and we understand what service is. So let's bear those two things in mind.

Dr. Bob's farewell speech at the First International Conference of Alcoholics Anonymous - July 1950, Cleveland, Ohio

As if I needed to research it, love is defined as an intense feeling of deep affection. I know what love is. I know what love feels like. You do too. My late wife Anne was the love of my life, and I knew it from the instant I first saw her. She was my soul mate, and still is, even though she died decades ago. Just typing these words makes me cry.

I still miss her each and every day with an intensity of sorrow I never knew could exist, which I hoped and imagined would disappear over time. It hasn't, but it no longer consumes me. The joy she brought me, and to so many around her, helps me appreciate that love will always be part of my code. My gratitude for the short time I had with her eases the grief I still feel for our loss.

I no longer curse the universe for having taken my wife from me, am no longer bitter over her death, and no longer drink to make me forget. My heart just hurts, even today. So I do what my new design for living suggests. I remain grateful that we were able to walk together, at least for a few moments in time, and so grateful that she showed me in such a gentle way what kindness and love were really all about.

Bill W. said that love and tolerance is our code in A.A., and Dr. Bob summarized A.A. by saying it was love and service. Love is the common denominator. So at the end of the day, what else matters more than love?

Sadly, some of us have yet to receive the gift of being truly in love with another, but all of us can love each other in the Fellowship. It's that difference between being in love and simply loving.

I've never been in love with anyone in the Fellowship, but I love everyone in the Fellowship because they are wounded souls just like me, evermore restless and discontented, brimming with divine dissatisfaction, simply trying to find a way to fit and grow into a world they don't quite understand and probably never will.

At the end of the day, in my selfish heart, what really matters to me the most is continuing to grow my relationship with the small handful of individuals in my life that I know love me unconditionally, as I do them. They are my family. You know who you are, and I will try my best to be fully present with you every second of every day. Thank you for being a part of my life.

NOTES

72731618R00242

Made in the USA
San Bernardino, CA
28 March 2018